IMI HANDBOOK *of* MANAGEMENT

Marion O'Connor
John Mangan
John Cullen

PENTAGON PRESS

First Indian Edition: 2006

ISBN 81-8274-164-5

Published in arrangement with
Oak Tree Press, Dublin
by

PENTAGON PRESS
A-38, Hauz Khas, New Delhi-110016 (India)
Phones: 011-51656996/7/8, 51517091
Telefax: 011-51656997

Sales Office: Flat # 105-106, 4262, St. # 3
Ansari Road, Darya Ganj, New Delhi-110002
Phones: 51563901/2, 23287705
email: pentagonpress@touchtelindia.net
Website: www.pentagon-press.com

Printed by New Elegant Printers, New Delhi.

This edition is for sale in Indian sub-continent only.

CONTENTS

FIGURES

EDITORS

MARION O'CONNOR is Management Researcher at IMI's Centre for Management Research. She holds primary and postgraduate degrees from NUI Galway, where she was a recipient of a postgraduate fellowship. Marion worked in AIB prior to joining IMI. She has recently published three major reports on management issues and is currently working on a doctorate at Trinity College, Dublin, in the area of management skill development in the marketing sector.

JOHN MANGAN is Director of Research and Programme Director of a number of degree and senior executive development programmes at IMI. He has BSc (NUI), MSc (Cranfield), and PhD (Cardiff) qualifications and he has published extensively in the areas of logistics and supply chain management. Prior to joining IMI, he worked at the Michael Smurfit Graduate School of Business at University College Dublin, the Irish Civil Service, Aer Rianta and Aer Lingus. In 2003/2004, he is also visiting lecturer in international logistics at the Massachusetts Institute of Technology and, in 1997, he was a Fulbright Scholar at Boston College.

JOHN CULLEN is Senior Management Researcher at IMI's Centre for Management Research. A librarian by profession, he has published in several academic and practitioner journals in Ireland, the UK and the US. His research interests include organisational and management learning, competitiveness, strategic intelligence and labour markets. He has Master's degrees from NUI Maynooth and University College Dublin, and is currently working on a doctorate on the relationship between organisational culture and management learning at Lancaster University.

CONTRIBUTORS

LYNDA BYRON is a management specialist at IMI, who specialises in general management, communications skills and customer service. Her client list includes companies in many European countries in a variety of sectors: public, private, blue chip and SMEs. She has extensive experience in developing large-scale interventions for high potential managers to ensure effective succession-planning in organisations. She is noted for her capacity to create a positive learning environment that is both challenging and enjoyable. She has a Master's degree from University of Dublin, Trinity College and is the author of a number of books and articles on presentation skills, assertiveness and managing customer service.

MARY CONDREN is a writer, academic and communications consultant. She contributes regularly to RTÉ, *The Irish Times* and to academic journals. She taught for seven years in the writing programme at Harvard University, and has also taught at the Michael Smurfit Graduate School of Business at University College Dublin and at the Royal College of Surgeons in Ireland. She has acted as consultant editor and reviewer for publishing houses and academic journals in Europe and the USA, and for the Irish Government in the preparation of major reports. She holds a doctorate from Harvard University.

GEORGINA CORSCADDEN has over 20 years' experience in the management development arena of training, coaching and consultancy. She has appeared in the national press and radio, both in Britain and Ireland, and on BBC TV. She is an experienced management development trainer, who specialises in organisational behaviour and personal skills. She has been involved in both public and private sectors, across a diverse range of organisations ranging from blue-chip multi-nationals, to government departments, the European Commission, insurance, banking, building societies, technology, etc. Georgina is a member of the British Psychological Society, the Chartered Institute of Personnel and Development and the Chartered Institute of Marketing. She holds an MBA, a Diploma in Business, a Post-Graduate Diploma in Marketing and accreditation for occupational testing and a variety of personality instrumentation. She is currently pursuing research in the area of management competences and has a particular interest in teams, coaching, and personal skills development.

KEVIN DAVEY is founder and Managing Partner of The Trinity Institute, a dynamic results-orientated business development and change management practice. He began his career as an electronics engineer, before moving into sales and marketing. He has over 22 years' experience in sales and general management, and 14 years' practical involvement in training, organisational change management and strategic development initiatives.

DERMOT DUFF is a management specialist at IMI, who uses his wealth of international business experience and a wide range of qualifications to help organisations achieve meaningful change. With a BE from University College Dublin and an MSc in Management Practice from University of Dublin, Trinity College, he works in the area of strategy, implementation, project leadership and all aspects of operations management, from product development through manufacturing and supply chain management to service delivery. A director and advisor in a number of companies, Dermot combines academic research with a pragmatic approach, and works with clients across a range of industrial and public sector organisations.

MARTIN FARRELLY is Director of Human Resources at IMI and responsible for the design and delivery of all HR programmes. Prior to joining IMI, Martin gained extensive experience in the HR function in the services, financial services, telecommunications and food manufacturing sectors. He holds the National Diploma in Personnel Management and a Master's degree in Organisational Behaviour.

ROBERT GALAVAN is a management specialist at IMI. He combines extensive management experience with a broad range of qualifications and credentials in the fields of strategy, management and psychology. Since joining IMI in 1999, Robert has brought his experience to a range of development programmes and initiatives, both through IMI public programmes, customised programmes and award programmes. He is also a visiting lecturer in Strategic Management at University of Dublin, Trinity College. He is currently conducting his doctoral research on strategic leadership in top management teams with Cranfield University in the UK. Robert is the author of a number of textbooks for the IMI Certificate in Supervisory Management and acted as series editor for several years. He is a regular presenter at conferences, writes for the press and conducts radio interviews.

DEIRDRE GARVEY is a management specialist at IMI. She has over 10 years' experience with software companies in the international environment. In Microsoft, she was responsible for worldwide vendor development for the outsourcing of international products. She has extensive experience in the localisation industry, having previously managed the localisation division of Stream International. She also has a number of years' experience in the training environment and in the management and training of new technology introduction. Deirdre has a BA (Mgmt) and MBS in International Business. She is currently completing a doctorate at University of Dublin, Trinity College, on the internationalisation of Irish software companies.

SIOBHAN McALEER is a management specialist at IMI, who has worked in numerous marketing positions in Europe, the US, Australia and Asia. Her areas of interest include: business growth strategies, international negotiation, e-commerce and models of e-business, international market entry strategies, and channel management and key account management. Siobhan holds a BA

(Hons) in European Business Studies and an MA in Marketing from University of Ulster.

TOM McCONALOGUE has a PhD in Organisational Change from Bath University and runs programmes at IMI in the areas of time management, communications and the management of change. As a private consultant, he works with Irish organisations engaged in managing organisational improvements and change and his experience includes overseas consulting assignments in Europe, the Middle East, Africa and the United States. He has published over 25 articles on management development and two books, *Eat the Elephants and Fight the Ants*, on time management, and *Dealing with Change: Lessons for Irish Managers*.

BRIAN McIVOR is a management skills training specialist with over 25 years' experience in the public service and financial service sectors. He has worked with a wide range of international organisations. His areas of professional interest include: career planning and development, interpersonal and communication skills, corporate communications, including corporate video and multimedia, and scientific management skills.

ANDREW McLAUGHLIN is Director of Training & Development at IMI. He leads courses on performance management, communication skills, negotiation and influencing skills, career development and team-building. He has written extensively on areas such as competency-based interviewing, work-life balance and stress management.

JOHN POWER is a management consultant who specialises in general management development skills, performance management and effective management teams. He has delivered team development interventions to both public and private sector organisations in Ireland, the UK and overseas and has also worked on behalf of the European Commission in South Asia and the Russian Federation. He has implemented management development projects and teacher training initiatives in Vietnam on behalf of the Grand Duchy of Luxembourg. John continues to work closely with international organisations and overseas governments on a range of consultancy projects involving change processes. He holds a Master's degree in management development from University of Salford (Manchester).

JULIA ROWAN holds a number of business and training qualifications. Working in Ireland and internationally, she delivers training courses in a variety of management effectiveness areas including time management, presentation skills and performance management.

MICHAEL SHIEL is a management specialist at IMI, where he teaches programmes in the area of strategy and leadership. He is an adjunct faculty member at University of San Diego, California, where he contributes to the doctoral programme in leadership. He is also a member of the Value Innovation Network based at INSEAD in Paris, where he participates in the development of novel practical and theoretical approaches to the strategic growth of firms. He holds an MBA in International Business from Fordham University (New York) and a Doctorate in Management from University of Hertfordshire for work on the application of Complexity Theory to the development of strategic leadership.

JILL STAMP is a business psychologist specialising in personal skills training to realise people's full potential. She holds a PhD in psychology from Queens University, Belfast and lectures for the Business School at University of Dublin, Trinity College. She is a Chartered Psychologist with the British Psychological Society, has published in a number of international journals and has featured on TV, radio and in press commenting on psychological issues. Jill is also a practising hypnotherapist, who believes in tapping into one's own inner resources to achieve success.

TIM WRAY is Director of Executive Education at IMI. Formerly Head of Internal Communications at *eircom*, he has over 10 years' experience in the field of organisational communication and has been invited to contribute as keynote speaker at national and international conferences on the subject. Tim has been responsible for the design and implementation of large-scale interventions within organisations that maximise participation and lead to faster and more effective change. He has extensive experience in developing the communication and interpersonal skills of managers so that they can become key influencers and effective agents of change within their own organisations.

DEDICATION

This book is dedicated to our families for their ongoing love and support in this, as in all our endeavours.

ACKNOWLEDGEMENTS

We wish to thank Barry Kenny, Chief Executive of the Irish Management Institute, for his help and support in the completion of this book. We also wish to thank the Chairman, Dr Chris Horn, and the Council of IMI for their ongoing support for research into the development of best management practice.

Our thanks are also extended to the contributors, our IMI colleagues, for the efficiency and expertise with which they produced the various chapters. We wish to also extend our gratitude to the numerous other people at IMI who supported us in many different, but important, ways throughout the editing process.

We wish to convey a special word of thanks to Kathleen Reardon, Distinguished Research Scholar at IMI and Professor of Management and Organisation, University of Southern California, Los Angeles, for prefacing this work.

Finally, we wish to thank Brian O'Kane and the staff of Oak Tree Press for all their encouragement and support.

PREFACE

Wouldn't we all do much better at an upcoming meeting, presentation, negotiation, or management decision if, before proceeding, we might glance at what experts have to say on those subjects? How useful it would be if, when faced with a tidal wave of work, we could be coached on time management techniques and methods of stress reduction without having to travel to a distant seminar. And wouldn't a considerable advantage accrue if, before writing an important e-mail, perhaps to a contentious colleague, we could read about ways to employ novel, effective influencing strategies?

These kinds of information that facilitate the management of others and one's own career on a daily basis are made available and accessible in this welcome compendium of management wisdom from Irish Management Institute experts. Each chapter offers both a chance to revisit knowledge previously acquired, but perhaps forgotten or neglected, as well as to acquire up-to-date, new and valuable information. This is a rare book, not only in its ambitious goals of covering so many important management topics, but also in how effectively it identifies key issues for each and explicates tactics by which managers can immediately improve.

The *IMI Handbook of Management* should be kept not on your bookshelf but in your briefcase, where you can refer to it over and over again.

Kathleen K. Reardon, Ph.D.
IMI Distinguished Research Scholar
Professor, The Marshall School of Business
University of Southern California

INTRODUCTION

Our objective in putting together this book was quite straightforward: to help good managers become even better. Management is neither a science nor an art, but rather a combination of these two domains and a role which, of necessity, draws upon a range of diverse skills, abilities and intelligences. Ivor Kenny, in his book on strategic leadership in Ireland[1], says

> *"... effective management is a combination of knowledge and intuition, of position and personality, of environmental constraints and human will, of time and chance .... Effective managers have to synthesise, to integrate different and conflicting theories and themes".*

In this *IMI Handbook of Management,* we have drawn together contributions from our IMI colleagues, covering 20 different aspects of management. While grounded in their respective academic disciplines, the focus of each contribution is on the practical execution of the topic covered. The individual authors are all engaged on a daily basis in the development of practising managers and this grounded, real-world orientation is evident in their writings.

Managers today face a mix of complex and diverse challenges and this book is designed to help you in some way to deal with these challenges. Recent IMI research[2] has shown that the top challenges that organisations and their managers are confronting include the financial issues of rising costs, coupled with the problems of managing change and retaining both customers and

---

1 Kenny, I. (1999). *Freedom & Order: Studies in Strategic Leadership,* Dublin: Oak Tree Press.

2 O'Connor, M. (2003). *Top Challenges for Managers,* Dublin: Irish Management Institute.

employees. On a personal level, managers are also experiencing difficulties in achieving a work/life balance, motivating and empowering staff and leading effectively. These issues are common to all managers and are awarded significant attention in this book.

Our handbook is divided into four complementary parts. **Part 1** covers you and your career. The focus is on managing oneself effectively and topics covered include: effective management of your time, getting things done, career planning, and managing stress and your health. In **Part 2**, the focus switches to managing others, a key requirement for all managers. Team-building, motivating others, negotiating effectively, and facilitating discussions and meetings are covered. In addition, key issues in both people management (HRM) and customer management (marketing) are also discussed. Communicating effectively is central to being a good manager and is the subject of **Part 3**. The areas covered include: presentation and communications skills for the individual manager, communicating internally within the organisation, asserting yourself and influencing skills, as well as chapters on gathering business information and report writing. In **Part 4** of the handbook, we turn to managing forward. Drucker's often-quoted statement that "*the only constant is change*" is more relevant today than ever. In the current business environment, characterised by intense competition, globalisation, rapid technological development and increasing communications capabilities, the ability of managers to think, analyse and plan effectively is critical. Topics covered include how to manage during times of change, managing outsourcing, strategic planning and becoming a leader.

We hope you enjoy reading, and learning from, this handbook as much as we enjoyed putting it together. It has been designed in such a way that you can dip easily into individual chapters for subject-specific advice. The job of the manager is today more complex than ever. We encourage managers to view their work, and in particular their own personal development, as matters of profound importance to themselves, their employers and the wider economy. More and more, managers are engaging in management development programmes in order to enhance their knowledge and skills. The use of methods that aid in awareness of self (such as psychometric profiling) and the use of mentors and coaches are growing in popularity. All of these trends are to be welcomed. The role and purpose of IMI is to improve the practice of management in Ireland. We encourage you to visit our website at **www.imi.ie** or to contact any of the editors or contributors if you wish to discuss or further your management development. In this regard, it is apt to consider some recent advice from Barry Kenny, IMI Chief Executive, in his preface to a major IMI research study on management development in Ireland[3]:

> *"All too often, training and development spend is an easy target in difficult times. If you really believe that people are your key asset, I would encourage you to continue to build management capability. After all, the economy is cyclical and we all know that we will return to growth, and to a renewed war for talent."*

Marion O'Connor, John Mangan and John Cullen
IMI Centre for Management Research
Dublin, Ireland
April 2004

---

3 O'Connor, M. and Mangan, J. (2004). *Management Development in Ireland,* Dublin: Irish Management Institute.

PART 1

MANAGING YOURSELF & YOUR CAREER

1: MANAGING YOUR TIME

Tom McConalogue

Key Learning Objectives

- ☐ Understand the need to make better choices with your time.
- ☐ Acknowledge some of the bad habits you may have fallen into with time management.
- ☐ Identify four strategies for achieving more focus on what you want to achieve.
- ☐ Let go of some of the reactive and routine tasks in the job.
- ☐ Have a range of practical tools for working on the short-term and long-term priorities in your job.

While the pressure of an increasing workload has sent many managers in search of a magic formula for getting more done with their day, this chapter looks more thoughtfully at why managers have problems with time and offers sound strategies for achieving better results. Although time management is essentially about getting more space for the important things in the job, it is also about letting go of some things that can take up a lot of time and contribute little to what you are trying to achieve. It sometimes means making tough, and reluctant, choices to let go of some things in favour of others, which is usually easier when you have clear direction and are committing time to the things that you really do want to achieve.

WORK PRESSURES & BAD HABITS

It is almost impossible to open a journal or magazine these days without coming across an article on stress management or an exposé of how to deal with increasing pressure in the workplace. But, are we really working that much harder than a decade or two ago? Not according to a recent report by the Chartered Institute of Personnel and Development, which suggests that the hours people work has changed very little over the years. What *has* significantly changed, however, are the increasing demands on our time for instant response to the demands of others and the availability of many more choices in our work and personal lives. Life was much simpler when there were only two television channels and a couple of breakfast cereals to choose from.

While managers are having to cope with more demands on their time, and a limited number of hours in the day, many have responded by drifting into bad habits as a way of coping with the pressures of time. One of the most common responses to time pressure is to look for ways to speed up the workflow in an attempt to get everything done. An increasing array of gadgets have come onto the market in recent years, such as the personal organiser, the hand-held palmtop, the mobile phone and voicemail, all of which have encouraged managers in the belief that they would get everything done in the day if only they were more efficient.

But, rather than ease the workflow, for many managers, the new technologies have simply added to the sense of urgency and a feeling that everything has to be done immediately and by them; as one commentator reflected wryly:

> *"I don't remember queues of managers outside telephone kiosks urgently needing to ring the office, before the mobile phone came along."*

The reality is that; no matter how hard you work, you will never get everything done. Not only is working hard simply hard work but, when you are up to your neck in work, you are not managing, you are being managed.

While there has been a great deal of comment and writing in recent years on the issue of reducing working hours and achieving a better work/life balance, a critical ingredient for managers in making it happen is getting the work/work balance right. What makes managing a difficult and complex discipline to master, and makes it so easy for managers to drift into bad habits, is that there are competing demands on the manager's time between what has to be done for today and what has to be made happen for the future. While several models illustrate the concern for managers, the importance/urgency framework (**Figure 1.1**) helps to simplify the issue.

Although a great deal of the manager's time can be taken up in dealing with trivial, urgent and routine tasks (box 1+2), those things get done because they are a familiar part of the manager's day. Not only do they get done, but managers enjoy the cut and thrust of crisis, urgency and reaction. Wouldn't it be a dull old day if the phone never rang or if there were no queries to resolve or crises to handle? Be honest.

FIGURE 1.1: THE URGENCY / IMPORTANCE MODEL

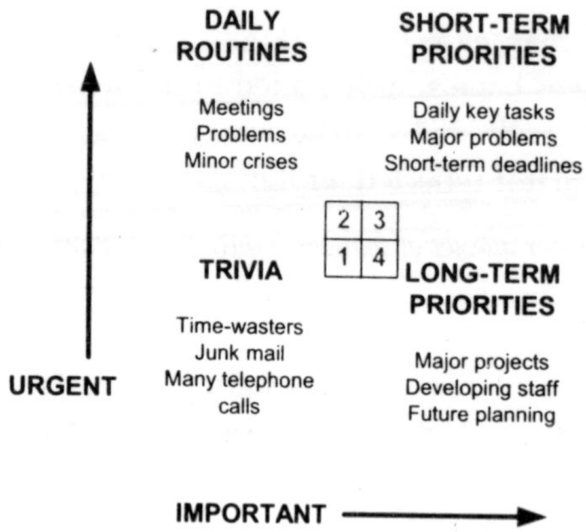

What mainly suffers in the manager's day are the short-term priorities (box 3), which often get pushed to the back-end of the day or left until tomorrow in favour of the longer-term challenges (box 4) that are difficult to start and hard to keep energy for over the long haul. Those things are different in nature – less tangible and not driven by urgency – and generally they don't get done unless they are made happen. Several surveys consistently identify planning and working on major priorities as topping the list of areas where managers need to give more time. But, human nature being as it is, the manager is no different from others in focusing on the things that are short-term and tangible, at the expense of tasks that are less tangible, harder to start and where results are only seen in the longer term. As *Gresham's Law* confirms:

> *"... in the normal course of events, urgency always drives out importance".*

MAKING WISER CHOICES WITH TIME

Against the backdrop of increasing demands on their time and the tendency to be driven by urgency rather than importance, how can managers redress the work/work imbalance in their jobs?

It is important first to recognise that time is a precious resource that needs to be managed wisely. Writers such as Peter Drucker, Edward Deming and Gareth Morgan agree that, if managers take away the amount of time in their day that they spend on distractions, interruptions, routine commitments and other imposed time, they probably have two to three hours within their control at most. And yet, two or three really productive hours in the day would make it a good and effective day for most people. Managers who use their time well realise that it is a scarce resource and they need to make wise choices to use those precious hours to pursue their own challenges and priorities if they are to be effective.

Four broad strategies can aid that process:

- Get direction through working to priorities
- Make time for the important things in the job
- Reduce the urgency and routine in your day through better delegation
- Minimise and manage the time-wasters.

Get direction through working to priorities

No one minds working hard, as long as they see it leading somewhere. Much of the stress and pressure at work today comes from feeling that you are working hard but not getting enough mileage from all your running. And yet many managers launch into their day by consulting their diary or e-mail, answering a few telephone calls or chasing up a few queries without so much as considering what they want to achieve with their day.

And while managing the things they need and want to get done for today, it is also important for managers to consider how to get mileage on the things they want to make happen for the future, which may not be so attractive or demanding of their time. Equally important to planning what you want to get done for today is having longer-term challenges in the job and finding ways to work on them in the short-term, by committing time to them.

Make time for the important things in the job

Most things in life get done if you give them time. You pass exams if you make time for study, you get fit if you make time for exercise and you develop relationships if you make time for the other person. While it is easy to justify the reasons for not getting into priorities in the job because we lack the time to do them, as with many other things, like playing in a golf competition or attending an overseas conference, we can always find time for things we really want to do by scheduling for them and not letting other things get in the way. While managers usually find time for the reactive things like meetings, handling interruptions and queries, because they are in the main driven by urgency and routine, it is also important to make time for the things that won't get done unless time is committed to them.

Reduce the urgency and routine in your day through better delegation

Some managers attempt to justify their lack of achievement in the job as a lack of trained staff and having to do everything themselves; others use comments like *"it is easier to do it myself"*, or *"I can't give them more work, they are already under pressure"*.

As a manager, it is important to recognise two realities:

- First, delegation is a process for "letting go" and there are several ways of letting go of work. For some managers, it means pushing more responsibility down to their staff, while for others it means pushing work back to colleagues or bosses who may have found them a convenient place to dump their unwanted problems. Reducing urgency and routine can also mean using the wastepaper basket as a practical tool in delegation. The elemental *Law of Calculated Neglect* (which counsels that many things, if left alone, will simply go away) suggests that much of the trivia in any manager's day could be reduced by simply giving it less time or not doing it at all

- Second, even managers who have staff are often reluctant to let go to them on the basis that it would be easier and quicker to do things themselves or that their staff are busy. But busy doing what? Everyone ends up being busy and much of what your staff are busily engaged in doing may be less important than taking on other responsibilities. As a part of managing your time, your staff may also need to learn that some things in their jobs are a priority and that others could be dealt with in other ways. Only by making quality time to appraise, coach and develop them in the job is it possible to build relationships where your staff begin to see their job as assisting you in achieving the results you are trying to achieve.

Minimise and manage the time-wasters

Much of the communications equipment now available to managers, such as e-mail and the mobile phone, has made them more open to distraction from clients, customers, bosses and colleagues, who expect an almost immediate response to their demands. But although it may not be possible to eliminate time-wasters altogether, because many of them go with the job, it is possible to manage and minimise them.

The most common time-wasters for managers include:

- Telephone interruptions
- Not saying "No" often enough to the demands of others
- Day-to-day crises and urgency
- Having to chase people up for information
- Drop-in visitors.

In dealing with time-wasters, it is important to recognise that, at the very least, we learn to live with distractions like the telephone and drop-in visitors and would miss them if they were absent. But more than that, we actually encourage many of the time-wasters and then complain about the effect they are having on our day. While managers complain about the constant distraction of the telephone, many are only too willing to be interrupted no matter how important the job on their desk, while others find it hard to resist getting into their e-mail and entertain drop-ins as a way of delaying tasks they don't want to start. As a consequence, many time-wasters become chronic and difficult to manage.

While it is usually easier to confront time-wasters if there are other things to which you are committed, it also helps to look for creative solutions on the basis that "*what we have tried so far hasn't worked*". In the case of telephone interruptions, some creative ideas for minimising them include:

- Hide in someone else's office when you need time to think or to plan
- Respond to queries when you expect to get other people's voicemail – this means you can deliver your answer, without engaging in a prolonged discussion
- Log your calls over several days and set a target to reduce them
- Use discussion-enders such as "*Are we finished then*?"
- Have a quiet time in the day when you are unwilling to be interrupted
- Leave a message on your voicemail as to when you will be available
- Rotate answering the phone between staff.

In essence, time management is about two things: getting more focus on the important things in the job (which are mainly the managerial tasks); and letting go some of the less important trivia, routine and urgency.

And while it may be tempting to think that, if you could get rid of some of the time-wasters, you would then have time for the more challenging things in the job, the place to start is where you want to focus. In the run-up to the Olympic Games, many of the athletes find it easy to let go of things in their lives such as their normal eating habits, their savings and even their jobs, because they are totally committed to getting to the games, achieving a good time and winning a medal. The more committed you are to the things you want to achieve, the easier it is to let go of the things that get in the way.

TOOLS & TECHNIQUES ON TIME

While understanding the issues in getting a better work/work balance, equally important is having strategies and techniques for making it happen. A few practical disciplines for getting more focus into what you are doing and for letting go of some of the work are elaborated below.

Do a monthly wish list

Managing, by definition, is not just about doing things for today but also about doing things today for the future. While managers may have all sorts of ambitions and aspirations in the job, it is all too easy to get sidetracked into daily routine and urgency at the expense of the longer-term challenges in the job. One way of consciously avoiding the treadmill of daily activity is to identify longer-term challenges in your job.

Setting long-term priorities can be as simple as designating one day each month when you are going to give five to 10 minutes to listing down all the things you would like to achieve, or get some mileage on, in the next three to four months. In a five-minute period, most people can come up with at least 10 potential challenges. Now choose two or three of them as priorities for the next month and let the others go.

Remember that priorities are, by definition, few in number. By trying to focus on too many things you typically end up by focusing on nothing: as management guru Tom Peters reflects:

> *"if you are working on 23 priorities, it's simple – you have no priorities".*

Energise the priorities with short-term tasks

While setting longer-term priorities is as simple as doing up a wish list and selecting two or three items as priorities, working to them is more difficult. Most long-term priorities are difficult to start, and hard to keep energy for, until you start to see the results. So we tend to procrastinate, or wait for a deadline to stimulate us into action.

Human nature is such that we usually have more energy for things that are immediate and demanding, one of the reasons that students suddenly find they have a great deal more energy for study a week before an exam. The key to getting into the bigger things in the job is finding ways to make them more like the things that do get done in the day such as drawing up a list, telephoning someone, arranging lunch, getting some information or planning time in your diary. Breaking priorities into short-term tasks and starting on the easy ones not only gives you an immediate sense of success but helps generate energy to go onto the next piece. While the analogy of eating an elephant suggests that you can't eat it whole and have to break it into bits, it also suggests there is no logic to where you start eating the elephant, except to begin on the easy bits as a way of getting some early success and the energy to go onto the next bit.

FIGURE I.2: PRIORITIES & SHORT-TERM TASKS

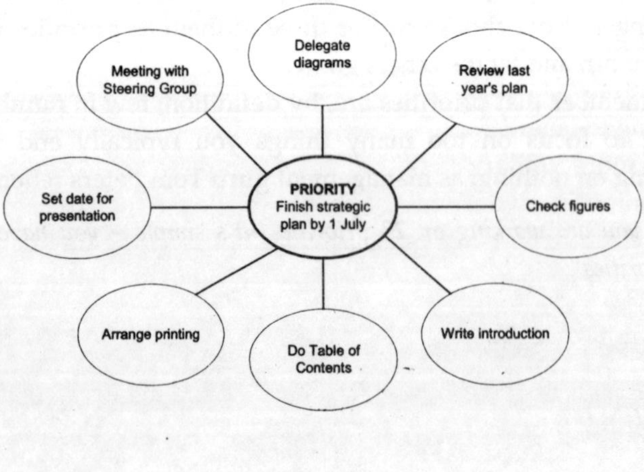

If you have a major report to complete in the next month, get the ball rolling this week by committing yourself to reading last year's report, writing an overall plan for the report, doing the introduction, delegating the diagrams to one of your staff or writing the table of contents. Use a bubble chart, as illustrated in **Figure 1.2**.

Get a few easy tasks done first and get the pleasure of crossing them off your list as you complete them. As you make progress, you may also discover other small things you could do, such as checking the Web for clip-art or asking one of your staff to proof read the report, so add further bubbles to the chart as you progress. There is no right place to start on most things; more important is doing something to challenge your procrastination about starting and finding small steps to fuel the journey

Block out time for the important things

It was once said that you can observe a great deal by just watching and, likewise, it is amazing how much you can achieve by giving time to things. One of the best ways of passing exams is to decide how many hours a week you need to study and block out those hours in your diary. Finding time for longer-term priorities like projects and more solitary activities like planning is often best managed by using a diary to block out chunks of time to get them done and not letting anything get in the way of those commitments. If that seems too adventurous, start by blocking out half-an-hour to do some thinking or planning on a task. Even the most intractable of jobs look easier when you give half-an-hour to breaking the inertia

On more solitary tasks, such as report-writing, which may need uninterrupted chunks of time in the day, it may help to work to the clock or to block out particular hours in the day or week. When writer James Thurber was having difficulty putting pen to paper, his long-suffering wife Althea helped him break the deadlock by insisting that he set an alarm clock to ring after 45 minutes and to force himself to have something written in that time period. It broke his writer's block.

Also work on the bigger and more important things at times of the day when you have most energy, which for most people is the mornings. Many managers are inclined to fill up their mornings with queries, correspondence and meetings and then try to get into the difficult things at times of the day when they have least energy. Try to get a head start on the day by getting rid of one difficult task first thing in the morning and, if possible, leave meetings or appointments that don't need all your attention for the afternoons.

Keep a "to do" list or weekly planner

While it is a common habit for people to keep lists of things they are trying to get done, there is a tendency for lists to get longer and longer as new things are added. And human nature is such that we tend to do the easy things first, the logic being that we will get rid of the easy things and then, once they're out of the way, we will get onto the bigger things. Unfortunately, it doesn't work that way. As the list gets longer and longer, we find more easy things as an excuse for not getting into the bigger things.

One of the most enduring stories on time management concerns Charles Schwab, one time President of the Bethlehem Steel Company in the US. Less than satisfied with his work output, he called efficiency expert, Ivy Lee, and offered him a handsome reward, if he could come up with something that would help Schwab get more done with his time. Lee suggested that Schwab make a habit each morning of writing down all the things he wanted to get done that day and to rank them in order of importance. He encouraged him to focus on his number one priority until it was finished, and then to concentrate on the next most important task, and not to worry if he only completed two or three tasks in the day, since he would always be working on the most important things first. He counselled Schwab to continue with the discipline until he was comfortable and to get his staff to do the same. Legend has it that Lee walked away with a cool $25,000 for the idea.

Keeping a "to do" list is a simple discipline for getting a sense of purpose into your day. It means taking three minutes at the start of each day to list down all the things you want to get done and to prioritise them, preferably as A, B, C and D with no more than three As on the list.

- **As** – things you must get done today
- **Bs** – things you would like to get done
- **Cs** – things you could put off
- **Ds** – things you want to delegate.

The secret of managing a "to do" list is to get into the As as early in the day as possible for two reasons:

- Most people have their best energy early in the day
- There is little more energising than getting rid of the As early.

On completing the As, simply reprioritise some of the Bs into As so that, as you go through the day, you are always working on the most important things. And keep the list on your desk so that, if there is a crisis or distraction that takes you away from what you were doing, you can easily get back to it again. Finally, when you get to the end of the day, review whether it was an effective day or whether you were sidetracked into less important things.

While keeping a daily "to do" list makes sense for some managers, there is an advantage for others in doing a weekly plan. The legendary Lee Iacocca, who brought the ailing Chrysler car corporation back from the brink, learned a habit at school that stood to him as a manager. Each Sunday, he took 15 minutes to list down all the things he wanted to get done in the following week and selected the three that would give him maximum leverage. He then broke each task down into bite-sized pieces and started into the easy ones on Monday so that, as he went through the week, he could keep track on what he had achieved and what was yet to be done. Starting into the week without a sense of what you want to achieve is a recipe for getting to Friday with that uncomfortable feeling that it was (yet) another unproductive and stressful experience.

Delegate some of the urgency and routine

Start to let go by finding out what your staff are doing with their time. Clarify their roles and key tasks and find ways to coach them on giving more time to their priorities and less time to what keeps them busy.

Avoid the trap of reverse delegation, by refusing to accept their "monkeys". Often, through our willingness to accept problems from our staff by giving them solutions or taking on their problems, we unconsciously encourage them to come with even more. Push the monkeys back by asking them what they would suggest or getting them to think about the options. Encourage and support them in coming with solutions rather than with problems.

Draw up a list of the tasks you should be trying to let go to others. Estimate the time they currently take up in your week. Pick one of the tasks as a challenge to reduce the time spent on it for the next month by pushing that task back to others, delegating responsibility to a key subordinate or simply giving it less time, and track your success over the month.

Also, consider keeping a Delegation Checklist. It is very easy as a manager to lose track of what you give to others, either forgetting when you gave it to them or when they promised to have the task completed. As you give jobs to your staff, note the tasks on a list with the person's name and the date you delegated the task. For some tasks that do not have to be completed immediately, agree a due date and note it beside the task. As staff complete jobs, you get the pleasure of crossing the tasks off your list and, at a glance, it is easy to see what your staff are doing for you, what has been completed, and what you may need to chase up.

SUMMARY

While managers are inclined to think of time management in terms of being better organised and in control, it is very easy to be highly organised around the wrong things – rearranging the deckchairs on the sinking ship. Being in control of the few precious hours in your day means getting more focus into what you are doing as a manager through having priorities and working to them. It also means scheduling around the things that are important in the job, so that these important things don't get sidetracked by other things that are driven by urgency and routine. But being in control of your time also means being flexible to the daily crises, urgency and distractions that need to be managed, without letting them dictate the agenda for the day. Some commentators have even described the job of the manager as one of "controlled chaos", suggesting that, while managers need to focus on their key tasks, they also have to retain the ability to respond to threats and opportunities as they present themselves. Rather than trying to control your time, start to manage it – if you don't manage it, then it can end up controlling you, both in your personal life and in the job.

CHECKLIST

- ☐ Recognise some of the habits you have drifted into with time management.
- ☐ Make time to manage yourself by having long-term priorities in the job.
- ☐ Work to priorities by breaking them into energising short-term tasks. Review your short-term tasks frequently and reset your priorities monthly.
- ☐ Schedule for the important things by using a "to do" list, a weekly planner or by blocking out time in your diary.

- ☐ Plan to let go of some work to your staff by clarifying their roles, keeping a delegation checklist and monitoring their performance.
- ☐ Manage the tendency to reverse delegation by pushing the "monkeys" back to your staff.
- ☐ Do something creative to manage one of your major time-wasters.
- ☐ Take time out to review and develop your own strategies for making better choices with time.

FURTHER READING

McConalogue, T. (2003). *Eat the Elephants and Fight the Ants*, Dublin: Blackhall Publishing.

2: GETTING THINGS DONE

Dermot Duff

Key Learning Objectives

- ☐ Learn the 25 lessons of getting things done.
- ☐ Manage yourself and others for greater impact.
- ☐ Recognise the power of simplicity.
- ☐ Realise that you have the power to change.
- ☐ Identify the key stages in project management.

Success depends on getting things done. Why then, is it invariably so difficult? Just what is the secret of getting things done? Is it enough to use your "to do" list better, or do you have to change your whole mindset and even personality?

TWENTY-FIVE LESSONS

"To do" lists are very necessary, but not sufficient, to really get things done. Changing your psychological outlook seems like drastic and unreliable medicine. So, what do high achievers do to be successful? What pitfalls of low achievers might usefully be avoided? How can I achieve more?

For those of you who have tried overly-simplistic and prescriptive self-help books and basic project management tools, you will know they help a little but, on their own, they are not enough. In this chapter, you will learn the key lessons in getting things done which will help to further your business goals or simply get more out of life.

Enjoy the many short lessons in this chapter, think about the underlying principles, decide what key tools you will use, and then start immediately to get more done.

Lesson 1: It's simple – keep it that way

Even the most complicated tasks are composed of simpler tasks. Keep it simple and KISS[4] complexity goodbye by asking yourself what really is the essence of this problem? What things will really get things moving? Who really is key to this project? The vital few can be crowded out by the trivial many – Pareto prevails!

Lesson 2: Eat the elephant a piece at a time

Promote simplicity, and overcome procrastination, by "eating the elephant" one piece at a time.

[4] KISS stands for "Keep It Short and Simple".

Divide and conquer problems by reducing them to simpler components that are easier to digest. Just starting to tackle the problem will help reduce anxiety and help plan the next steps.

Lesson 3: Be an abominable "No-man", not an obsequious "Yes-man"

To get more done, do less. Less, ironically, is more, because you will get more done when you stop juggling the extra tasks, the last-minute requests, the special favours and all the other time 'monkeys' that you let stick to you.

It may seem alien and strange initially but, if you have a need to do more than your clock or calendar allows, you will have to reduce your load to the level where you have fewer fires to fight.

But do remember, it ain't what you say, it's the way that you say it. If the boss wants you to do yet another little job, say "Yes", but negotiate for some other job to be dropped, or additional help to be given.

It's said that you don't get what you deserve, you get what you negotiate. In fact, if you don't assert yourself, you do actually get what you deserve – a heavy workload is often the price of submissiveness.

Lesson 4: Talk to yourself

All day, every day, there is a little voice in your head, talking to you. It never stops carping on about things not done, and terrible things that might happen as a consequence. This persistent nagging little voice helps keep us safe, by worrying about eventualities and alerting us to danger. It is, however, a pernicious internal monologue; turn it into a constructive *dialogue* by putting positive topics on that inner agenda. Get balance into the subconscious argument by rising above the worry tape playing constantly in your head.

Talk to yourself about the good things that might happen, and start to make them happen. Don't go *out* of your mind – go right *in* to your mind, and control your thoughts before they control you.

As Mark Twain said:

"My life has been full of terrible calamities, none of which actually happened!"

Talk yourself into a positive outlook, and imagine yourself in the zone of accomplishment.

Lesson 5: Don't just talk to yourself

You have friends, talk to them. Don't bottle it all up, or you will eventually explode with frustration or worry. Almost every challenge you face will be similar to one already overcome by someone in your social network. The wheel was a great invention; don't re-invent it needlessly.

Lesson 6: Bank on it

Relationships are like bank accounts; you can only get from them what you already put in. Cultivate friendships – by doing something (good!) for other people before they might have to do something (good!) for you.

Lesson 7: Dream a little, live a lot

We've all got to have dreams; envision your future so it can begin to happen.

If you don't know where you are going, you will never even leave the bus station, never mind arriving at the destination of your choice.

If you simply want to stay where you are, maybe you need to dream some more? Or quite possibly, your dream is already fulfilled, you just haven't realised it yet?

If your dream is not fulfilled, find the star that's right for you and hitch your wagon to it.

Lesson 8: Make believe

Mahatma Gandhi said:

> *"Vision without action is merely a daydream, and action without vision is just being busy, but vision with action can change the world."*

Energise your long-term vision by setting short-term goals. Figure out your route, and plan the milestones along the way. If you want to lose 6kg in 6 months, plan on losing 1kg every month (but before you set your goals, do a deep reality check!). Measure your progress along the way. Congratulate yourself on reaching your milestones, and take the opportunity to re-plan your way forward.

Lesson 9: Be emotionally intelligent

IQ, intellectual quotient, is important, but so is EQ. Emotional intelligence is the capacity to know what makes people tick. Reduced to its essence, it means you walking in the other person's shoes. Even more fundamentally, it means having empathy and being polite – the stuff you were told at school was correct, after all, but it is easier said than done. For further insights, see the work of my colleague at IMI, Mike Fiszer.

Lesson 10: Know who you are

You can't do everything; in fact, if you think about it, you probably can't do very many things well! A great musician might also be a great plumber, but it's unlikely, just as a great brain surgeon probably can't programme a video-player correctly! Not simply because of lack of time and lack of motivation but because such combinations of temperament and interests don't often occur; different types of people have differing skills and perspectives. Happiness (and a sense of accomplishment) comes from knowing what you are good at. So do what you are good at, and become great at it.

Know your weak points, but don't try to eradicate them. Instead, play to your strengths and work around your weaker aspects. Every coin has two sides, so keep your better side up.

Lesson 11: Know who they are

Perhaps you, too, have been told, without a trace of irony, that you are unique, just like everybody else?

Folks do differ, thankfully. Some are more outgoing and friendly – but often a bit impulsive. Others are reflective, and maybe loyal, but perhaps awfully picky. You probably feel if they were more like you, the world would be a better place: please note that it surely wouldn't! Without diversity, there would be simply monotony and bland sameness.

You can't change other people, so you will have to change yourself – or at least, change the way you approach them. With the slow, deep thinker, go equally slow. With the quick-thinking fox, talk the fox's language. To know one type from the other, just listen; people, being social animals, will eventually yield to their innate desire to express themselves.

Lesson 12: Don't just do it

A colleague of mine has a wonderful piece of reflective advice:

"Don't just do something – stand there!"

This means taking the time to think about the issues, weighing up the consequences, looking for alternatives, researching the background, having a fallback position, and planning the work. Failing to plan is planning to fail!

Lesson 13: Just do it – now

Having planned the work, now work the plan. You have thought the idea through, so act. Now! Yes, right now! The world is full of good intentions – don't just be a contender, a might-have-been, be a champion.

Lesson 14: There are risks out there – plan for them

No sensible person undertakes a journey without checking what the hazards are. No plan is really a plan until the danger points have been identified. At the same time, not all risks are equally likely, or have high impact. Decide which risks are worth paying attention to, then work to avoid them, to reduce their impact or to get reparation when they occur. Like travelling by car, wear a seat belt, keep the spare wheel prepared, and do buy insurance; it's the same with real life.

A French proverb says:

"To those who cannot or will not see, all things seem sudden."

Be prepared and plan ahead.

Lesson 15: Yes or No?

We don't like to disappoint people, nor do we like to be found wanting. As to whether a job is done or not, we tell white lies. Avoid the syndrome where jobs are said to be 90% complete but which stay that way well past the deadline. Parcel the work so that it can be completed as a deliverable package. Not just done, but also be verifiably done. This avoids the "nearly there" syndrome, by making the work more discrete and measurable so that it can be seen to be complete – or not. Similarly with your own milestones; plan your work so that it can be done, then carry it out as a defined task, with a beginning and a clear end.

Lesson 16: Travel light

Travel light, live long. If it's not simple, then make it simple. If it's complex, it will break. Take with you only what you need; the rest is just baggage.

Lesson 17: Fight, not flight

Feel the fear, and do it anyway. That which we most dread, is what we most need to do. Avoidance tactics may delay tackling the issue but the fundamental problem will grow instead like a weed, prompting a vicious circle of avoidance followed by guilt. The end result can border on self-loathing, turning a simple task into a personal guilt-trip.

Lesson 18: You, Inc.

You are the owner of You, Inc. You are your own managing director, your own brand, your own balance sheet. Build your self-worth by investing in yourself. Assess *you* regularly. Produce your annual plan, and do quarterly reviews. Enhance your personal value and reputation by working on others' perceptions of you! Perception is reality in this case.

Lesson 19: Solicit feedback

Eat the breakfast of champions! Great achievers actively seek feedback, filter the useful from the dross, and then act accordingly. Learning can be expensive, even painful, but ignorance is possibly fatal.

Lesson 20: Wow!

Go on, surprise yourself! Do the thing you most want to do. If it's a trip to Hawaii, or even just filling in your tax returns, get the wow factor that comes with the excitement of chasing something worthwhile, something exciting.

If the project you are running or the goal you have set for yourself doesn't excite you or your team, get a goal or a project that does. You owe it to yourself and your team.

Lesson 21: How long is a piece of string?

To make a schedule, you will have to estimate how long each task takes.

Usually, people are overly optimistic in their estimation: if you double your original estimates, you will probably still be conservative. This is because of the tendency to overlook tasks completely, to ignore start-up and set-down tasks, to avoid including rework times and other hidden activities.

Lesson 22: Order matters

Start with the end objective in mind, map out the chain of events in logical, time-sequenced order. Look for opportunities to improve the schedule so maybe you can kill two birds with the one stone or save time or money by grabbing a head start. Scan the schedule for omissions – what is missing? Invariably, a key resource will be scheduled to be in two places at once, so check for bottlenecks and inconsistencies.

Lesson 23: A "to do" list is not a plan

A "to do" list is usually a powerful mechanism for crunching through short-term tasks. To make the "to do" list a regular habit, use a pre-printed form and keep the list prominent.

Turn a "to do" list into a plan by scheduling when you will do each item. Not all will need to be done today. Do the items that are urgent and important as a top priority. For big tasks, extract the important tasks that must be done now, and schedule the rest. Eventually, some slack time will emerge in your calendar. Keep working to stop the important items becoming urgent as well! Use the freed-up time to get ahead on the important tasks. Use the time to improve your system of working.

Lesson 24: Meetings, eternal meetings

Many managers spend half their time in meetings, fuming inwardly at the waste of time involved. Some possible remedies include:

- **Don't go**: Especially if it is not a decision-making meeting. Just send your update or information instead.
- **Go, but don't give more time or attention than necessary:** Use the time to think, plan, review your "to do" list, read a report. Alternatively, ask for a slot early in the meeting.
- **Go, but only if there is a proper agenda**: A good agenda is really a meeting plan. Structure meetings so that a meaningful outcome is produced. A good meeting is really a micro-project, and so needs a miniature project plan.

Lesson 25: Goals

"A goal is nothing more than a dream with a deadline."

Without a goal, energy and direction will be missing. Setting goals is not easy, but it helps if you work back from where you want to be or how you want to see yourself at some future date. But be careful what you wish for, because your dreams are likely to come true, especially if you apply yourself.

Is That All There Is?

Getting things done is all very well but just doing things is not enough. Sorry to say, but even achieving all your dreams mightn't be enough, after all. The world is full of people who appear to have it all, and then end up asking *is that all there is*?

Maybe it is enough just to be, not to always to do? In any case, oneness with the environment – in other words, harmony – must be the bedrock of constancy, so live in the moment, and enjoy each moment. We work to live, not live to work.

CAN YOU REALLY CHANGE?

Yes, you can, and in a single moment, even – but only if you really want to badly enough, and decide to take the necessary steps.

As the saying goes:

> *"Whether you think you can, or think you can't, you are probably right."*

In the final analysis, only you can set an upper limit on your possibilities. To paraphrase Eleanor Roosevelt, nobody but yourself can undermine your self-respect.

FURTHER READING

Peters, T. (2003). *Re-imagine!* London: Dorling Kindersley.

Appendix: Key Phases in Managing a Project

To help you get thing things done in formal projects, use the following structure.

Definition Phase

The definition phase of managing a project may include the following steps:

- Idea generation
- Needs generation
- Concept screening
- Feasibility study
- Statements of requirements
- Objective-setting
- Budgeting.

Questions to be asked in this phase	Source of Answers
What is the purpose of the project?	Project Statement
How will we know when the project is complete?	Objectives
How will we decide how to do the project?	Options
What are the key pieces of work to be done?	Work Breakdown
What do we need to accomplish the task?	Resource Requirements
Does everybody involved in the project agree with the first five issues?	Project Definition Meeting

Planning Phase

The planning phase of managing a project may include the following steps:

- Solution selection
- Impact and opportunity analysis
- Estimation
- Scheduling
- Diarying
- Milestone-setting

3: Managing Stress & Your Health

Andrew McLaughlin

Key Learning Objectives

- ☐ Understand the nature of stress.
- ☐ Learn the basics of stress management.
- ☐ Recognise the effects of stress on the body.
- ☐ Realise the importance of physical exercise.
- ☐ Practise relaxation techniques.

Organisations and individuals worry about stress. For organisations, the costs are considerable in terms of absenteeism, burnout, early retirement and general loss of efficiency and effectiveness. For the individual, stress means lack of satisfaction at work, loss of productivity and difficulties with relationships both at work and at home.

Stress is now accepted as being crucially related to our total health – physical, mental and emotional. According to doctors, the majority of visits are stress-related. Stress and strain are known to cause, or worsen, many medical conditions. As a result, stress is used to describe many of our modern ills.

If we have poor coping skills, deficient social support and high stress, then the internal balance of our bodies may be easily upset and our resistance lowered. The more vulnerable we are, the more risk we run of getting sick. The factors that place us at risk range from our attitudes in coping with stress to the kind of food we eat and the genes we inherit. The way we react to the daily hassles of life or to specific stressful events can mean the difference between coming down with an infection or remaining symptom-free.

The Nature of Stress

Stress is a non-specific response to stimuli, called stressors. Although life itself depends on certain forms of stress, it is only when stress is handled poorly by the body or mind that it becomes a health hazard. Stress occurs when there is an imbalance between the stressor (either real or perceived) and the resources that a person has available (again viewed subjectively) to cope. What seems to be important is the idea of control. When you do not feel in control, you experience distress. Stress that is expressed negatively can be linked to many physical complaints from headaches and high blood pressure to symptoms affecting a person's mental state. Anxiety, depression and feelings of anger, fear, helplessness or hopelessness and other emotions are often linked to stress. Stress can also contribute to obesity because of its action on the body.

EVOLUTION OF STRESS THEORIES

In the early 1900s, Walter Cannon, a physiologist, related stress to the inner balance of the body. He noted the effect of the hormonal (endocrine) system on metabolism and the effect of emotions on physiological processes. Cannon used the term "emergency response" to describe the "fight or flight" stress mechanism that is commonly experienced during the stress reaction. Through his work, a greater understanding of the link between stress and the nervous system was observed. This has now developed into psychoneuroimmunology, or the study of the impact of the mind on the immune system.

In the 1940s, Austrian-born Hans Selye, an endocrinologist, working in McGill University in Montreal, presented a broader view of stress. He perceived stress as an adaptive mechanism that is not always necessarily negative. In addition to physical stress, Selye considered psychosomatic aspects of stress.

He made distinctions between good and bad stress. Selye described "eustress" as the good or positive stress, such as rewarding or creative work, and "distress" as the negative stress from harmful or potentially-harmful stimuli.

The same stressor may be a source of eustress in one person, but a distress in another. The deciding factor appears to be the individual's perception, interpretation or tolerance of the stressor (see **Figure 3.1**).

Selye defined stress as the "non-specific response of the body to any demand made upon it." The stress response could be elicited by a broad variety of potentially-harmful factors such as physical injury, temperature extremes, physical exercise or exertion, emotional stimuli, fasting, illness, noise and nervous stimuli. **Figure 3.2** highlights the potential outcomes that can occur in the individual, which are directly linked to the onslaught of pressures and the resources required.

FIGURE 3.1: POTENTIAL STRESSORS

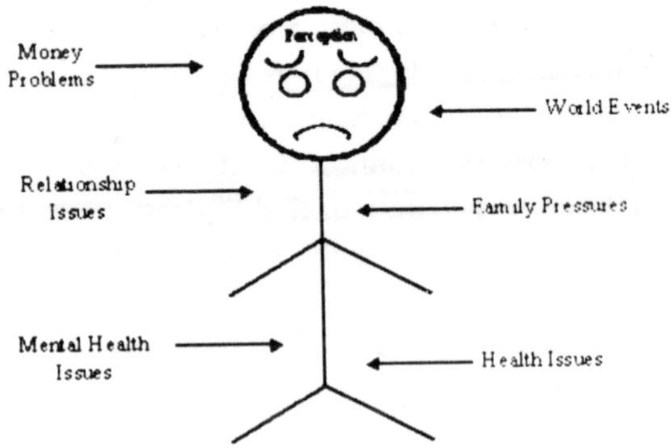

FIGURE 3.2: THE INDIVIDUAL & STRESS

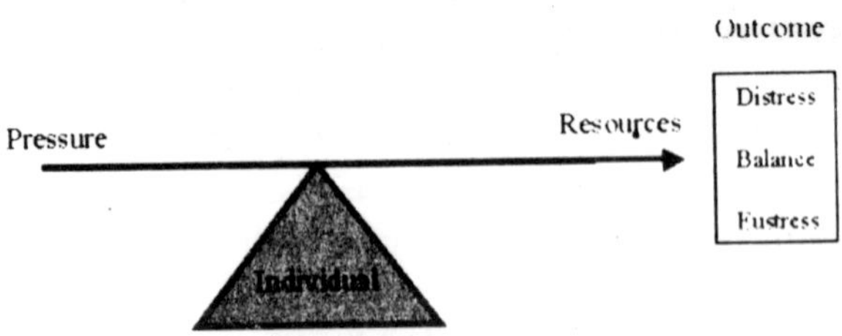

Additionally, Selye found that animals have identical responses to stress as humans. Stress prompts hormonal responses linked to harmful health changes. The following is a description of what happens to the body:

- **Alarm reaction:** As stress is experienced, the body is aroused into a defence "fight or flight" response. At this stage, the adrenals release adrenaline, a stimulant. In turn, this response causes the pituitary gland to release certain hormones (ACTH) and the adrenals to release cortical hormones – cortisol
- **Resistance Stage:** During this stage, the body attempts to maintain balance as stress continues. Powerful hormones,

including cortisol, continue to be excreted, as alarm responses continue or are reversed

- **Exhaustion Stage:** Continued cortisol secretion occurs, prompting detrimental changes in circulation, digestion, and immunity. As the body's adaptive mechanisms weaken, adrenal exhaustion, poor immunity and other "diseases of adaption" begin to occur.

PERSONALITY TYPES

In the 1970s, Dr Meyer Friedman and Dr Ray Rosenman found that specific personality types have different responses to stress. The classic competitive, hard-driving, time-urgent and often hostile Type A individual appears to experience more harmful effects of stress than the easygoing, even-tempered, Type B counterparts. The Type A person is much more likely to suffer a heart attack than the calmer Type B personality.

Friedman and Rosenman also found that, during the workday, Type A individuals tend to excrete higher amounts of stimulating stress chemicals than Type B individuals. Type A people also appear to have higher amounts of these chemicals in their blood and tend to have higher blood pressure.

Further research has shown that hostility and anger are the two components of Type A that are implicated in damaging the heart. Type As need to manage their lifestyles to ensure that the burning drives that they have do not lead to burn-out. [A review of the progress of the Type As in the research shows that the Type As did much better than expected – by and large, because they took advice on behaviour modification, changing their lifestyle and reaping the benefits.]

Of course, under-stimulation (so called "rust-out") is as much of a problem as over-stimulation. Executive stress may be a myth because executives have better education, more resources and more control over their environment. Un-employed people suffer from stress just as much and probably more than executives.

THE EFFECTS OF STRESS ON THE BODY

Today, we know that two powerful systems of the body cope with stress. The nervous (sympathetic) system controls the rapid body changes in response to stress, while the endocrine (hormonal) system regulates the longer-term patterns of stress response by releasing hormones into the blood.

During stress, the autonomic nervous system is activated. Chemicals activate a part of the autonomic nervous system called the sympathetic branch, thereby reducing the normalising effects of body functioning. This makes sense in evolutionary terms, as there is little point in repairing tissue and excreting growth hormones when a sabre-toothed tiger is panting at our heels – what we require at that time is increased alertness, strength, visual acuity and aggression.

The stimulation results in increased metabolic rate, heart rate, circulation and blood pressure. In addition, the effectiveness of the digestive system is diminished and disturbances in sleep patterns become more common. When we are stimulated, we do not secrete melatonin and serotonin – the sleep hormones. Sleeping in the presence of sabre-toothed tigers was probably life-limiting.

The effects of stress on an individual's nutritional status start with a reduced digestion. When this occurs, enzyme production is reduced and absorption of vitamins, minerals, protein, fat and carbohydrates is diminished. As stress continues, the adrenals produce stress hormones, cortisol being the most prominent. As the level of cortisol increases, so too does the metabolic rate – often up to 10 times the normal resting level.

When metabolism increases, there is an increased need for calories. Cortisol also appears to increase blood sugar (glucose), while placing greater demands on the pancreas (insulin response) to keep the blood sugar stable. Many people become more susceptible to disturbances in blood sugar during stress and can put on weight – particularly, in men, around the abdomen.

Cortisol also speeds the breakdown of protein and muscle – a catabolic process. It decreases the build-up of muscle. Amino acid imbalances can occur, resulting in depression and poor sleep. One of the best indicators of stress is either inability to sleep or waking very early and not being able to get back to sleep.

Just as proteins are broken down, so too are fatty acids. Cholesterol and triglyceride (fats) levels may also become elevated, creating more links between stress and heart disease – specifically, atherosclerosis.

How Emotions Affect the Body

Understanding the mind-body influence is a vital consideration in stress management. Selye's work emphasises the need to cultivate a sense of inner peace in order to maintain inner balance amid the events of life. Through research, it is being shown that emotions – including love, hate, happiness, sadness, fear and anger – are all interpreted by the body, affecting the nervous system, the immune system and the cells themselves. You cannot afford the luxury of a negative thought.

Biochemist Candice Pert has also found that our thoughts and feelings are experienced on a deep cellular level. Pert's book, *The Molecules of Emotion,* explains how tiny cellular protein messengers, called neuropeptides, appear to be produced by the brain and certain other body cells, including the immune and endocrine cells.

Understanding the profound influence of the mind upon the body also leads to understanding how we can create healthier "self-talk". It begins with the recognition of the inner dialogue we have with ourselves.

Dr Stanley Baxter of UCLA has shown under advanced tomography that words can elicit the same changes in brain chemistry as anti-depressants. Words can heal – for example, love, support, understanding – or wound – for example, bitch, idiot, blame. Sometimes, in our inner dialogue, we speak to ourselves in ways that we would not speak to our worst enemy. In such circumstances, you might ask yourself *"Whose side are you on?"*.

In stress management, one method that assists in this process is cognitive therapy, based on a theory that draws the connection between our thoughts, feelings and behaviour. Developed by Aaron Beck, this approach considers exaggerated fears, erroneous beliefs and attitudes and impractical goals, all of which may create unnecessary levels of distress. Examples are saying things are "awful" or a "catastrophe" when they are nothing of the kind. For example, if you describe the loss of a customer as a catastrophe, how would you describe the loss of both of your legs? It is about getting life events in perspective, in order to react at an appropriate level.

Another Beck classic is saying *"I can't stand it"*, when something unwelcome happens. The reality is that you can stand it and probably have done so many times before.

Through counselling and other self-help work, individuals can learn to see the relationship between their thinking and their stress, and learn to correct their cognitive, "thinking" errors.

Relaxation & Biofeedback Therapy

Relaxation and biofeedback therapy are other complementary stress management techniques. As intellectual feedback continues, perhaps within a counselling setting, individuals may also choose to learn special skills to improve their ability to relax.

Relaxation

Specific relaxation techniques can diminish harmful stress responses, with benefits in as little as 20 minutes a day. With increased levels of relaxation, respiration rate and heartbeat slows down, muscle tension diminishes, and digestion and biochemical activity normalises. Many cases of high blood pressure are improved as the whole system relaxes.

Through various relaxation methods, the effects of our modern-day stressors such as traffic jams, tight schedules and financial pressures can be reduced. One of the most accessible relaxation techniques is diaphragmatic or abdominal breathing. Proper breathing requires the use of the diaphragm, the layer of muscle that separates the chest cavity from the abdominal cavity. **Figure 3.3** shows how to do it.

When you breathe properly, the diaphragm contracts and the abdomen protrudes slightly, allowing the lungs to expand and fill with air. To get the maximum benefit from the 2,500 gallons of air you take in daily, learn to breathe from the bottom up. Through slow, deep breathing, the body and mind can quickly become calm and relaxed.

Meditation is another method of relaxation that provides stress reduction benefits. There are hundreds of scientific studies proving the benefits of meditation. Research has shown that skilled meditators can reduce their level of cortisol by 25% with just 40 minutes of meditation. This may be particularly important, since chronically high levels of cortisol damage health by depressing the immune system.

Herbert Benson, who wrote *The Relaxation Response* and *Beyond the Relaxation Response*, recommends the following technique:

- Choose a quiet place
- Sit in a comfortable upright position (lying down is not recommended as it is easy to fall asleep)
- Repeat the word "one" silently
- Breathe easily
- Continue for 15 to 20 minutes
- Let thoughts pass on
- Practise once or twice daily.

Figure 3.3: Guidelines for Diaphragmatic Breathing

1. Choose a location where you do not expect to be disturbed. If disturbances occur, so be it.
2. Dim the light in the room. This encourages focus, concentration, imagination and perception. Tuning inwards is achieved better. The senses are not distracted.
3. The room should be slightly warm, but not too warm, since that again is a hindrance for the proper execution of the exercises.
4. Wear light clothes, so that you feel comfortable in them. Take off your shoes.
5. Choose quiet surroundings. Children can be asked to keep quiet for 10 minutes. You can put up a notice on the door, saying you will be available in a few minutes. The telephone receiver can be laid off the hook for a short while.
6. Put one hand on your belly and one on your chest.
7. Inhale through your nose and allow your abdomen to gently expand.
8. Imagine that you have a balloon below your navel and it is expanding.
9. Continue breathing to expand your ribs and chest area – wide and deep.
10. Finally bring the air into your upper chest and fill out the area below your shoulders. Be careful not to tense your shoulder – just imagine the air filling the space beneath.
11. Pause and begin the exhale either though your mouth or nose (breathing is easier to control through your nose).
12. Exhale in the opposite order, first empty below your shoulders, then relax the ribs and chest area and, finally, gently press your abdomen towards your spine as you completely empty your lungs. Pause and begin the cycle again.

It may help you to think of four stages: Inhale, Pause, Exhale, and Pause, with three steps during the Inhale: Abdomen, Ribs and Upper Chest.

Another tip is to think that you are being breathed rather than breathing. Take the effort out.

A last tip is to imagine a feather resting on your nostrils. Try not to dislodge it.

Biofeedback

Biofeedback is a way of using medical devices to show the impact of different states in changing indicators, such as heart rate and blood pressure.

Introduced in the 1960s, biofeedback has been shown in clinical studies to be a valuable tool in behavioural medicines as a method to help individuals integrate the body and mind. With regular training, biofeedback can further assist people by helping them fine-tune their relaxation skills and learn more about how the body responds to stress.

Biofeedback is often aimed at changing habitual reactions to stress that can cause medical consequences. During the biofeedback session, the therapist assists the individual in achieving the desired goal of increased relaxation at will. Various monitoring tones, lights and gauges feedback information to the individual regarding the extent of stress or relaxation they are experiencing. The most frequently-used methods of biofeedback are skin temperature and muscle tension. Skin conductance and brain wave biofeedback are other modalities used in special settings. Home options include checking your pulse, using a commercial blood pressure monitor or bio-dots that respond to skin temperature.

With more proficient relaxation and biofeedback skills, people can gain greater ability to relax on demand. When relaxation exercises are combined with biofeedback training, even greater stress management benefits can be achieved.

Benefits of Aerobic Exercise

Lungs

The lungs are where the air you breathe is processed and the oxygen is removed and transferred to the bloodstream for distribution throughout your body.

The amount of air that lungs can process is the first limiting factor. If your lungs cannot process enough air, they cannot extract enough oxygen to produce enough energy. Two factors limit the lungs' ability to process air:

- The lungs have no muscles of their own and are completely dependent for expansion and contraction on the muscles of the rib cage and diaphragm. A conditioned person has the capacity for inhaling more air for longer periods and exhaling more waste, because the muscles around their lungs have been trained to do more work
- The condition inside your lungs: how much of the capacity is usable is more important than the size or total capacity of the lungs. This usable portion is called the vital capacity and is measured in the laboratory by the amount of air that can be exhaled in one deep breath. A conditioned person's vital capacity is about 75% of their total lung capacity.

If you allow your lungs to deteriorate, you'll be living your life with two handicaps in the lungs alone. When you need more oxygen in a hurry, the muscles controlling your lungs will not be in condition to force high volumes of air through, and the usable space of the lungs may be seriously reduced.

Aerobic training can reverse both trends, exercising the muscles surrounding the lungs, increasing their strength and efficiency, and helping open up more usable lung space.

Blood

The limiting factors for healthy blood include the number of red blood cells and the amount of haemoglobin the cells carry. Even if your lungs could process more oxygen, your body tissue still would not receive more unless you have experienced the training effect of aerobic exercise.

An average-sized person may increase his/her blood volume by nearly a quarter in response to aerobic conditioning. And, of this amount, the red blood cells may increase proportionately more. Sit around and do nothing, and it deteriorates.

Heart

The heart takes oxygen-filled blood from the lungs and pumps it throughout the body. It also takes carbon dioxide-filled blood back from the body and pumps it into the lungs.

A person who exercises regularly will have a resting pulse rate of 60 to 70 beats per minute. A de-conditioned person will have a heart rate of 80 or more. Even at complete rest, a non-exerciser forces the heart to beat nearly 30,000 times more every day of life. Healthy hearts will peak at 190 beats per minute or less without strain. Poorly-conditioned hearts may go as high as 220 beats or more during exhaustive activity – dangerously high. Your maximum heart rate can be calculated by using the formula 220 less your age.

Aerobic training benefits the heart in several ways. It develops it into a strong and healthy muscle that works effortlessly, whether during moments of relaxation or moments of peak physical exertion. By doing so, it maintains large reserves of power to handle whatever physical or emotional stress is imposed upon it.

ATTITUDES & EMOTIONS

Your heart rate can be changed by your attitude and emotions. The adrenal glands produce the "fight or flight" hormones. This starts the heart pumping more oxygen around, before you even make a move. Some people are stressed or worried all the time and create a message to the heart, "keep going". In some circumstances, a de-conditioned heart can take off, beating at excessively fast rates, possibly leading to a heart attack.

Ancient yogis believed that a human was allocated a certain number of heart-beats and breaths and, when these were used up, the person died. This is a way of reminding us that a lower heart rate and deeper breathing probably prolong life.

THE SIX SECOND MODEL

Remember that you would not be here if your ancestors had not developed the stress response. The key insight in stress management is that there is a gap between stimulus and response. All human freedom lies within that gap. So let me introduce you to the six second model of stress management.

Notice stress in your body as it occurs. Ask yourself what is going on. Give yourself six seconds to consider the logic of the situation. Is it helpful to respond this way? There are very few experts who teach you to do something by beginning "Now tense yourself". In other words, physical tension is usually unnecessary. Now do yourself a favour and "just let go". Say to yourself "relax". If a thought is bothering you, say "stop" in a commanding voice. Then replace that thought with a more pleasant one.

Remember it is *your* mind and *your* body. Stress management is about taking over the controls again. And relax ... just do it.

CHECKLIST

- ☐ **Identify the stress triggers:** With awareness, we can better anticipate many stressful situations.
- ☐ **Learn to say "no" more often:** Refuse to accept unfair or excessive demands.
- ☐ **Get sufficient sleep:** Proper rest – seven to eight hours of sleep every night – can help protect the immune system and general health while improving productivity, stress tolerance and recuperation.
- ☐ **Get fresh air:** Clean, fresh air is a basic requirement for good health. Allow fresh air into your office and home. Deep diaphragmatic (abdominal) breathing in fresh air can calm and invigorate the body and mind.

- ☐ **Get physical exercise:** Physical exercise on a regular basis can help to reduce the effects of harmful stress hormones and reduce muscle tension and anxiety. But remember moderation. Excessive amounts of physical exercise can create excessive stress by stimulating cortisol and lactic acid.
- ☐ **Eliminate sugar and caffeine:** More stable blood sugar and a stimulant-free diet are crucial to mind-body balance. Caffeine in people who are not sensitive is fine in reasonable quantities and should be consumed before lunch. After lunch, it can remain in the body until bedtime when it may interfere with sleep patterns.
- ☐ **Nutritionally support the body:** The adrenals and the immune system can take a toll during stress. Vitamin C and other antioxidant nutrients, B complex and minerals help offset the harmful effects of stress and keep the body strong. Eat nutrient-rich foods and consider supplementation. Working with a professionally-trained nutritionist can help to pinpoint specific needs. A multivitamin tablet is a reasonable insurance policy.
- ☐ **Deal with emotions constructively:** Don't stifle feelings; emotions need to be channelled in positive ways to prevent potential negative health effects. Seek professional assistance if necessary.
- ☐ **Develop meaningful relationships:** Close fulfilling relationships including a significant other is important to good health.
- ☐ **Give life purpose and meaning:** Learn to slow down and see life with a more spiritual outlook. Focus away from materialism and develop the spiritual side of life.

- **Buy a pet, especially if living alone:** People with pets show better resilience than those who are completely alone. Stroke your pet regularly and watch your blood pressure fall.
- **Learn time management and delegation techniques:** Learn how we create stress through our own thinking errors. A stress management program or working with a therapist can provide a clearer understanding of this skill.

REFERENCES & FURTHER READING

Benson, H. (1994). *Beyond the Relaxation Response: How to Harness the Healing Power of Your Personal Beliefs*, New York: G. P. Putnam's Sons.

Pert, C. (1999). *Molecules of Emotion: Why You Feel the Way You Feel*, London: Pocketbooks.

4: PLANNING YOUR CAREER

Brian McIvor

Key Learning Objectives

- ☐ Understand what a successful career means for you.
- ☐ Undertake an inventory of skills, expertise and traits.
- ☐ Identify career drivers and anchors.
- ☐ Consider career options.
- ☐ Set meaningful goals and action plans.

This chapter is about finding your ideal career. However, our careers need to be examined in the light of the balance between our work and the other elements of our life. The areas of working, learning, playing and giving are examined with the objective of finding the correct proportion and overlap between them. What we can do (our skills) and our knowledge (expertise) need also to be factored in, together with an understanding of the elements that will give our career meaning and satisfaction.

WHAT DEVELOPS YOUR CAREER?

What is a Career?

A career might be defined as a time-based plan of your working life. However, such a definition might be too limiting, because of the focus on the working element. To make a career plan more meaningful, we will examine the elements of career and life balance under four headings:

- Working
- Learning
- Playing
- Giving.

Key questions here include:

- What's going on in your life and career?
- Are you thriving or just surviving?
- What's your role?
- Have you reached your potential?
- Have you all these elements in balance?
- Do you have vision?
- Do you have sustainability?
- Do you have a network?

A strict definition of career implies a progression upwards, but we need to consider other options such as plateauing, disengaging or interrupting a career path so that other critical elements in our life that need precedence (such as family) can be allowed to do so.

What is "success" – for you?

Before you proceed any further, take a few moments to write out a Success Statement for yourself, starting as follows:

> ***My career would be a success if it were one in which the following happened:***

What we really need is a reliable direction. To do this, we need to have a clear understanding of what success is for us – since, for different people, success means different things. We all have individual and particular wants and needs. Unless we factor these into our career plans, we will experience long-term dissatisfaction.

POINT FOR REFLECTION

Surveys in Ireland and the United Kingdom have shown that between 55% and 70% of people feel that they are in the wrong job but very few of them do anything about it. If this statistic is true, then over half the readers of this chapter will need to examine their careers seriously.

Obstacles to success

As part of your career plan, you might like to consider also what would stand in the way of your career plan.

List the potential obstacles:

My career plan would be vulnerable to the following factors:

1 External factors (economy, environment etc.)

2 Internal Factors (self-limiting beliefs e.g., perfectionism etc.)

Then ask yourself:

- Which of these are within my control?
- What action do I need to take to clear them?

The answers can then be used as a basis for your own personal action plan (see the section later in this chapter on exploring your options and making things happen).

CAREER & LIFE PLANNING ESSENTIALS

Before planning to move from your current career or role, you need to identify, with some precision: What, Why, Where, How, Who and When, in the context of your career.

What helps you to identify the core skills you have built up over your life and career to date and to identify any skills gaps you may have to close in moving forward. This also means taking a look at what you have done to date in your life and work and taking stock of yourself.

Traditionally, this means identifying your:

- Ideal life-style, combining working, learning, playing and giving
- Key skills
- Areas of knowledge or expertise (professional and organisational)
- Traits or attributes (how you operate).

A useful idea to work with here is the notion of transferable skills – identifying the skills you have developed to a very high level and which you enjoy using. Research shows that the higher the level of skills, the greater its transferability into other roles.

Why involves understanding yourself and what drives your career. It also involves understanding what rewards and motivates you and what the relation is between reward and motivation. Research suggests that people leave jobs because of working conditions rather than for reasons of pay and rewards extrinsic to the job. What are the things that need to be in place in your organisation for you to perform at your best?

Where identifies the location, the type of organisation, outcomes, salary, and people you want to work for. Marry **What** and **Where** to your research about your target field(s) to get the job or career move *you* want.

How identifies what strategies you will use to move forward in your organisation – or outside of it, if both your needs and the needs of the organisation are not being met. Once you have identified your transferable skills, your drivers, your fields of interests and optimal working conditions, you need to analyse your options:

- Staying within the same organisation (in a different role)
- Moving to a new organisation (in a new or different role)
- Moving to a new way of working.

You will also need a Plan B.

Who identifies your network, the people who will be your eyes and ears for information, opportunities and jobs. The network will be something you will put time into – to support others in their own journey.

Identify the time scale: **When**. Get used to setting goals and taking small risks.

Set goals that are SMART:

- Specific
- Measurable
- Achievable
- Relevant to your agenda and not to others
- Time-bound.

Career and Life planning can be regarded as a cyclical process (**Figure 4.1**).

Who you are is a complex combination of skills, motivations, learnings and aspirations. To do a complete analysis of such items may take a very long time. Some authorities in this area consider career development and life-long learning as part of the same process.

FIGURE 4.1: THE CAREER & LIFE PLANNING CYCLE

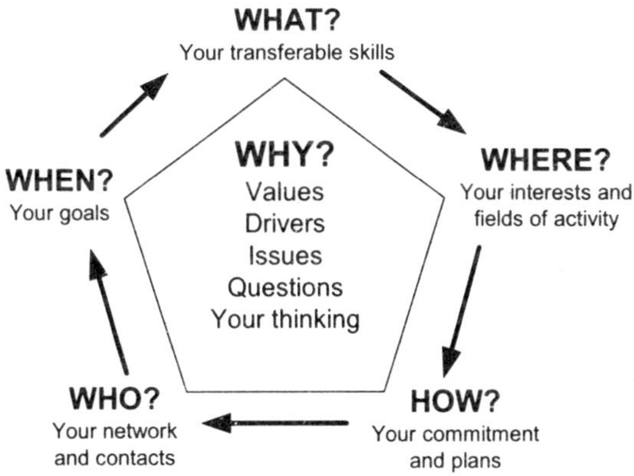

CAREER & LIFE BALANCE: WORKING, LEARNING, PLAYING & GIVING

What's your work / life balance?

For most people, work dominates our waking time in any week. In considering a healthy work/life balance, we should consider the amount of time the other components occupy.

Is learning getting enough time – both on and off the job? How much learning is taking place on the job – informally and in formal training? The prime responsibility for managing the learning lies with the jobholder – in order to ensure that necessary learning takes place.

The four components of career and life balance are:

- **Working:** What we do in the hours of 9 to 5 (or 7am to 7pm?). This is where you combine your best skills, knowledge and traits to produce your life's work. To get more out of life, we may need to approach it in a complete new frame of mind and move away from the traditional ways of looking at these four components of our lives.

- **Learning:** Revising current levels of skills, acquiring new knowledge, dealing with change, managing your stress, coping with the increasingly complex environment and growing in your own wisdom and learning.
- **Playing:** Sports, pastimes, amusement and just plain fun! Where you re-create yourself and keep body and mind active.
- **Giving:** Your relationships: the people in your life – family, friends, community and the world at large – helping them meet their special needs through your special gifts.

How the four aspects of work / life balance integrate

It is useful to draw a work/life balance diagram for yourself – as it is at present and as you would like it to be. **Figure 4.2** shows such a diagram.

FIGURE 4.2: THE WORK / LIFE BALANCE DIAGRAM

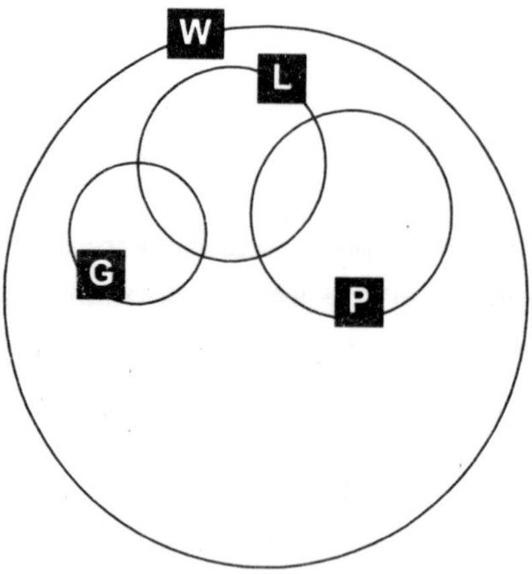

How do the elements of your work / life balance overlap?

Here are some examples of different WLPG combinations:

- **The Workaholic:** The work element predominates. No learning takes place on the job – because there is no time for it. Whatever learning or play happens is almost by accident. There is no form of giving. There is no integration or overlap between the various components. **Future:** Poor – burnout is inevitable

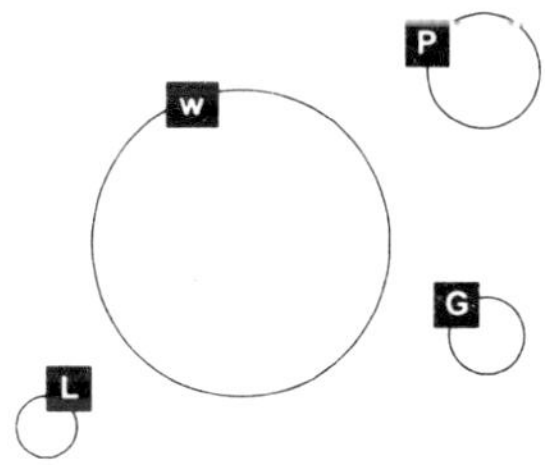

- **The Corporate Employee:** The classic position of someone who is owned by their company. Everything takes place within the context of the workplace. **Future:** Fair – if this arrangement really suits you. There is a danger you may become disconnected from the real world – and see the world through the eyes of your organisation

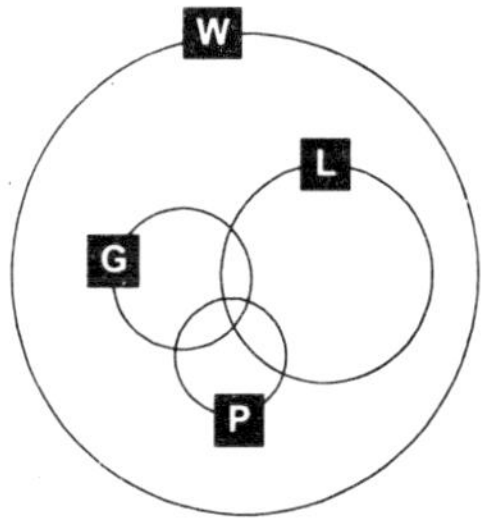

- **The Philanthropist:** Everything takes place within the context of giving. This is not a typical profile of a professional manager. **Future:** Good, within an organisation that has a service or community element

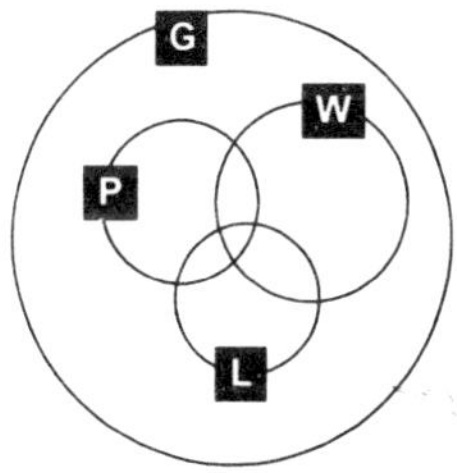

- **A Balanced Life/Style:** The aim here is to get the relative components in balance with each other and to ensure there are healthy overlaps and boundaries between the elements. **Future:** Good but needs constant monitoring.

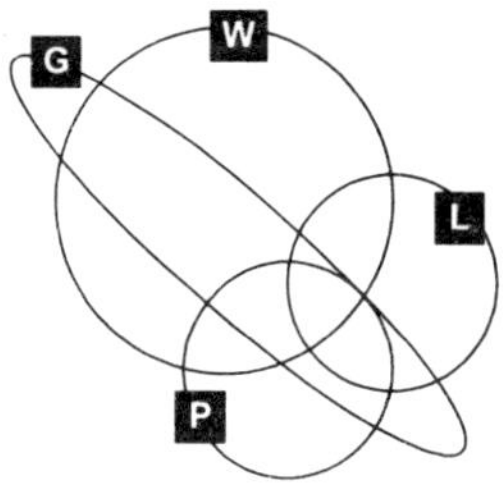

Managing boundaries

In most companies, hours of work for non-management staff are clearly defined, paid for by overtime and subject to control. For managers, however, usually hours worked per week or month are open-ended and never discussed. It is tacitly accepted that this is part of the price that needs to be paid for promotion in many organisations. This is an idea that needs to be challenged.

Increasingly, career management is being seen as something that both the organisation and the individual need to have input into.

When is the last time you had a conversation with your boss about the boundaries between work and the rest of your life? When did you last discuss the direction of your career with your organisation? Are there elements of work life balance that need maintenance or serious attention?

Working: Identifying Your Transferable Skills

What is a skill?

A skill signifies or denotes action of some sort. A skill is an action that will produce results with people, information or things. Skills may be very broadly defined as in "communication skills", which covers a multitude of sub-skills, or as precisely defined as you can make it.

Note the differences between skills, objects and attributes:

- **Skill:** What you do
- **Object:** What you use the skill with
- **Attribute:** How you apply the skill, the quality you bring to the skill

For example, writing is a skill; writing letters is a skill with an object; writing letters humorously is a skill with an object and an attribute.

Level of skills

As you inventory your skills, you will notice that certain skills, such as recording data, are not as complex or as difficult to acquire as higher-level skills such as analysing data.

It is a central principle of career and life planning and job search that you need to:

- Maximise the list of skills that you have
- Sort your skills into those that are at the highest level.

Some higher-level skills involving people, like leading, mentoring or guiding, comprise dozens if not hundreds of other skills. It is very easy to get lost in a forest of skills, so prioritisation is essential.

Skills clustering

Most people are dimly aware of their skills – and to what level they can deliver. However, a thorough skills analysis can reveal up to 1,000 skills for any individual.

There are three "families" of skills:

- **Mechanical Skills:** Skills with Things: The first major family of skills is that dealing with technology, equipment, plants animals or skills involving our senses. *Typical skills words in this category: making, repairing, installing.*
- **Information or Data Skills:** The second family of skills deals with collecting and analysing data of all sorts. *Typical skills words in this category: recording, comparing, calculating.*
- **People Skills:** This deals with all our interpersonal skills, which we use with others one-to-one or in groups. *Typical skills words in this category: listening, persuading, selling.*

The first step in the process, then, is to identify in which of these three categories your skills are strongest.

The second step is to arrange your skills into families. For example, the skills of coordinating, controlling and directing could be categorised into the cluster skill of managing.

Another approach is to take a commonly-used skill such as leading and ask yourself:

- What am I doing, typically, when I manage?
- What am I best at in this area?
- Where and how have my best results been achieved in this area?

The need for objects

Identifying a skill, no matter how precisely it is done, is only one third of the work. If you list *presenting* as a skill, this ignores the range of subjects where your presentation skills may be applied. Therefore, there is a need to identify the precise object of the skill or range of objects. For example:

- Imprecisely defined object = presenting anything
- More precisely defined = presenting financial data
- Most precisely defined = presenting quarterly sales reports for items in stock on 1st January last.

In skills inventorying, skills can be considered high or low level.

Low-level skills are typically:

- Simple in essence
- Highly-prescribed
- Specific to a particular function or industry
- Repetitive.

Examples of low-level skills include: lifting, listing, and assembling.

High-level skills are typically:

- Complex in essence
- Less prescribed
- Generic
- Variable and characteristic to the individual.

Examples of high-level skills include: creating, innovating, leading, motivating, and designing.

The main reasons for focussing on high-level skills is because:

- They are more transferable across function or industry and thus are more marketable.
- More discretion and creativity is required in how you use them.

Organising the "master skills" set

Once skills have been organised under the main headings (Mechanical Skills, Information Skills and People Skills), you will need to decide which are your "master skills".

Master Skills are skills that incorporate other skills under them. For example, managing sales includes the skills of monitoring performance, motivating staff, setting goals. Try to identify a small number of master skills which, between them, identify your key contributions to your organisation.

To be considered as a master skill, the following criteria should be considered:

- Is this a high-level skill?
- Do I have a facility for this skill?
- Do I produce valued results (for my organisation / industry) in this area?
- Do I really like using this skill?
- Will I be sufficiently rewarded for using this skill (extrinsically or intrinsically)?

Case Study: Putting Career Planning into an Organisational Context

One of the benefits of the introduction of Performance Management Development Systems (PMDS) into organisations in Ireland is that it has focussed managers' attention on the primacy of skills identification. PMDS systems identify the contribution that skills inventorying can make to the identification of skill gaps and the development of meaningful training and development plans.

LEARNING: YOUR EXPERTISE

Part of your personal inventory should also include subjects, both professional and technical. Knowledge gained through formal qualifications is one thing but organisational effectiveness also includes the following:

- Knowledge of how the organisation operates
- Product knowledge
- Knowledge specific to the organisation itself such as insider knowledge of industrial processes
- Knowledge of the industrial environment
- Contacts and networks.

All these elements of professional knowledge are useful in your own professional inventory but also in determining where you should go both in terms of location and role. Simple examples in a medium-sized engineering firm might be:

SUBJECT	LEVEL of KNOWLEDGE	AREAS of APPLICATION
Computer Packages	ECDL Advanced	All Administration Departments
Product knowledge	In the top 1% in industry	Marketing Product Development Industrial design

Another question here might be – in which areas or roles in your organisation could these items be combined?

This type of analysis might be sufficient on its own to help you in developing future career paths in your organisation.

CASE STUDIES

INDUSTRY KNOWLEDGE

Over the years, many managers build up formal and informal networks of contacts. These informal networks may be useful to competitor companies and be sufficiently attractive for a manager to be head-hunted. For example, in recent years, staff from the semi-State sector who have taken severance packages have easily found employment in the same field of activity advising organisations that have critical contacts with their previous employers.

CRITICAL KNOWLEDGE

A number of years ago, the dot-com bubble burst and many managers lost their jobs. Some managers found themselves being sought out and hired into other IT companies because they had been through a company collapse and could warn their new companies of the signs of imminent disaster.

PLAY: RECREATION AS RE-CREATION?

On one level, the traditional view of play is of sport or recreation. However, the concept of play should include elements of how we bring a light approach to our work and to our relations with colleagues. Playing is both a recovery space for us and a way in which we can help reduce stress for ourselves and others at work – for example:

ACTIVITY	NATURE	IMPACT
Hill-walking	Physical	Keeps me fit; Relaxes me; Presents challenges

FOOD FOR THOUGHT

Survey after survey of stress management lists aerobic exercise as the great de-stressor. Three periods of half-an-hour per week of aerobic exercise is sufficient. However, there is a hidden benefit – time spent off the job and spent playing means that the unconscious mind has an opportunity to deal with the solution to problems. Long walks are an excellent way to keep fit and reflect on problems away from a stressful working environment.

GIVING: VALUES & GOALS

Values are the principles by which you act every day, in your job, in your life, in your work, with your friends and relations. Your values permeate everything that you do and should be a reflection of them. In your chosen career, you should be working in a place where the value system is in harmony with your own. This is not to imply that all of your values should be expressed through your work, but there should be an area of common overlap. Here are some sample values that may help you start your own search:

- **Justice and fair play:** Ensuring that everybody's rights are respected in the workplace and elsewhere
- **Inclusion:** Making sure that the circles you move in are not exclusive or limiting
- **Service to the community:** No one is an island. Many of our actions have implications, directly or indirectly for others. The community is a collection of people with different value systems, different goals, but with common interests
- **Excellence:** Striving for the best in everything that you do
- **Empathy:** Sensitivity to the feelings, needs, wants and desires of others.

A useful exercise is to draft a personal Values Statement and to consult it from time to time.

Key relationships

As part of the holistic examination of your career and life balance, you should consider the key relationships in your life and your impact on each other.

COMBINING LEARNING & GIVING

A powerful option for managers in combining learning and giving in their lives is to offer mentoring to their colleagues or to outside bodies. There have been a number of very successful mentoring schemes in Ireland in recent years. The process can have significant effects for the mentor themselves, as it gives an opportunity to reflect on self-development away from the work-place.

CAREER SATISFACTION

Identifying your own career drivers

A career driver is something that is very innate and special to you. A certain field of activity, ways of working, results or values will have a different resonance for you than they will have for others. For this reason, it is important to produce a prioritised list of what your drivers are so that you can identify what is at the core.

Well-meaning friends may advise you with regard to your career but, in doing so, they are talking from their own experience and from their own deep-seated (often unconscious) drivers.

Needs and wants

A fundamental distinction has to be made between what you *need* out of work or out of life and what you *want* out of work and life. Some wants manifest themselves as needs and, once they are met as needs, they then become secondary. For example, at the basic level of survival, there is a need for physical wellbeing, security. Once these needs have been met, other needs apply – for example, approval by others, self-esteem and finally, realising your own potential. This list is a restatement of the classic needs hierarchy identified by Abraham Maslow, although Maslow's model is only one of the many that might be applied. However, it is useful in identifying the "hygiene" factors that need to be taken care of before other work can proceed.

If you talk to some people about what drives their career, they will tell you that it is the need for money, security, a place to live, or an education for their family. And there is an element of truth in this because, for those people, they are the current realities. But what happens when there is sufficient money in the bank, the house is built and paid for, and the children are educated? Is the need then to build another house – just for the sake of it – or to take on again other activities that were historically so important? The search in career drivers is for the core elements that determine our preferences and choices.

Dave Francis's classic book, *Managing Your Own Career* (1985), building on the work of Edgar Schein, identified nine career drivers (**Figure 4.3**). This particular classification has been of tremendous help to thousands of job searchers and career seekers over the years, here and abroad.

FIGURE 4.3: NINE MAJOR CAREER DRIVERS

1	**MATERIAL REWARDS**	Seeking possessions and a high standard of living.
2	**POWER and INFLUENCE**	Seeking to be in control of people and resources.
3	**SEARCH for MEANING**	Seeking to do things which are believed to be valuable for their own sake.
4	**EXPERTISE**	Seeking a high level of accomplishment in a specialised field.
5	**CREATIVITY**	Seeking to innovate and to be identified with original output.
6	**AFFILIATION**	Seeking nourishing relationships with others at work.
7	**AUTONOMY**	Seeking to be independent and able to make key decisions for oneself.
8	**SECURITY**	Seeking a solid and predictable future.
9	**STATUS**	Seeking to be recognised, admired and respected by the community at large.

Source: *Managing Your Own Career* (Francis, 1985).

What drives me?

To direct your career effectively, you need to understand what you want and need from your working life. Different elements of work motivate different people in different ways. Classic studies of motivation identify the hygiene factors that need to be in place to ensure that we are not dissatisfied at work – factors here include pay and working conditions. However, the studies show that recognition, achievement and self-development are powerful motivators.

Other studies by Edgar Schein (among others) revealed values that anchor a person's career. If these factors are not present in their working life, there will be a constant feeling of lack of fulfilment and restlessness. Many people are only dimly aware of their career drivers, and tend to take critical decisions based on other people's influence, or mere expediency; such choices prove to be unfulfilling.

Once you have identified your primary career drivers then the other elements fall into place. Research shows that most people tend to have only two or three major drivers.

Case Study: Dara's Dilemma

Dara has had a number of safe, secure and pensionable jobs – including stints in teaching, the civil service and financial services. But Dara is restless and wonders why careers, which satisfy others, lose their appeal within a year or two. On examining his drivers, Dara discovers that what he is looking for in his ideal career is a combination of creativity, autonomy and the ability to influence others. Dara is now working as a successful consultant in the field of change management.

Optimum working conditions

European research in the area of job satisfaction shows that working conditions is one of the three major determinants in ensuring career satisfaction. (The other two determinants are the identification and application of the appropriate skill sets and the identification of the correct field in which the skills can be used.)

Studies on motivation establish that intrinsic factors in the workplace such as recognition, advancement and the intrinsic value of the work itself are key motivators. Extrinsic factors such as pay and perks are hygiene factors for most people. If not dealt with, they de-motivate; if dealt with, they do not, of themselves, motivate but only eliminate potential sources of de-motivation.

In order to arrive at an inventory of optimum working conditions that you need, you must first identify the things that make the work life difficult for you. These are OBSTRUCTORS. Then, explore the opposite – ENABLERS. Examining opposites of enablers might identify a range of options, which you can then choose from.

In the example below, select the option that best suits you.

OBSTRUCTOR	POSSIBLE ENABLERS	REALISTIC PROSPECT?
Technology that keeps breaking down, is slow or inaccessible at critical times.	No technology.	*Unrealistic.*
	Well-designed and maintained office systems.	*Adequate, reasonable.*
	Technology whose design I am consulted on and over which I have appropriate control.	*Realistic, if I am pro-active.*
	State of the art technology with world-class delivery.	*Possibly unrealistic.*

Rewards

Rewards are both complex and characteristic. They are complex, because they comprise a number of both intrinsic and extrinsic elements. They are also characteristic, because no two people will want to be rewarded in exactly the same way.

A common misconception is that salary is the best and only reward but studies of people who change career show that salary is *not* a major consideration in their decision-making. Recognition, advancement and opportunities for development are likely to play a much greater role in considering rewards.

Apart from values, you might like to consider other factors here such as:

- **Extrinsic rewards:** Outside the job, for example, pay, company cars, personal laptops, staff discounts etc.

- **Intrinsic rewards:** These come with the job, and include:
  - o **Advancement:** The level you would like to attain in any organisation
  - o **Recognition:** In your organisation or professionally
  - o **Self-Development:** The opportunity to learn on the job or to develop your potential fully
  - o **Activity:** The nature and perceived value of the work itself
  - o **Lifestyle:** What your work enables you to do in the outside world (travel, etc)
  - o **Profile:** Public visibility, both inside and outside your organisation
  - o **Access:** To customers, colleagues and other valuable contacts
  - o **Resources:** Resources (e.g., access to information or research) that will help you.

CASE STUDY

Two leading supermarket chains in Ireland differ considerably in pay rates for staff. Supermarket Chain A pays more but has lost staff to Chain B, which pays less but has a better reputation for looking after its staff. Staff in A talk about having a job. Staff in B talk about having both a career and a life!

PUTTING THE ELEMENTS OF THE CAREER PLAN TOGETHER

By now, you should have some clarity on the following:

- **Work / Life balance:** Combining WLPG
- **Skills:** What are the four or five core skills that you have to a high level and which enable you to produce your best results?
- **Knowledge/Expertise**
- **Career Drivers:** What gives your career meaning?
- **Optimum working conditions:** Where and how you will produce your best results?
- **Rewards:** What are the significant payoffs for you?

Remember that an ideal career is one that meets the needs of both the jobholder and the organisation they both belong to.

EXERCISE

Copy all the data from the previous sections onto a large sheet of paper and ask yourself the following questions:

- Does my current career contain all or most of these elements?
- What role, organisation or environment would be best for me?
- What level should I be aiming for in the medium to long term?
- Am I going to specialise or become a generalist?
- What is the most developmental path for me to take?
- What changes do I have to make in my life and work?

EXPLORING YOUR OPTIONS & MAKING THINGS HAPPEN

There are four major options to consider here:

- Expanding the horizons of your current job
- Moving to a new role or new organisation
- Moving to a new role in a new organisation
- Engaging in further development to add to your knowledge or skills.

Given the data you have identified above under skills, interests, drivers and values, you might consider doing a decision table based on a SWOT (Strengths, Weaknesses, Opportunities and Threats) analysis of each of the options. Which of these options seem to meet your needs, the needs of the significant people in your life and those of your organisation?

Note that changing **either** job or organisation is easier than changing **both** job and organisation. It may be easier to find a different role **inside** your organisation than to find the same work **outside** it. To do this, you need to be proactive and to consider the potential contribution you can make to other parts of your current organisation.

It is easier to act yourself into a new way of thinking than to think yourself into a new way of acting. (Goethe)

How do you make the future happen?

There are three ways:

- Visioning the future
- Networking
- Goal-setting.

Visioning

An effective way of bringing your career plan forward is to construct a set of visions or scenarios of your future. These scenarios are a description of your WLPG (working, learning, playing and giving) at some point in the medium term (three or five years from now). The scenarios should include all the elements discussed above – including your knowledge, skills, rewards, and working conditions. You should see your vision as one in which your career drivers have become central.

VISIONING & THE 1970S OIL CRISIS

In the early 1970s, Shell Petroleum had constructed four alternative scenarios of what would happen the oil industry in that decade. In the event, they correctly identified a scenario in which the oil-producing nations imposed embargos on the exports of oil. This exercise meant that Shell was uniquely positioned to take advantage of the situation.

Networking

It is useful to regard your network as a medium of exchange of information. Inventory your main contacts and identify what you can do for them and what they can do for you.

Note the strength of weak ties: self-employed consultants report that some of their best business contacts and referrals come from people who they know only vaguely. How often has that happened in your life?

Goal-setting

Goals are what you want to achieve as the expression of your values.

If you fail to set goals, you will not move very far:

Failing to Plan means Planning to Fail.

If you wish for the best – you usually get it. (Somerset Maugham)

THE HARVARD EXPERIENCE: A CLASSIC CASE OF GOAL-SETTING

In a classic study (which has been replicated elsewhere a number of times) a survey was taken of the graduation class of 1955. Only 14% of these had set goals for themselves. When this group was surveyed 20 years later it was discovered that each of the 14% were either Chief Executive or owner of their organisation – and their combined net worth far exceeded the other 86%.

CHECKLIST

- ☐ Are you clear about the relative amounts of working, learning, playing and giving in your life?
- ☐ Are you clear what your key skills are?
- ☐ What are your areas of expertise and how do they combine?
- ☐ What are your values and goals – how are they reflected in your life at work and outside it?
- ☐ What drives your career and gives you satisfaction?
- ☐ What working conditions allow you to produce your best results?
- ☐ What will reward you?

- ☐ Who will help you – and who can you help?
- ☐ What long, medium and short-term goals do you need to have to make your career happen?

REFERENCES & FURTHER READING

Bolles, R. N. (1977). *The Three Boxes of Life*, California: Ten Speed Press.

Bolles, R. N. (2004). *What Colour is Your Parachute?*, California: Ten Speed Press.

Francis, D. (1985). *Managing your own Career*, London: Fontana/Collins.

Hawkins, P. (2004). *WLPG - The Windmills Approach to Working, Learning, Playing and Giving*, Liverpool: Liverpool University.

Lees, J. (2003). *How to Get a Job You'll Love: A Practical Guide for Unlocking Your Talents and Finding Your Ideal Career*, New York: McGraw-Hill Higher Education.

Tieger, P. D. and Barron-Tieger, B. (1992). *Do What You Are*, Little Brown USA.

PART 2

MANAGING YOUR STAFF & CUSTOMERS

5: MOTIVATING OTHERS

Georgina Corscadden

Key Learning Objectives

- ☐ Understand the principles of effective motivation.
- ☐ Recognise your role in motivating others.
- ☐ Learn how to use positive motivation versus criticism.
- ☐ Appreciate the psychological contract and its applicability to work.
- ☐ Become aware of the value of equity in motivation.

Motivation is about building a repertoire of skills as a manager that can be used on a daily basis. The kernel of motivation is using the 10 key principles of motivating others. Motivating others must also take account of the psychological contract that exists in a work domain. This chapter not only explains the techniques to use, but also looks at why they are valuable and the benefits to be gained.

INTRODUCTION

Ever wondered what happened to your highly-motivated and enthusiastic new recruit? As a manager, you are the linchpin for motivation. Do you champion the individuals in your team, section or department? Do you catch them doing things right, or pride yourself on catching them out? Check, by taking a minute to answer the questions in this mini-quiz.

QUIZ

Please answer honestly "Yes" or "No" to these questions.

1. There is only one way, my way?
2. Nobody showed me, they can work it out?
3. I pay them to do the job; they should know what it is?
4. Do you pride yourself in catching them out when they get it wrong?
5. Do you think personal feelings, emotions and key life events should be dealt with by Human Resources?
6. Do you avoid any real clear communication of expectations, they should know?
7. Are you always right?
8. Do you constantly have to check up on them?
9. Do you feel you are the only one with initiative?
10. Are you the only person who seems to make decisions, can no one think for themselves?

If your answers are predominantly "Yes", then perhaps the lack of motivation in your team might be due to your management style.

THE BEGINNING

Why do most of us work? Cast your mind back to when you first received news of your current job ... It's likely you felt proud, elated, energised, excited, renewed in vigour, enthusiastic to begin, grateful for the opportunity, etc. Surely, these are qualities employers want to harness. Yet, often highly-motivated individuals become less so, if they are unable to use their knowledge, improve their skills and have the freedom and responsibility to make decisions.

Yes, most definitely we all have to earn money, but how much depends on our own internal motivation, values and life perspective. If we are honest, and money was our sole motivator, then we would all be doing different jobs. The role of motivation is much more complex than money alone. Look around at the people who work in a variety of fields where money is often distinctly lacking, yet populated by motivated individuals. This suggests there is something deeper at the heart of motivation. Why do we choose one organisation over another? The answer is ... Values.

ALIGNING THE VALUES

The core of our own motivation and of managing others means that we consciously, and subconsciously, join an organisation that to some degree aligns with our own work motivation and perspective. If an organisation doesn't know what it is trying to align in its recruitment and selection process, then the likelihood is a misfit for both the organisation and the individual, with costs to them both.

Aligning the individual and the organisation is the most successful way of sustaining motivation. The key to success is ensuring that individuals are matched to the right management style. For example, a person who wants and needs clear direction when they begin a new role may flounder if their manager delegates first, in an attempt to be developmental. The foundation blocks of motivation are clear expectations and agreeing a route map forward. The manager's role is initially to help with navigation, to build up the knowledge of using certain instruments and skills and then to delegate when these are in place, not before.

The most important step with your staff is to clarify goals and expectations. This means giving a clear way forward so that they know what to do and to what level or standard they will be measured. There is nothing more debilitating for an employee to find out that what they have been doing for the last six months is wrong. This can have lasting damage for motivation that is hard to repair and also dents the trust the employee may have had for you.

Role clarity

Clarify what is expected of the person in the role in a certain time frame. If they are new, what is the expected point they should reach in job maturity by 3 months, six months? For an experienced person, you may have different expectations, but make them clear. Do not rely on assumption, or hope that they will learn it the hard way, or allow them to be taught potentially bad habits by others. If you want to accelerate productivity, then make clear what you want from the beginning. Ensure the standards or competencies used to measure what is expected are transparent, clear and understood.

Praise & Recognition of Work

Ask any random selection of people what motivates them and you are likely to find the same points are self-selected:

- That positive reinforcement of what people do well works more than continuously finding fault
- That praise and recognition are powerful tools, not only for increasing an individual's self-esteem but also impacts on the quality of their work.

Praise and recognition creates a fertile ground for development, enabling a willingness to strive for more. This allows the manager to cultivate an environment where individuals internalise the competence of connecting and aligning to the organisation's goal and purpose.

The secret ingredient for a manager's repertoire of skills is to leverage the strengths, or as the song says:

> *"... accentuate the positive, eliminate the negative ...".*

The alternative is to be critical and notice only what does not get done – not the effort, but only the output. This loses its balance over time, as people may decide to live to the label of getting things wrong. However, more dangerous over time is that low morale is palpable! It is also contagious, lowering over time the quality and standards of what is offered. When you go into an organisation, or even talk on the phone, it is not difficult to see and experience whether the individual is motivated and attached to the importance of their job.

Poor performers are rare, as usually there is the other side of the coin ... their manager. People leave managers not organisations, as many exit interviews demonstrate. If this sounds unrealistic, then sit in on some exit interviews and listen to why people are moving jobs. Often a variety of reasons are offered, with a rising frequency for slightly more money, but the main reason is to be away from their current manager:

> *"... they dampen my energies regularly; nothing is ever good enough; he/she never notices the hundreds of things I do well, just the one I didn't do."*

I remember a manager who sent me an email on a job, with a double-handed compliment. He had congratulated me on making 99% of all my targets, but asked for 100% next time! This just diminished the hard work and effort and seemed to belittle what I had achieved. Far from motivating, it made me realise that my manager did not understand the effort that was required for what was achieved. In addition, feedback via email lost the power and impact that a face-to-face may have had; face-to-face, the request for 100% could have been presented and accepted as a joke; whereas I interpreted the tone of the email negatively.

Negative criticism as a style of managing creates a myopic view for any business. Real competitive advantage can be gained by enabling everyone to value their internal and external customers all the time. Good motivation is when you enable others to keep "hitting the high notes of service offering" by encouraging them to embrace and add value to their job daily.

Building your "goodwill bank account"

Economists say that human capital is one of the few assets that can appreciate, yet organisations systematically depreciate their human capital. Many businesses pay millions for "goodwill" embedded within an organisation and yet continue to squander currency in not cultivating all the good talents most people have to offer.

By taking time to notice what people do, they will offer a myriad more in return for recognition of their effort. Positive feedback makes us all feel good, even if, on occasion, a little embarrassed. It provides fuel and impetus to want to continue to do well; just as giving negative feedback that is not constructive lowers the desire to try harder next time.

If you take the time to notice that John has worked hard out of hours to finish a report, and that Mary postponed a personal event just to attend a crucial meeting, then you are banking goodwill. When the time comes where you need John and Mary's support, then it is easier to make a withdrawal as you have been paying dividends in by recognition. If you haven't recognised them openly, but just in your head, then you will be in the red and likely to have a section or department running on empty.

The seeds of greatness are within us all, but few are encouraged to take root and grow. How many managers treat their employees in a way that encourages presenteeism, that is, they are there in body but certainly not in spirit and attitude? This results in game-playing, with optical illusions of being there but delivering poor productivity.

PSYCHOLOGICAL CONTRACT

Maslow suggests that motivation is about a hierarchy of needs, leading to self-actualisation and that lower levels – for example, safety – must be met before another need becomes pressing.

Herzberg talks about "hygiene" factors, such as environment, as being extrinsic or external motivation. According to Herzberg, the motivators are the intrinsic or internal factors such as a sense of achievement.

Motivation has had many theorists presenting different views, but all essentially agreeing that well-motivated people are those with clearly-defined goals who take action to move towards these goals. Do you regularly communicate with your staff about their goals and the relevance and, indeed, importance to the wider organisation?

The psychological contract provides a mutual clarity of expectations of what an individual offers an organisation and *vice versa*, over and above what is contained in the formal contract between them. This offers a mutually beneficial arrangement for most people, but what are the building blocks of providing the right work environment? What is it that enables people to give of their best in an organisational context?

There is a changing environment that affects this contract, like education standards and expectations, which are different to, say, 50 years ago. There are additional legal implications now for how people are treated at work. **Figure 5.1** offers a model to map out some of the points to think about in the context of motivation and a checklist to ascertain where you might be.

FIGURE 5.1: THE PSYCHOLOGICAL CONTRACT

Psychological Safety	Role clarity	Employees know what is expected of them and have clear standards or competencies by which they are measured.
	Role support	Employees are given authority and decisions are supported by their boss. They have the right resources, materials, etc to do the job.
	Recognition	Employees are given praise for what they do and effort is noted regularly.
Meaningfulness of work	Feedback	Employees receive regular feedback on their performance and guidance and development on areas that need to improve.
	Contribution	Employees are encouraged to offer their ideas and initiatives and to know that their individual effort makes a difference.
	Achievement	Employees are encouraged to use "stretch" goals to increase their sense of achievement and maximise potential.
	Diversity	Employees are enabled to express their own personality at work and that this is safe to do so. This in turn allows potentially greater creativity, initiatives and the employee to be more committed to their work and organisation.
Organisational Style	Management style	Supportive or non-supportive.
	Culture	Competitive individualistic or group culture, blame culture or learn from mistakes and collaborative culture.
	Relationships	Accessible colleagues or competitive.

PARETO'S LAW

This asserts the 80/20 rule that 20% of the effort often gives 80% of the dividends. In the case of motivation, it's interesting to note that most people may be getting 80% right, but are encouraged or indeed convinced that the 20% that they need to work on contaminates the 80%. The successful managers motivate by focussing on the 80% and leverage the strengths to bring the other areas up, not the negatives.

But you might say, "If I give continuous feedback, then it means I am pressured to give pay rises, or that people won't take me seriously and will be suspicious of my motives?". We give positive feedback to enable people to know what it is they did well and most importantly to repeat it. Equally, giving constructive feedback, which is helpful to the other person, is grounded in fact and gives some pointers on how to improve.

FEEDBACK PROTOCOL

The feedback protocol should offer timely, positive feedback, but be counter-balanced by constructive developmental feedback. The ying and yang of feedback is to encourage the behaviours and performance you want more often by praising and recognising it when you get it.

The need to cultivate an environment allows people to build up an internal competence, or "autopilot" of getting things right. The dynamic of this works by building up trust and respect. The prize component should be equitable feedback, that is, feedback which is positive but also offers developmental constructive feedback. The simple truth of this allows people to develop and improve and repeat the good performance not poor performance.

A Cameo Scene

There are three types of performers, high, good and poor, so where do we concentrate effort? Most likely, we are hooked at the lower end as they take up the focus and attention. But it may be that these low performers are simply in the wrong department or section: a transfer, a different task, or a different manager can help some people blossom.

For example, a department manager, Brenda, was having a regular monthly meeting with her team. Well, it was regular for her, as she had been doing the job for five years. The team, however, had a different perspective as this little cameo shows.

One manager, Aisling, was very experienced and always delivered good results, though perhaps was a little bored. Her summary was always clear and in synopsis point form that suited the format of the meeting and the manager's short time to read and be updated.

A new manager, Niall, who had only a little management experience, was struggling to find time to attend the meetings, never mind prepare a summary. However, the anxiety of being newly appointed and wanting to make a good impression and give justice to the appointment meant that he had spent hours on the report, perhaps to the detriment of other tasks. Still, it was worth it. It was detailed and thorough and he was proud of it, even though it had taken up a lot of time and energy over the last few weeks. If truth be told, he was glad to be able to hand it in finished.

Another manager, Brian, was very experienced but never seemed sure when making decisions and frequently used these meetings to get closure on outstanding projects.

Scene A

Aisling handed in rather confidently her one page report. Targets were reached easily.

Department manager Brenda's reaction: Thanked her publicly and suggested that Aisling was the role model to follow. Brenda thought she was so easy to manage.

Negative motivation: This potentially could have a negative impact on the other managers by heralding publicly that Aisling was the role model to compare to, even before hearing what they had achieved. This might damage their own belief in their ability to do the job. "Targets are reached easily" might suggest that Aisling is able to give and do more.

Action to motivate: Brenda could ask Aisling to coach or mentor one of the others, depending on her other skills like communication and patience. Positive encouragement is good, but some *constructive* suggestions as to her ability not being fully used would be a more powerful way of highlighting that her *potential was greater*. Agree some *stretch goals* and review them in a suitably short time appropriate for the job – for example, three months.

Scene B

Niall gave in his 50-page report that he had expended a good deal of effort on.

Department manager Brenda's reaction: Looked in astonishment at the larger-than-life document that seemed to resemble *War and Peace* more than a management report. Brenda made a reference to Aisling's style of reporting as being more appropriate and that maybe they needed to have a talk after the meeting. This last statement suggested a threatening tone to Niall.

Negative motivation: The opportunity for "a talk, after the meeting" sent Niall into a panic (we all know that wonderful butterfly feeling in the stomach!) and now he is no longer psychologically present in the meeting as he is concerned with the meeting to follow. In addition, he feels undermined publicly and made to look foolish and now feels his fragile credibility in the new role is pretty non-existent.

Action to motivate: Brenda first could ask Niall if now is a good time to have a conversation around his *role*, allowing him time to reflect whether he needs to re-group his thoughts. Brenda could offer a *disclosure* about her first meeting that didn't go well and how devastated and low she felt. This might give some small comfort to Niall, and make him listen in a slightly more open way. Brenda could suggest that they get a coffee and come back. All the while, Brenda gently could be asking how Niall was finding the new role and his team.

Brenda should reassure Niall and clearly make the point that everyone needs time to settle in. She also should remind him why he got the promotion in the first place and reiterate how much confidence she has in his abilities. Brenda should apologise if she had made him feel uncomfortable and should suggest that they have a regular weekly meeting to help *clarify the goals* and tasks necessary. Brenda also could suggest that Niall might like to look at any *training and development* that might help him in the role. Finally, Brenda should close the meeting by *recognising* the time and effort Niall had put into the report. She also could suggest that Niall try to synopsise the key points to one page that she could review.

Scene C
Brian, looking rather embarrassed, fumbled with his notes and then said that he didn't have his report. When asked why, his reply was," You said ASAP and, so far, it just hasn't been possible. And, anyway, there are a couple of obvious projects that I need to talk to you about to finalise some points".

Department manager Brenda's reaction: Brenda had to work hard at controlling her frustration, but became agitated and started to suggest that Brian wanted her to do his job as well as her own. He was being paid to make those decisions, but was creating havoc by leaving things build up. Suppliers had now started to call her, along with other regions in the organisation, complaining.

Negative motivation: Be public with praise, of course the caveat being not if it is done in a way that undermines other's efforts. Be *private with criticism.*

Action to motivate: Brenda should apologise for "letting off steam" and should suggest they have a meeting about the urgent projects and to give more *clarity on his role*. They also should agree where Brian could have *full authority to make decisions*; if he needed a sounding board, he could talk to the other managers or indeed her, but the final decision was to rest with him. She should re-iterate that she had confidence in his experience and capabilities and knew he was *capable of achieving results*.

The reality of time pressures and deadlines affects us all. Managing others requires recognition that a blanket approach and one-size-fits-all doesn't work. In many organisations over the years, the biggest bone of contention for individuals is lack of role clarity with no feedback other than criticism. Indeed, most people would say that it is the people who don't perform that get the most attention, even if it is of a negative kind, whereas the high performers are ignored. It is assumed the high performers will always remain with little investment. Not so, everyone values recognition and it does promote growth and development.

The Inverted Pyramid of Motivating Others

Are you expected to remember all these details each time you have a dialogue with your staff? Not all perhaps, but remembering the inverted pyramid (**Figure 5.2**) might help the skills to become an unconscious internalised competence, so that you do the following in "autopilot" mode:

- **Step One:** *Role clarity and expectations* has to be the starting point. What is the role and what are the standards, competencies expected and how are these measured?
- **Step Two:** *Recognition.* Tell them what they are doing well, celebrate it, announce it, be public with praise and private with criticism. This is laying the foundation for any feedback to be heard, the positive and the constructive. It will also, if done well, create a platform of people wanting to do well for you, simply because you take the time to notice.
- **Step Three:** *Feedback protocol* is about using positive feedback and constructive, then positive again. Remember the key is about using constructive feedback that centres on the behaviour or skill not the person. Constructive feedback has to be more than just *what* needs changing and include some suggestions on *how*. Make sure the constructive feedback is grounded in fact, evidence and observation, not hearsay.

Figure 5.2: The Inverted Pyramid of Motivating Others

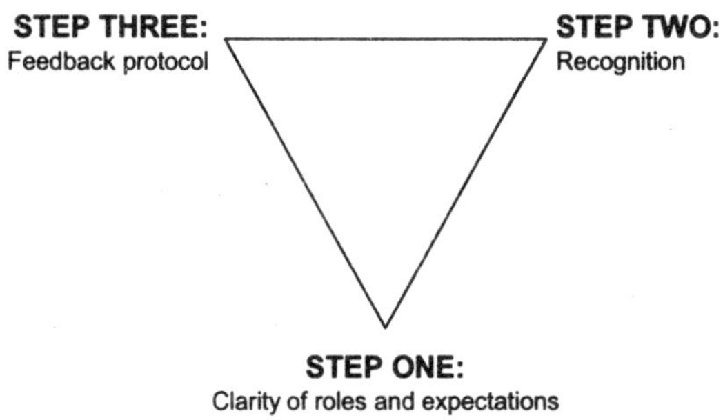

PARABLES, STORIES & FABLES!

Many centuries passed before Napoleon's secret emerged, that his men would die (or, at least, risk death) for ribbons! Not extra rations, or money, but strips of coloured cloth that symbolised they were noticed – by Napoleon. As a result, it was said that, in battle, having Napoleon on the field was the equivalent of having 25,000 extra men.

When you walk around your organisation do you lift the spirit level to inspire even greater energy or mistakes! Do you dampen the spirits significantly that no one is capable of producing more, as they are concentrating their energies on staying out of your way, or having endless destructive conversations as to your management style. No organisation can afford this reduced minimal competitive advantage if the energy is not focussed towards the customer, but towards managing emotions about the boss!

Parable: Effort = Performance = Reward & Equity

A long time ago, a farmer saddled six donkeys to a heavy hay wagon to be taken up a steep hill. Two of the donkeys were not achievement-orientated and decided to just drift along and let others do most of the work (management diminish all performers if this is left to happen). Two others were relatively young and inexperienced and had never had any induction training or clear description of what a donkey was supposed to do (they should know!). Therefore, they had a hard time pulling their share. One of the others suffered from a slight hangover from consuming fermented barley the night before. The sixth donkey did most of the work, because delegating a task to a busy donkey means it always gets done!

The hay wagon arrived, finally, at the top of the hill. The farmer got down from her seat, patted each of the donkeys equally on the head and gave the proverbial six carrots (not sticks) to each donkey.

On the next hill climb, the sixth donkey ran away!

This story is about equity: if one person underperforms, and the manager doesn't ask why, the result is simple – the sixth donkey, or the people who are carrying the workload, will

- Leave and find another employer who will value them more, or worse
- Stay but will down-gear, creating a bigger problem as your high performers now become underperformers

The key principles for motivating others are presented in **Figure 5.3.**

Remember to be human. We all make mistakes, but the value is in what was learned. Ask "Why?" first, followed closely by "What have you learned?", and "What can we do to remedy the situation?". Then look to the future to prevent further issues.

FIGURE 5.3: TEN PRINCIPLES OF MOTIVATING OTHERS

	Key Principles	Tips for Motivating Others
1.	**Clarity of Goals**	Clarity of goals and expectations is cited as the most important factor in being able to do any job well. Clarity takes time to communicate, so ensure a regular dialogue to ensure clear objectives and agreed route map. Don't leave people floundering.
2.	**Recognition**	Recognition is crucial to continued motivation, if you don't recognise you jeopardise future performance. If you don't recognise effort then people may interpret that you are not interested, or even worse don't even know the effort put in. If you don't pay attention and recognise effort, then effort will simply diminish.
3.	**Feedback**	**F**ollow through on commitments, promises, especially on delegation and be flexible. **E**ncourage and champion people to be capable of more. **E**quitable in your feedback, people expect to hear what they have done well and also want to know what they can improve upon. **D**irect and guide towards the goals and route map for success. **B**elieve in others and continually tell them you have confidence in them. **A**cknowledge their strengths and leverage this potential versus what they haven't done. **C**elebrate their successes, be public with praise and private with criticism. **K**ernel is to utilise the feedback protocol, which should be timely, positive, constructive, and close on a positive.
4.	**Value Individuals**	The Pygmalion effect: A well-known experiment with children at school resulted in them achieving higher grades when their teacher believed in them to succeed. The moral of the story is that motivation and subsequently performance increases when an individual is made to feel valuable. Treating people with dignity, importance and worth increases self-esteem. Make your team feel important and imbued with a 'can do attitude', resulting in a continuous positive outcome

	Key Principles	Tips for Motivating Others
5.	D ... is for Delegate, not Dump!	Delegate the full responsibility of a task and real authority. This doesn't mean abdication or abandonment, but developing the decision-making skills of your team. Delegation takes time initially but pays dividends, not just in the task, but in developing high performers and allowing you time to manage
6.	Tools & Resources	What do you need to give to get excellent performance? What are the tools of the trade? How can you help your staff navigate forward and what is the route map and compass? Do they need training, time, or other resources to ensure success?
7.	Contribution	Cultivate a culture that encourages people to contribute and be involved. Allow ownership of projects large or small. Feeling important motivates, so ask for opinions and ideas and listen to them. Give credit whenever you use someone's idea or suggestion.
8.	Positive Attitude	Positive thoughts motivate. Catch people doing things well and tell them. Don't wait to catch them doing something wrong.
9.	Allow mistakes	Allow a culture that accepts mistakes happen, but insist on, and encourage, learning.
10.	Raise expectations	Develop the standard of expecting the best from others and you may get your wish! Champion your staff and they may surprise you.

SUMMARY

Good motivators encourage people to retain the vitality and enthusiasm they first brought to the job. They give direction, support and enable staff, so they can meet their objectives. They focus on three key themes of valuing the individual, agreeing clarity of goals and giving continuous positive and constructive feedback.

Rudyard Kipling's sentiments have often been used as an analogy for good management:

"I kept six honest serving men, they taught me all I knew – their names where What, Why, When, How, Where and Who."

In terms of motivation, it could be changed to:

"I have six honest serving men, they taught me what to do – to value people, give feedback, recognition, praise, set goals, and give clarity of what and when."

If you want to build up the structural capital of your people, then accentuate the positive and give continuous feedback.

CHECKLIST

Do:

- ☐ Value the individual.
- ☐ Clarify goals, expectations and standards to be measured.
- ☐ Agree a route map forward of objectives within a timescale.
- ☐ Give responsibility and authority.
- ☐ Be consistent.
- ☐ Delegate 'real' authority.
- ☐ Acknowledge achievement and effort.
- ☐ Communicate regularly and clearly.
- ☐ Allow mistakes but insist on learning.
- ☐ Encourage initiative and contribution.
- ☐ Use a feedback protocol.
- ☐ Be accessible, non-judgemental.
- ☐ Use challenge and stretch goals.
- ☐ Celebrate the positive, savour success.
- ☐ Raise your expectations.
- ☐ Ask for help in problem-solving.

Don't:

- ☐ Use a blanket approach and one-size-fits-all.
- ☐ Leave them to work it out for themselves. This is highly unproductive and may result in people becoming demotivated or leaving.
- ☐ Leave employees floundering.
- ☐ Over-ride decisions unless crucial.
- ☐ Be inconsistent in behaviour, expectations or standards.
- ☐ Use delegation to dump the jobs you don't like. It is not about abdicating responsibility. D in Delegation is for development.
- ☐ Diminish this by not noticing.
- ☐ Use throw-away or ill-thought-out comments.
- ☐ Tolerate mistakes and create a blaming culture.
- ☐ Jump to conclusions, listen.
- ☐ Criticise.
- ☐ Humiliate, bully or use aggression.
- ☐ Tell, but agree goals with them.
- ☐ Take it for granted and move to next task.
- ☐ Expect poor performance.
- ☐ Give the benefit of your wisdom by solving others problems for them all the time and don't pretend you have all the answers.

REFERENCES & FURTHER READING

ADL Associates (2003). *Back to Basics, Tried and True Solutions for Today's Leaders*

Smithson, K. and Sikanas, D. (1998). *Priceless Motivation; Quick Tips to Excite and Inspire Your Most Valuable Asset –People,* Grand Rapids, MI: Baudville Inc.

Sproul, R. C. (1999). *Stronger than Steel,* San Francisco: HarperCollins.

Thomas, K. (2003). *Intrinsic Motivation at Work – Building Energy and Commitment,* New York: Berrett-Koehler Publishers Inc.

Younggren, L. and Sikanas, D (2000). *The Joy of Recognition – Designing and Implementing Successful Recognition Programmes,* Grand Rapids, MI: Baudville Inc.

6: BUILDING EFFECTIVE TEAMS

John Power

Key Learning Objectives

- ☐ Understand why teams fail.
- ☐ Know the five stages of group development.
- ☐ Identify key components of teams.
- ☐ Resolve team conflict.
- ☐ Lead teams effectively.

Teams can be defined as working arrangements that bring together a number of individual employees with the purpose of working collaboratively to achieve a shared goal. In fact, teams are considered to be able to achieve a higher level of performance than individuals working alone. However, for many managers and employees, much mystery surrounds what actually needs to be done to drive a team to this higher level of performance. The purpose of this chapter is to demystify some of the confusion that frequently surrounds the use of teams.

Why Do Teams Fail?

Although the idea of teamwork sounds like a great way to achieve goals in theory, the reality can be a different story – fractured working relationships, conflict, frustration, poor results etc.

So rather than beginning this chapter with advice on how to make teams work, it may be better to first gain an understanding of why teams fail.

The main problems that can lead to poor teamwork and their associated causes are listed in **Figure 6.1**.

The causes of the problems listed can be cured. However, it is important to realise that in many cases, if you do not immediately address a problem when it first occurs, it can quickly spread into other problems and the situation rapidly worsens. The case study on page 104 illustrates this point.

Figure 6.1: Problems & Causes that can Lead to Poor Teamwork

Problem	Cause
Weak vision	Leadership is unclear what it wants the team to achieve.
No team culture	The organisation is not committed to, or ready for, the concept of teams.
Mismatched needs	Team members have their own private agendas.
Confused goals	Team members do not know what they are supposed to do.
Wrong tools	No training, or appropriate facilities, have been provided to team members.
Poor feedback	Poor communication from management and no consideration of team performance.
Unresolved roles	Members are confused as to what it is they are to do.
Poor policies & procedures	Lack of thought put into the team manual/handbook.
Poorly-designed rewards	The team is not rewarded for team performance.
Lack of trust	Members will not commit to the team because they do not trust each other.
Unwillingness to change	The team is stuck in past methods of working.
Personality conflicts	Team members do not get along.

Source: Adapted from Robbins & Finlay, 1998.

Case Study

Widget Plc brought together a number of their functional managers to review the performance of the organisation. At their initial meeting, they decided their mission was to find and implement process improvements in their organisation. At first glance, it appeared that they had a good mix of talents.

The project team comprised of:

- The Production Manager
- The Marketing Manager
- The Finance Director
- The Human Resources Manager
- A senior engineer from the research and development department
- Other team members, including employee representatives.

At face value, this team composition appeared to be ideal. They were multi-disciplined and had diverse backgrounds. Resources were supplied and a project leader was appointed and given the team's mandate of "improving organisational performance at Widget Plc.".

However, the team began experiencing difficulties immediately. Disagreements broke out at their fortnightly team meetings with regard to which issues were most important. Quite often, these disagreements were unresolved and meetings ran on for hours, without any concrete decision being made. As a result, the members of the team were unsure as to what they had to do on a daily basis. This fractious behaviour continued for two years, until eventually one by one the team members became increasingly frustrated and uncooperative, causing senior management to order the dissolution of the team.

In hindsight, we can see in the case above that the team was doomed from the start. Initially, they failed to set any specific goals and objectives. As a result, team members put forward their own idea of what was necessary to "improve organisational performance at Widget Plc.". This eventually resulted in conflict and disagreements that were not resolved. This spiralled into a situation where people developed their own agendas and did not trust other team members. Poor communications existed between team members and their fortnightly meetings were ineffective and tiring. This ultimately led to the dissolution of the team.

What is a Team?

Many different definitions of the team concept exist. Therefore, rather than defining a team, it is better to describe some of the key concepts associated with the use of teams:

- The primary reasoning that supports the use of teams in the workplace is that teams generally outperform people working on their own
- Modern work environments generate complex problems that can only be solved through using a wide variety of skills
- Teams with members possessing different skills offer a logical method of dealing with such problems
- Teams consist of a number of people who rely on each other to achieve their mutual goals
- Team members develop a better understanding of organisational issues than individual employees working alone
- Teams bring about a sense of belonging, trust and acceptance amongst employees.

Are teams and groups the same?

Many people consider groups and teams to be pretty much the same thing. I can recall a recent conversation during which a work colleague commented to me *"... you and your team did a good job there!"*.

Naturally, I (modestly) accepted and acknowledged her praise but, on reflection, I realised her description of what had happened was inaccurate. Although she was correct in that I, and a number of my fellow workmates, had been successful in achieving some targets – we did not do so as a team!

In fact, we rarely even worked together and had only officially met together three times in the previous eight months. When I reflected on the situation more, I realised that, in many ways, we had not been as efficient as we could have been. We had duplicated each other's effort; had failed to communicate with each other on a regular basis, and had worked essentially as individuals while trying to achieve a group goal.

The situation described above highlights the common misperception that teams and groups are the same thing. The primary difference between the two is that ***teams deliver extra performance***. To avoid any misunderstanding, the key differences between teams and groups are highlighted in **Figure 6.2**.

FIGURE 6.2: GROUPS *VERSUS* TEAMS

Groups	**Teams**
Have a strong, focussed leader.	Have shared leadership roles.
Members are individually accountable.	Members are mutually accountable.
Run efficient meetings.	Encourage discussion and problem-solving.
Have individual work-products.	Have collective work-products.
Measure performance by its influence on others.	Measure performance by assessing collective work-products.

Source: Adapted from Katzenbach and Smith, 1986.

To summarise, a team consists of a **number of employees** who work together in a **highly collaborative way** to achieve **shared goals**.

TEAM ROLES

Due to the fact that teams involve people with different aptitudes working together, managers must understand that the central part of ***team management*** involves linking these different aptitudes together. So, what is meant by linking?

Linking involves leadership, decision-making, and communication skills that can only be learned by experience and practice. These skills are the glue that holds a team of disparate individuals together. Each of these individuals is likely to fulfil a different role in the team. For example, a marketing employee may fulfil a more creative role, whilst an accountant may perform a more analytical role. These may sound like stereotypes but a number of common roles have been found to occur in effective teams.

Margerison-McCann (1990) developed the Team Management Wheel (**Figure 6.3**) to illustrate the different roles involved in teamwork.

FIGURE 6.3: TEAM MANAGEMENT SYSTEMS

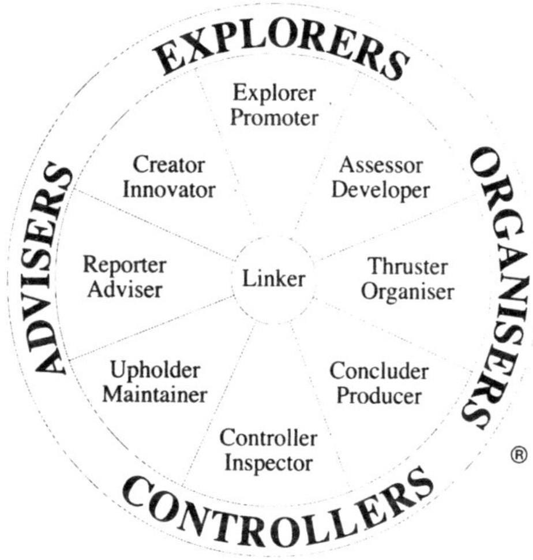

The roles are:

- **Reporter-Advisers:** Prefer to operate in a beliefs-oriented and flexible way. They may also be introvert and creative, or extrovert and practical. Reporter-Advisers are good at generating information and gathering it together so that it can be understood. They are usually patient and are prepared to delay decisions until they know as much as they can. To others, they may seem indecisive. The Reporter-Adviser, however, thinks it is better to be accurate than to put forward advice that may later prove wrong. They are important support members of the team, but are unlikely to have a strong preference for organising. Their concern is to make sure the job is done correctly and that all the relevant information is available

- **Creator-Innovators:** Prefer a creative and flexible role. They may be either extrovert and beliefs-oriented, or introvert and analytical. Creator-Innovators have ideas that may contradict and upset the existing way of doing things. They can be very independent, wishing to experiment regardless of the current system and methods. It may be best to let them pursue their ideas without disrupting the present way of working until their new approaches have been proven. Many organisations set up R&D units to allow people with ideas the chance to see if they can make them work
- **Explorer-Promoters:** Prefer a creative and extrovert approach. They may be either analytical and flexible, or beliefs-oriented and structured. Explorer-Promoters are usually excellent at taking up an idea, getting people enthusiastic about it, and pushing ideas forward. They will find out what is happening inside and outside the organisation and compare new ideas with what is being done elsewhere. They are good at bringing back contacts, information and resources which can help move innovations forward. They are not always good at organising things or controlling details, but will see the wider picture
- **Assessor-Developers:** Prefer an extrovert and analytical approach. They may be either creative and structured, or practical and flexible. Assessor-Developers will look at how to make ideas work in practice. They are concerned with seeing if there is a place for innovation in the market, and they will test ideas against practical criteria. Very often, they will produce a prototype or conduct client research. Their interest is in taking innovation to the next stage and when they have done this, they will probably be less interested in producing things on a regular basis. They will prefer to move on to the next project
- **Thruster-Organisers:** Prefer an analytical and structured approach. They may be either practical and extrovert, or introvert and creative. Thruster-Organisers like getting things done and may be impatient. They will set up procedures and systems to turn ideas into working reality. They like to establish clear objectives and ensure that everyone knows what

is expected of them. They will push people and systems to meet deadlines

- **Concluder-Producers:** Prefer a practical and structured approach. They may be either introvert and analytical, or extrovert and beliefs-oriented. Concluder-Producers place emphasis on producing a product or service to a standard. They will do this on a regular basis and feel that their work is fulfilled if plans are met. They like procedures and doing things systematically. They prefer to perfect their existing skills rather than continually changing and learning new ways of doing things
- **Controller-Inspectors:** Prefer an introverted and practical approach. They may be either beliefs-oriented and structured, or analytical and flexible. Controller-Inspectors enjoy detailed work and make sure that the facts and figures are correct. They are careful and meticulous. They can concentrate for long periods of time on one task, and like to do things in depth to make sure that things are done according to plan in an accurate way. This can be very valuable in auditing, contractual work and quality control
- **Upholder-Maintainers:** Prefer an introverted and beliefs-oriented approach. They may be either practical and flexible, or creative and structured. Upholder-Maintainers can be good at ensuring the team has a sound basis for operations. They take pride in maintaining both the physical and social side of work. They may be the conscience of the team and provide support for team members. They often have strong views on how the team should be run, based on their beliefs. When upset, they can be determined in defending their interests. They can also be a tremendous source of strength and energy and often make excellent negotiators.

As you can see from these descriptions, many of the roles have complementary attributes that, when combined, make for an effective team. For example, Creator-Innovators are supported by Explorer-Promoters, who in turn are supported by Thruster-

Organisers and so on. The key to successful teams lies in getting these different roles to support each other. Effective leadership is crucial to this task.

EFFECTIVE LEADERSHIP IN TEAMS

There are three key elements to leading teams effectively. As a leader, you need to:

- Facilitate team development
- Free the potential of each team member
- Inspire the team to achieve its goals.

Facilitating team development

It is important that the team leader does not confuse his/her role as team leader. Sometimes, team leaders feel they need to be involved in every team activity and thus they stifle the creativity of team members. At an early stage, they should clearly communicate that it is the team effort that counts and that they are present in a coaching/mentoring capacity rather than in a supervisory capacity. It is their responsibility to develop the team and ensure that it quickly becomes a cohesive unit that generates high performance.

At this stage, the leader should:

- Establish a common vision for the team
- Communicate the team action plan
- Clarify individual roles and objectives
- Gain commitment to plans and strategies
- Build trust between team members.

Free the potential of each team member

Once the team members are clear as to what they have to achieve, it is then up to the team leader to understand the potential of each team member. By recognising the attributes each member brings to the team, the manager can understand how these different attributes can be combined to obtain maximum performance.

To free the potential of individuals, you need to remove organisational and personal barriers to performance. Removing organisational barriers requires genuine empowerment – encouraging risk-taking and entrepreneurship within a no-blame culture. In order to remove personal barriers, the leader needs to:

- Work with team members to develop aspirational goals
- Coach and develop individuals, focusing on their positive potential
- Be a role model in everything they do.

Inspire the team to achieve its goals

Professor Lynda Gratton of the London Business School comments that *"inspirational leaders capture hearts, minds and souls".*[5]

Inspirational leadership is a combination of vision and trust. Great leaders have the capacity to convey a vision that their people want to belong to and the integrity to capture their commitment to achieving it. Nobody can be a leader without followers and nobody will follow a leader they don't trust. With trust comes the potential to inspire people to achieve your vision.

In order to inspire or motivate team members to achieve the highest levels of performance, leaders must be adept at identifying and solving problems at the earliest opportunity. If a leader fails to deal effectively with problems that their team's members have identified, then they run the risk of causing frustration and conflict in the team.

General Colin Powell has been quoted as saying that:

> *"The day soldiers stop bringing you their problems is the day you have stopped leading them. They have either lost confidence that you can help them or concluded that you do not care. Either case is a failure of leadership."*[6]

---

[5] Source: http://www.inpharm.com/static/intelligence/pdf/MAG_7300.pdf.

[6] Source: http://www.govleaders.org/powell.htm, Harari, 1996.

This sentiment is equally relevant to effective team leadership. Team members must be confident in your ability to help them achieve their goals. It must be reinforced by the provision of continuous feedback as to how they are progressing.

Feedback to team members serves a dual purpose:

- First, it acknowledges the hard work of the team
- Second, it reinforces the goals the team are trying to achieve and prevents team members from deviating from them.

Finally, it is essential that, once a team achieves its goals, they must be rewarded as a team. There is nothing more disheartening to a team than if their leader takes all the credit for their hard work. Rewards should reflect the collaborative effort that the team has put into their work activities.

MANAGING CONFLICT IN TEAMS

Conflict is a natural part of the process of working in teams. By their nature, teams bring together a number of people with different skills from diverse backgrounds and throw them into a process where their ideas, attitudes and opinions will be challenged. Sometimes, managers who enter a team situation are left dismayed when a process, designed to improve inter-organisational communications, degenerates into conflict. Therefore, it is crucial that team members have the capacity to resolve conflicts when they occur.

There are a number of typical managerial responses to handling conflict:

- **Denial/withdrawal:** Sweeping the conflict under the carpet
- **Suppression:** Smoothing conflict over, by preserving working relationships despite minor conflicts
- **Dominance:** Using power to resolve the conflict
- **Compromise:** Bargaining, negotiating, conciliating, etc.
- **Integration/collaboration:** Where emphasis is put on the task, individuals must modify their behaviour for its sake, and group effort is seen as superior to individual effort.

An integrative/collaborative approach to conflict resolution is seen as the ideal way to handle disagreements in teams. Conflicts cannot be left to fester, but must be handled immediately. A "10-step approach" to handling conflicts is outlined in **Figure 6.4**.

FIGURE 6.4: THE TEN-STEP APPROACH TO CONFLICT RESOLUTION

1	Present the issue objectively – this involves describing the conflict in such a way so as to appear "neutral" to both opposing sides.
2	Actively listen to the other party's view – if a participant to a conflict feels they are not being listened to, they are likely to become unco-operative. Therefore, it is essential that you listen, and try to understand, where the other party "is coming from".
3	Explain your viewpoint – this involves presenting your opinions in a non-judgmental way. Try to avoid using phrases that allocate blame to the other party – "What you should be doing is ..." or "What you cannot understand is ...".
4	Clarify the issue in terms of both sets of needs – ensure that all parties to the conflict understand what the conflict is really about.
5	Develop objectives through collaboration – work together to identify areas that must be tackled in order for the conflict to be resolved.
6	Brainstorm possible alternative solutions – remember to take on board all proposed solutions.
7	Select the best solution for both sides.
8	Develop a realistic plan of action to resolve the conflict.
9	Implement the plan.
10	Evaluate success based on the needs of both parties and revise if necessary.

Source: Adapted from *Organisation Management and Development*, 1998.

It is clear from the steps that a collaborative approach is needed. By encouraging people to understand their differences, it is possible for them to see how alike they really are. Quite often, conflicts escalate because the parties involved refuse to acknowledge that there may be a valid contrary viewpoint.

The key to resolving conflicts in teams is to gain consensus on what the team wants to achieve, and then identify the ways in which conflict between team members prevents the team from achieving its goals. By keeping the goals of the team foremost in everyone's minds, the team becomes more focused on positive, progressive activities rather than on harmful disagreements or conflicts.

When developing the use of teams in an organisation, it is important to realise that any incidence of conflict between different teams is handled appropriately. Glenn Parker, co-author of *Team Workout*, says:

> *"It's not uncommon for a company to have two teams which seem to be at odds with each other".*

The reasons why conflict can arise between teams include:

- There is a dispute over resource allocation decisions
- One team relies on another team's output to carry out their task effectively – for example, a production team may need an indication of expected customer orders from a sales team in order to develop effective production scheduling
- Competitive rivalry can result in jealousy and conflict
- One team is deemed to have an easier task than another team.

Parker and Kropp (2001) identify nine ways to handle *inter-team* conflict:

1. Get teams to agree to come together to resolve the problem – at the beginning of the session, explain that the purpose is to resolve the problem, and make sure to set some positive norms for the session, such as agreeing to listen to each other, not interrupting, and to keep the focus on the issues
2. Ask one team to move to another room. Give each team a few sheets of flip-chart paper and ask them to prepare a list of answers, in about 20 to 30 minutes, to the following questions:
   a) What does the other team do that inhibits our ability to get our job done?

b) What do we do that inhibits the other team's ability to get its job done?
3. Team members reassemble together and post their flip-charts on the wall
4. Team members are encouraged to ask questions for clarification of the items on the flip-charts
5. Identify key issues standing in the way of effective inter-group teamwork. If there are a lot of issues, make sure to rank them in order of importance
6. Subgroups composed of members from each team form to develop action plans for each issue – write each issue on a separate sheet of flip-chart paper and post them around the room. Make sure that each subgroup contains a reasonably equal number of people from each team, and that the groups are not too large – perhaps a maximum of six people
7. Subgroups are asked to come up with a problem statement that includes causes of the problem, and an action plan, including responsibilities and a timetable
8. Each subgroup presents on its plan. The other subgroups react
9. Conclude with a summary, debriefing and a review of the next steps based on the action plans.

This procedure is similar to the "10-Step Approach" outlined in **Figure 6.4**. However, one of the important keys to effective team performance is highlighted in this process. Co-operation, and communication, amongst members of different teams can be improved by forcing members from different teams to work together to solve issues that they have raised.

STAGES OF TEAM DEVELOPMENT

Tuckman (1965) identified a number of stages of development that teams go through (see **Figure 6.5**).

Initially the team goes through a **forming** stage, during which the team members are introduced to each other. The goal that the team is trying to achieve is also clarified at this stage.

Figure 6.5: The Stages of Group Development I

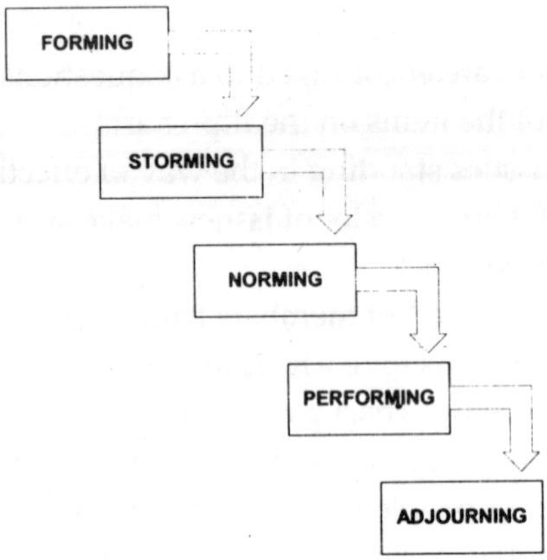

Source: Tuckman (1965).

Then the team progresses through a **storming** stage, where team members have conflicting ideas as to how their objective should be achieved and what pattern of behaviour the team should adopt.

This conflict is resolved during the **norming** stage, where a pattern of cohesive team behaviour emerges. Norms are established either formally or informally and conflict lessens with disagreements taking the form of constructive criticism.

As the norms the team have established become widely accepted, the bond between the members will strengthen. This provides the team process with the momentum it needs to begin **performing** and making steady progress towards its goals.

Finally, the team achieves its objectives and the time has come for the team to **adjourn**. Often, team members will form informal relationships with each other that stretch beyond the life span of the team. This is even more likely to occur if the team has experienced success.

Figure 6.6 clarifies the behaviour and feelings exhibited by team members at each stage of team development.

FIGURE 6.6: STAGES OF GROUP DEVELOPMENT 2

	STAGE	FEELINGS	BEHAVIOURS
1	**Orientation (Forming)**	Excitement, anticipation, suspicion, fear anxiety.	Define task and group behaviour, complaints.
2	**Redefinition (Storming)**	Resistance, negativity, questioning team potential.	Arguing, defensiveness, tension, distrust, disunity.
3	**Co-ordination (Norming)**	Acceptance, constructive criticism, relief.	Conflict avoidance, trust, unity.
4	**Formalisation (Performing)**	Personal insights, attachment, satisfaction.	Positive self-image, problem-solving, success.
5	**Termination (Adjourning)**	Sense of loss, reflection.	Informal networks, confidence.

Source: Adapted from Tuckman (1965).

Again, it is the responsibility of the team leader to ease the transition of the team from one stage to the next. By recognising the feelings and behaviours that can occur at each stage, team leaders can be prepared to facilitate the team members' progression from their initial coming together to their eventual performance of their desired task and eventual adjournment. The ultimate goal is to create a high-performing team – one that achieves its goals with the most efficient usage of resources.

HIGH-PERFORMING TEAMS

Wheelan (1999) identifies the following characteristics of high-performing teams (HPTs):

- **Goals:** Team members should be clear about what they have to achieve and also should agree that their goal is reasonable and attainable

- **Roles:** The selection of team members is crucial. Firstly, each member of the team must be clear about the role he/she is being asked to play. Secondly, the member must have the ability and skills to accomplish their assigned task. Finally, each member must agree with and accept that role assignment
- **Interdependence:** HPTs require team members to work together as a unit, and in subgroups. Team members will rely on each other at different times to accomplish different tasks
- **Leadership:** The team leader's style should be adapted to the needs of the team. For example, it will be more directive in the forming stage, and become more consultative in the later stages of team development
- **Communication and feedback:** HPTs have an open communication structure that allows all members to participate in team discussion. Regular feedback is provided both to team members, and to the team as a whole, regarding their performance. This allows the team to become self-regulating and continuously improving
- **Discussion, decision-making and planning:** HPTs spend time planning how they will solve problems and make decisions. This enables their decision-making strategy to be more effective as it has already met with member approval
- **Implementation and evaluation:** High performance teams follow through and implement the solutions and decisions made by team members. Team members should also hold each other accountable for acting on those decisions
- **Norms and individual differences:** Successful teams encourage norms that encourage high performance, quality and achievement. These teams usually have norms that encourage creativity and innovation. Members are permitted to differ from team norms as long as their behaviour is perceived as helpful to task accomplishment
- **Team structure:** HPTs usually contain the smallest number of people necessary to achieve their task. The team usually works in sub-groups to accomplish different parts of the task. It is important that these sub-groups are valued and accepted for

their contribution to the team. Both the team and its sub-groups must be given sufficient time to accomplish their task
- **Co-operation and conflict management:** HPTs tend to be highly cohesive and contain cooperative members. Also high performance teams manage conflict well. Usually they have frequent, but brief, periods of conflict that tend to be creative and proactive.

The Margerison-McCann High Energy Teams Model (TMS Development International Ltd, 2004) is shown in **Figure 6.7**. It can be used to prepare a team action plan by answering the following questions:
- **Who are we?** What values do we hold dear? What values do we aspire to?
- **Where are we now?** What is our current situation?
- **Where are we going?** What do we want to achieve? What is our team goal?
- **How will we get there?** What is our planned strategy? What do we have to do?
- **What is expected of us?** What performance is necessary? What behaviours do we have to adopt?
- **What support do we need?** What help/resources are out there? Are they readily available?
- **How effective are we?** How will we measure performance? Are we up to scratch?
- **What recognition do we get?** What form will these take? Will we be rewarded as a group?

FIGURE 6.7: THE HIGH ENERGY TEAMS MODEL

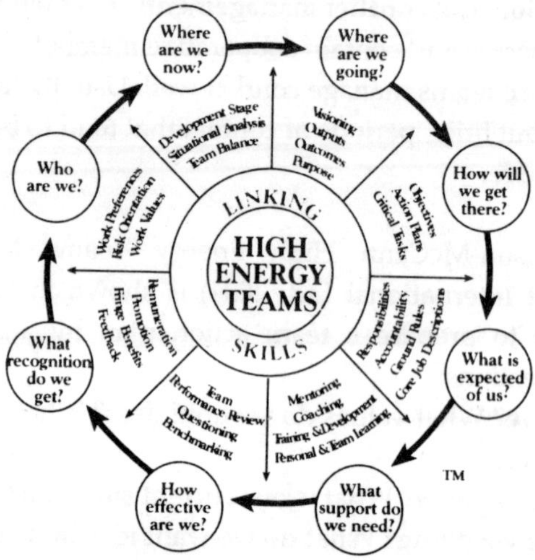

By spending the time necessary to produce clear, and agreed, answers to the above questions at the beginning of the process, much time can be saved later on because everyone will be "singing from the same hymn sheet".

PROVIDING ACCURATE FEEDBACK

The provision of accurate feedback is the key to achieving higher levels of team performance. Nothing is more de-motivating than spending time on a team exercise, only to receive no feedback regarding your performance. It is important to realise that feedback is not only given at the end of the team project. Feedback should be provided at all stages of the implementation of the team action plan and should flow freely and openly from one team member to the next. Some guidelines for giving, and receiving feedback are shown in **Figure 6.8**.

Figure 6.8: Guidelines for Giving & Receiving Feedback

Giving

1. Offer your feedback as information, and check that the receiver wishes to receive it.
2. Be descriptive rather than judgmental, or critical.
3. Describe the person's behaviour not personality.
4. Ensure balance by giving positive and negative feedback.
5. Give feedback at the time the behaviour occurs, not ages later.
6. Deal with aspects of behaviour that can be changed.
7. Offer only as much as you think will be useful at the time, do not overload.
8. Give the receiver an opportunity to clarify what has been said.

Receiving

1. Accept feedback when it is given in a spirit of cooperation.
2. Listen actively to what is said.
3. Ask for clarification if you do not fully understand feedback.
4. Avoid arguing, denying or justifying.
5. Thank the giver, and reflect on the information you have received.
6. Check out the accuracy of the feedback with others.
7. Decide (a) whether you want to do something about it and (b) what you will do.

Within high performing teams, this type of proactive feedback helps both individual, and team performance. The process of effective team communications can be illustrated through a model called the Johari Window (**Figure 6.9**).

The Johari Window model helps us realise our degree of self-awareness and gives us direction to explore how we might increase this awareness. The Arena quadrant of the window contains all information that is known by both you, and your colleagues in the team. The idea of using the model is to increase the amount of information in this quadrant.

FIGURE 6.9: THE JOHARI WINDOW

		SELF	
		Known	Unknown
OTHERS	Known	ARENA	BLIND-SPOT
	Unknown	FAÇADE	UNKNOWN

Source: Originally developed by Luft and Ingham.

For example, if you ask for feedback from your fellow team members, the Blind Spot might decrease as the Arena area increases. If you disclose information about yourself, the Facade area will decrease and feed into the Arena area. The idea is that the Arena area is the biggest area. The others decrease as you go on and, as a result, you will become aware of aspects of the Unknown area that you can then feed into the Arena area.

This can be a useful exercise to carry out at the forming stage of team development, as it increases the team's awareness of individual members' strengths and weaknesses. It can also be a good exercise to revisit during the life of the team, as it can clarify the team's situation whilst also illustrating the team's progression towards a more cohesive unit.

CONCLUSION

Teams can offer organisations a highly productive way of achieving goals. However, for teams to be successful, much depends on developing, and sustaining, proactive team dynamics. This can only be achieved if team members feel that they are part of the team and that being part of the team will be of benefit to them. The management of the team environment will be crucial in this regard: the right facilities, supports such as training, interpersonal skills and management attitude must be present if teams are to be effective.

CHECKLIST

- ☐ I understand why teams sometimes fail?
- ☐ I can identify the central characteristics of teams?
- ☐ I understand the differences between teams and groups?
- ☐ I can identify different roles that members play in teamwork?
- ☐ I understand the importance of effective leadership to team success?
- ☐ I understand the importance of managing conflict in the team process?
- ☐ I understand the different stages of group/team development?
- ☐ I can identify the characteristics of high-performing teams?
- ☐ I understand the importance of providing feedback to team members?

REFERENCES

Anon. (1998). *Organisation Management and Development*, London: BPP Publishing.

Katzenbach, J. R. and Smith, D. K. (1986). *The Wisdom of Teams*, Boston: Harvard Business Review Press.

Luft, J. (1969). *Of Human Interaction*, Palo Alto, CA: National Press.

Margerison, C. and McCann, D. (1990). *Team Management Wheel*, TMS Development International Ltd.

Margerison, C. and McCann, D. (2004). *High Energy Teams Model*, TMS Development International Ltd.

Parker, G. and Kropp, R. (2001). *Team Workout: A Trainer's Sourcebook of 50 Team-building Games and Activities*, New York: Amacom Publications.

Robbins, H. & Finlay, M. (1998). *Why Teams Don't Work*, London: Orion Business Publishing.

Tuckman, B. W. (1965). Developmental Sequence in Small Groups, *Psychological Bulletin*, vol. 63.

Wheelan, S. (1999). *Creating Effective Teams*, London: Sage Publications.

7: NEGOTIATING EFFECTIVELY

Kevin Davey

Key Learning Objectives

- ☐ Understand the term negotiation.
- ☐ Learn the five phases of negotiation.
- ☐ Adopt the 10 keys for planning a negotiation.
- ☐ Acknowledge the six principles of negotiation.

A better understanding of ourselves allows us to communicate better with others. Negotiating is about achieving the best possible outcomes for each party. This depends on the parties involved and the needs of both at the time of the transaction.

WHAT IS NEGOTIATION?

"Getting people with differing views to reach consensus!"

Negotiations are part of our every day lives, whether we like it or not. From the moment we throw the rattle out of the pram, we are negotiating. Every day, we are required to negotiate either personally or professionally – trying to agree on the price of a car or a house, or where you and your partner are going for dinner or on holiday. As children, we often tried to negotiate with parents *vis-à-vis* our bedtime or the time we were due home from a party or a night out. In business, we often negotiate around an increase in salary or in the case of acquisitions or mergers.

Negotiations and concessions are an integral part of our everyday lives, therefore the better we understand the skills and techniques, the greater our chances are of getting what it is we want. By reading this chapter, you will learn the five stages of negotiation and a number of skills and techniques, which will assist you in future negotiations.

The five phases of negotiation

1. Preparation and planning
2. Opening
3. Proposing
4. Bargaining
5. Closing.

PHASE 1: PREPARATION & PLANNING

As with any project, presentation, meeting or indeed sporting challenge, the key to success is through preparation, practice and visualisation.

All successful professional negotiators carefully consider the wants, needs, goals, expectations and aspirations of both parties. They take time to consider many "what if" scenarios, coupled with as many "then what" strategies and tactics, which will increase their chances of getting agreement on terms closest to the goals and targets they have set. The aim here is to avoid surprises and therefore put them in a position to quickly decide on the most appropriate course of action and reduce the risk of a knee-jerk reaction or making overly generous concessions.

It is often said that you cannot hit a target you cannot see. Therefore, it is critical to have clear unambiguous goals set prior to entering into the negotiating process.

Consider an archer taking part in a competition. The target remains static and is usually made up of four circles moving from the outer circumference of the target and ending up with the centre or bull's eye. The closer the arrow comes to hitting the centre, the greater the reward. However, it is unlikely that the archer will strike the centre every time and sometimes they have to accept a lower score or indeed, in some cases, they may miss the target completely.

When planning outcomes, a framework that mirrors the archer's target can be defined as:

- **The Ideal:** The ideal, of course, is the centre. In other words, if you could wave a magic wand over the negotiation, what exactly is it that you believe is your ideal agreement or outcome
- **The Realistic:** The realistic outcome will involve some form of compromise or concession that may have to be made when it becomes clear that either (a) you are not going to get all that you had hoped for, or (b) you may have been too greedy or ambitious with your opening offer or entry point

- **The Acceptable:** The acceptable is the minimum offer that you feel you can accept and live with both yourself and the consequences
- **Walk-away:** The walk-away is also referred to as the exit point – it's where the archer misses the target completely. This is the point where you score nothing and the deal makes no sense.

Some years, ago the Harvard Negotiating Institute developed what it calls **BATNA** – the Best Alternative To a Negotiated Agreement – which defines what alternatives you have if you can't close a deal. This means that you should develop your first, second and third best alternatives to a negotiated agreement. It suggests that you list all the alternatives available to you should the negotiation fail to close on the terms you want. Decide on what your options are if you walk away from the deal.

Figure 7.1: Ten Keys to Planning a Negotiation

1. Assess needs and objectives of the other party.
2. Assess your own needs and establish your objectives.
3. Identify major areas for negotiation.
4. Assess costs and values of concessions on both sides in each major area.
5. Assess the scope for broadening the negotiations (co-operative mode).
6. Assess the power and skills on both sides.
7. Assess the actual and possible stated stances of the other party.
8. Decide your own actual and opening stances.
9. Plan tactics
    - How to build your own power.
    - How to minimise the other parties' power.
    - How to handle concessions.
    - How to handle your own concession pattern.
10. Prepare agenda.

PHASE 2: OPENING

The opening offer is nothing more than the first statement of what you are looking for from the negotiation. After you have set your goals for the negotiation, you can consider the opening offer. There are no firm rules for this process.

To determine your opening offer, you should consider the goals you have set and the information you have gathered while preparing for the negotiation. Obviously your opening offer should be higher than the goals you have set for yourself. But it should not be so outrageously high as to be off-putting to the other side or make you look foolish or inexperienced. Whether the amount you state in your opening offer is higher or lower than the amount of your goal depends on whether you are the buyer or the seller (you determine how much higher or lower through good preparation):

- If you're the seller, your opening offer should never be lower than the goal you set
- If you're the buyer, the opening offer should never be higher than the goal you set
- First few items for negotiation should be relatively unimportant
- The danger of deadlock is highest at this early stage.

Many people tend to get quite anxious about the opening offer. They are fearful that they will mess up the entire negotiation by putting forward a demand that is too modest or even too ambitious. Use your anxiety level as a measure of how well-prepared you are. Part of being well-prepared is knowing relative values. If you know the value of what you are offering, the opening offer is easy to deduce. You just decide how much negotiating room you want to leave yourself.

The acronym below can be used as a preparation framework.

Needs & Expectations

Goals & Objectives

Tradable Items

Always Think in Ink

Envisage Success

Needs and expectations

In principled negotiation especially, it is well worth considering not only the needs of both parties but most importantly their expectations. Consider the last time you experienced anger or frustration in your business or personal life. You can be sure that, somewhere along the line, it stemmed from disappointment or a gap in your expectations.

For example, you purchase some simple piece of equipment from a shop and arrive home to find that a critical accessory is not in the box and the sales person did not point this out. Another example is that you delegate work or a task to someone whom you know is capable and he or she makes no effort or no commitment to deliver on time.

Goal-setting

Goal-setting is the single most powerful way of ensuring ideal outcomes. Research suggests that negotiators with clear, specific, written objectives are responsible for more successful negotiations.

The three areas of focus in goal-setting are:

- The Client
- The Company
- Yourself.

Goal-setting time frames can be:

- Short-term (one to four weeks)
- Medium-term (one to two months)
- Long-term (two to 12 months).

Use the SMART Formula for clarifying outcomes:

- **S** : Specific
- **M** : Measurable
- **A** : Achievable
- **R** : Relevant
- **T** : Timed.

Tradable items

Brainstorm a list of all items from both parties' perspective that could be considered tradable. It's important at this point not to restrict your thinking. Be imaginative and allow thoughts to flow freely. Studies from Harvard suggest that the most successful negotiators generate the greatest number of creative variables. Therefore, do not dismiss any ideas. Include people in the session who may have very little knowledge of the negotiating parties or the situation – objective creativity can often be the key to developing that one idea which can win the day.

Creative Negotiation

Some years ago, I witnessed a scenario where a capital equipment salesperson was selling a small personal copier into an accounts office. The buyer was pushing for several hundred euro off the €2,000 machine. After some discussion, the salesperson said,

> *"Ok, here's what I will do for you. I will hold my price and provide you with 3-year service cover, that's over 1,000 days, free running costs. Imagine you did not have to pay for petrol, tax or insurance for your car for three years".*

He continued:

> *"That's 5,000 sheets of copy paper".*

The comparison and perceptions were so vast that it seemed pointless to still be discussing a few hundred euro. The reality, of course, is that the supplies included cost about €60 and, most importantly, the value of the machine was not compromised.

Therefore, after you have listed all that could be traded, put careful thought and consideration into what items you are actually going to trade and their cost to you *versus* the perceived values to the other party.

Always think in ink ...

Thinking in ink does several things:

- It clears the mind and captures good ideas and strategies on paper
- Due to the preparation and the written plan, your confidence will build and you will become emotionally more stable
- It creates what is called the "power of legitimacy". It automatically instils within your psyche that this has been thought out and is tangible, practical and workable.

Envisage success

The purpose of preparation is to build confidence and, ultimately, to ensure success; therefore, it is very helpful if we can take time to run through in our minds what success will look like.

Increasingly, sports people are employing sports psychologists; this is because, when all the external factors are equal or maximised, the only place left to create advantage is the inner or mental game.

Mental preparation gives you a distinct advantage in a negotiation situation. Mentally preparing and deciding your "what if'" and "then what" avoids all sorts of surprises and as already mentioned, avoids knee-jerk reactions.

PHASE 3: PROPOSING

When you know how to set limits and have confidence in that ability, the entire negotiating process changes. You can hang tough or walk away from a negotiation when necessary.

Kenny Rogers may have sung it best in his hit song *The Gambler,* which was about the high stake negotiations that take place around a poker table. Rogers croons this important truth:

You gotta know when to hold 'em
Know when to fold 'em
Know when to walk away, and
Know when to run.

Notice that the word "know" appears in each line of the chorus. Being able to set limits is directly tied to knowledge, and knowledge is the result of preparation.

The "Four Knows" are:

- Know that you have other choices: "There is always a better deal around the corner"
- Know what the other choices are: BATNA (Best Alternative To a Negotiated Agreement)

- Know your "or else": Decide what you want to do if the deal doesn't close
- Know how to enforce your limits. Be careful about setting limits because if you set limits and go back on them your credibility may be compromised.

PHASE 4: BARGAINING

Silence

Saying nothing can be as powerful as saying something, provided it is used at the right time and in the right way. Silence usually requires conscious effort and can be very useful. Silence can imply certainty on your part and prompt uncertainty in the other party. Therefore having made a clear suggestion, "So what do you think?", wait and do not allow the silence to push you into elaborating on what you have just said.

Summarise regularly

Negotiations are complex and involve juggling a number of variables. It is easy to loose the thread of the discussions; therefore, summarise regularly. Linking this to words like "Suppose ..." or "What if ..." keeps the conversation organised and allows you to explore possibilities without committing yourself.

Note-taking

Taking notes is a helpful method of keeping your negotiations on track. Remember information is power, so don't leave yourself confused about what was said. Reviewing notes also gives you time to think. Remember the old Chinese proverb,

"The palest ink lasts longer than the most retentive memory".

Promote good feeling

Negotiation tends to build up agreement progressively. As you proceed, make sure you emphasise that each stage is positive, preferably for both parties but in particular for the other person.

Key phrases to use include:

- That's a good arrangement
- That will work well
- That's fair
- That's a good suggestion
- Let's do it that way.

Slow down

Build-in time to think. Silence and note-taking have already been mentioned. Use these as ways to think ahead. It's quite legitimate to request a break to consider what has been discussed so far. Other tactics may involve working something out on a calculator or making a telephone call.

Variables

Nothing is agreed until everything is agreed. Do not make an offer or final offer until everything that needs negotiating is out on the table. Statements like "Yes, I'm sure I can help you there" or "Is there anything else you want to consider" are ways of getting all variables out in the open. Almost anything the other side presents as fixed can be made into a variable. Fixed is as likely to mean "not wanting to negotiate" as "not able to be negotiated".

Constraints and deadlines

There was never a deadline that wasn't negotiable. In the negotiation process, keep in mind that all aspects of timing are variables:

- How long will things take?
- When will they happen?
- In what order will they happen?

Trading concessions

Never give a concession: Trade it reluctantly

The first part of this rule is important because the number of variables is finite and you want your share.

The second part is also crucial because perception is as important as fact: we must appear to be driving a hard bargain. This is the "if … then approach"

Optimise your concessions

Build up the value and significance of anything you offer to trade by:

- Stressing the cost (financial or otherwise) to you ("Well, I could do that but it would involve a lot more work")
- Exaggerating – credibly. Do not overstate and, if possible, provide evidence (" Well, I could do that but it would involve at least twice as much work: I have just been through …")
- Referring to a major problem that your concession would solve ("Well, I suppose if I were to agree, it would remove the need for you to …")
- Implying that it is an exceptional concession ("I would never normally do this, but …")
- Implying that it is not only exceptional but beyond the call of duty ("I really don't know what my boss would say but …")
- Maximise the perceived value of everything you offer.

Minimise their concessions

Reduce the value the other party puts on anything offered to you:

- Do not overdo the thanks. Avoid a profuse "Thank you so much" but be brief even dismissive, "Thanks" (your tone of voice is as important as the phrase you use)
- Depreciate, or reduce the value of the other person's concession ("Right, that's a small step forward, I guess")
- Amortise the concession where appropriate. Divide it into smaller units that will sound less impressive ("Well, at least that saves me X every month") rather than quoting the total figure

- Treat concessions as given but don't put a value on them. A brief acknowledgement may be all that is necessary ("Right, let's do it that way")
- Take concessions for granted – in other words, treat them as if they were always a foregone conclusion. ("Fine, I would certainly expect that")
- Accept, but imply that you are doing the other person a favour ("I don't really need that but let's arrange things that way if it helps")
- Link value to time by suggesting that it is now not worth what is implied ("Well, that helps a little, but it's not of major importance now that we are done").

PHASE 5: CLOSING

A deal closes when both parties agree on enough terms that they can move forward and "seal the deal". For some people, a handshake is sufficient. For others, the deal will not be considered closed until all commitments and agreements are documented.

The elements of an agreement include:

- What you are getting.
- What you are paying for what you are getting.
- How long the contract will last.
- Who the parties involved in the contract are.

When to close

Some people do not appear to be in any hurry to close the deal. They just go on and on enjoying the process, taking up time and neglecting to bring the discussion to a close.

The key to closing is **"early and often"**. The common thread running through all negotiations is to bring the negotiation to a mutually acceptable solution.

You have a closing opportunity, when:

- An acceptable solution is on the table
- The other side wants to close

- A deadline is approaching
- All the negotiation goals are met
- You have no better alternatives.

Studies reveal that:

- Weak closers get stuck on position; strong closers focus on solution
- Weak closers often procrastinate; strong closers stick to deadlines
- Weak closers feel a sense of loss after the deal is struck; strong closers celebrate.

If you want to end/postpone the encounter:

- Watch for shifting of papers, looking at watch, distracted answers
- Consider a break
- Consider a further meeting
- Never let the meeting become boring
- Summarise and involve the other party
- If the meeting is long, use interim summaries.

There is no doubt that we are all more comfortable using our own words and style, therefore, once you have internalised the ideas and concepts in this chapter, be sure to translate them into your own language and wrap your own personality and style around them. Good luck in the future!

Figure 7.2: Six General Principles of Negotiations

1	**People who ask for more get more.**	Large initial demands improve the quality of success, but they also increase the possibility of deadlock.
2	**No deal is better than a bad deal.**	While this is true in general terms, it is important to be able to break through deadlock to reach agreements, which satisfy both parties.
3	**Concession will break a deadlock.**	You will be less likely to do well unless you get something in return. Large concessions, the first concession and last-minute concessions will detract from your success unless you make them contingent on a concession from the other side.
4	**Compromise will break a deadlock.**	While the above is true, the definition of compromise is that both parties will get less than what they've hoped for, and the agreement may not be as strong as it would have been otherwise. "Splitting the difference" may be a well-established tradition for breaking deadlocks, but it represents a mutual agreement to give up the fight and to settle for less. You cannot afford to split the difference.
5	**Finding alternative "currencies of exchange" can help break deadlocks by meeting the needs of all parties.**	For example, shorter working hours may be non-negotiable but longer breaks might be. Can you think of any labour dispute where the resolution hinged on a similar redefinition of terms?
6	**The use of negative power weakens a negotiator in the long run.**	The effect of negative power is that trust is reduced and hostility is increased, destroying the communication, which is the keystone of any effective negotiating process.

REFERENCES & FURTHER READING

Dawson, R. (2001). *Secrets of Power Persuasion*, Englewood Cliffs, NJ.: Prentice Hall.

Fisher, R. and Ury, W. (1983). *Getting to Yes: Negotiating Agreement without Giving In*, London: Hutchinson.

Kennedy, G. (1998). *The New Negotiating Edge, The Behavioural Approach for Results and Relationships*, London: Nicholas Brealey Publishing Ltd.

Shell, R. G. (2000). *Bargaining for Advantage: Negotiation Strategies for Reasonable People*, London: Penguin Books.

Thompson, L. L (2000). *The Mind and Heart of the Negotiator*, London: Prentice Hall.

8: FACILITATING MEETINGS & CHAIRING DISCUSSIONS

Julia Rowan

Key Learning Objectives

- ☐ Diagnose the problems at meetings you chair or attend.
- ☐ Identify what to do at each stage of the meeting life-cycle.
- ☐ Clarify objectives that direct the meeting.
- ☐ Use ground rules to facilitate better participation.
- ☐ Select an appropriate chairing style.
- ☐ Understand how group dynamics can help, or hinder, group performance.

Most managers spend between 25% and 75% of their time in meetings – and they estimate that 60% of this time is wasted. So what puts meetings at the bottom of the corporate activity popularity stakes – and, when the success of meetings depends on all of the participants, is it fair to place responsibility for the success of the meeting in the chairperson's hands? Yes, it is!

From the formal meeting with an agenda to the "What do we need to discuss?" facilitated discussion, this chapter looks at what it takes to run fantastic meetings – and also includes some ideas that might help when you're "merely" asked to participate.

Why Bother with Meetings?

Good question. Most of the readers who have turned to this chapter will know exactly why we need to bother. For those of you that don't know, let's start with some research: managers spend between 25% and 75% of their time at meetings. And the more senior you become, generally, the more meetings you attend. This means, of course, more preparation time, more follow-up time and more time spent sitting at meetings.

With managers spending so much time at meetings, it would be reasonable to expect that the "practice makes perfect" principle comes into play. Unfortunately, it does not. Managers estimate, on average, that 60% of the time they spend at meetings is wasted.

How does that apply to the manager working a 40-hour week?

- Managers spending 10 hours (25% of their time) at meetings, feel they have wasted six of those hours
- Managers spending 20 hours (50% of their time) at meetings, feel they have wasted 12 of these hours, and
- Managers spending 30 hours (75% of their time) at meetings, feel they have wasted 18 of these hours.

So apart from the waste of salary – which must run into billions of euro – there is the waste of energy, the growth of cynicism and the loss of morale, and sometimes even, the acceptance that "this is just the way things are done around here – so I'd better join in".

What goes wrong at meetings?

Lots of things go wrong:

- Discussions that seem to go nowhere
- Unclear decisions that nobody follows up on
- Minutes (if there are any) arriving 10 minutes before the next meeting begins
- The opinions (and voices) of a few people dominating
- No follow-up
- Annoyingly-detailed PowerPoint presentations, containing a whole load of stuff that everybody knows, and sending you to sleep before the interesting material is reached.

What can you do?

Transforming your meetings into "fantastic" meetings is quite straightforward, but not necessarily easy. The management of meetings can be divided into three phases:

- Planning fantastic meetings
- Running fantastic meetings
- Following-up on fantastic meetings.

PLANNING FANTASTIC MEETINGS

Many meetings fail before they ever begin, simply due to poor planning and lack of thought.

Here are some key things to do before you hold a meeting:

- Hold a meeting for the right reason
- Formulate and circulate a clear objective or objectives for the meeting
- Circulate the agenda and any working papers in advance
- Make the right arrangements.

Hold a meeting for the right reason

Like much of the good practice on meetings, this sounds obvious – but isn't always thought through.

Meetings should be held:

- When there is a decision to be made – either by the people at the meeting, or by the decision-maker who wishes to consult others before deciding
- When a discussion would enhance understanding of subsequent decisions to be made
- When they foster team effectiveness and harmony.

Meetings should not be held:

- Just because they're scheduled
- Only to share information that could be circulated in another way and will not benefit from discussion
- When key people cannot attend.

CASE STUDY

Mary is an independent website design consultant who is amazed at the number of meetings to which she is invited that are not necessary.

"I might submit a proposal to a company and would be delighted to be invited to a meeting, only to find that they needed some further information that could easily have been supplied over the phone or by e-mail. I'm amazed at this meetings culture – people seem to hold meetings at the drop of a hat. I've now learned to ask – nicely – what the purpose of the meeting is, and then deal with queries over the phone. Calling meetings at the drop of a hat might be OK for people working in the same building but, when you're the one who has to travel, you learn to be a bit more discerning about the meetings that you go to."

Formulate and circulate a clear objective or objectives for the meeting

Too many meetings are derailed by general chat that doesn't seem to go anywhere. Just having a general chat doesn't give participants any "grip", so the conversation wanders.

In order to have a fantastic meeting:

- **Consider exactly what you want to get out of the meeting:** This could be one, or all, of the following:
  - Exploring issues relating to a subject
  - Learning the background to something – for example, to improve the quality of future decision-making
  - Generating ideas about how to approach something
  - Making a decision or refining numerous options
  - Generating commitment by consulting and listening to interested parties
- **Set expectations:** Let people know in advance what will be expected of them at the meeting. Do you want them to participate in making a decision or to contribute ideas that will inform your final decision? Do you want them to appraise critically a plan or to brainstorm ideas? People often attend meetings wondering what exactly is expected of them, or feel frustrated when their expectation of what was required was not met.

CASE STUDY

Carl is Production Manager of a pharmaceutical company in the South-West. The CEO regularly calls meetings of the senior management team in order to "talk about" issues.

"It could be recruitment, quality, waste – any issue at all. We used to sit for hours talking 'about' issues, with nobody knowing what was expected or what result was wanted. The CEO used to start discussing all sorts of issues, going into detail that really wasn't useful. Now I always clarify in advance what the CEO wants from the meetings. Sometimes, this means that I have to spend time with him, clarifying what he wants to achieve by talking about things. This isn't my job – but it means that the meeting is much more focussed and we get a better result in less time."

Circulate the agenda / working papers in advance

When no agenda is circulated (or it's circulated, but not read), two problems occur:

- First, half of your participants will do their "preparation" *at* the meeting, thinking out loud and formulating opinions as they go along.
- Second, the other half will only contribute to the meeting if they have had time to reflect and formulate opinions before the meeting.

Quick Tip: Write your Agenda as a Series of Questions

So, instead of listing your agenda like this:
* Website
* Sales
* Finance

It could read like this:
* **Website:** How do we generate 50% more hits by end June?
* **Sales**: How do we increase sales in Region X by 15% by Q4?
* **Finance:** What are the issues involved in changing our accounting practice in X area?

This kick-starts your meetings because, once participants read the questions, their brains will automatically start to reflect on the issues.

Make the right arrangements

Making the right arrangements means thinking ahead:

- **Invite the right people:** What often happens is that a discussion about a particular issue is in full swing when it becomes obvious that input from somebody not present at the meeting is required. This means that the discussion has to be rescheduled – often leading to a loss of energy for an issue. Walk through the agenda in relation to the objectives, reflect on the type of discussion that might ensue and invite the right people to the meeting (consider just inviting them for the specific agenda item for which they are needed)

- **Book the room and equipment needed:** Get the right size room. Check technical issues such as PowerPoint compatibility with the projector

CASE STUDY

John was the regional manager in charge of a team of 21 sales representatives. The team used to meet monthly – generally in the company's Boardroom – a very formal room with an impressive mahogany table, leather chairs, crystal glasses ... or in a hotel where the tables would be arranged in a big 'U' shape. John found that he did most of the talking, asking questions that nobody would answer, trying to encourage discussions, with very little response.

"*The layout of the rooms, was all wrong and people just felt intimidated in front of so many of their peers*".

Eventually, John started organising meetings for six to eight sales managers at a time in small meeting rooms or in one of the company's training rooms. The difference was startling –

"*They took ownership, got involved in discussions, instead of just criticising management decisions, offered to help each other with issues*".

While John now attends three meetings a month instead of one, (plus a quarterly meeting which everybody attends), he reckons that the improvement in the quality of the meetings is worth the extra time commitment.

- **Organise refreshments:** At the very least, ensure that water is available
- **Prepare your room:** A prepared room sends a message to participants that the meeting is important. Preparation can be very simple – the right size room, a round/oval table if possible, enough chairs for all participants (and extra chairs moved out of the way), water/cups. Write up the timed agenda on a flipchart or whiteboard. Write out the meeting objectives to keep the focus
- **Invite the right number of people:** Psychologists tell us that, once there are more than about nine people in a room, the chances are that the group will start to split into factions and/or

some people may coast. Therefore, if making a decision, say, about a new supplier or a new policy, you may wish to have one information-gathering meeting to which everybody concerned is invited and then a separate meeting with fewer people to make a decision as to how to go forward.

RUNNING FANTASTIC MEETINGS

What counts as a well-run meeting? Is it one where good decisions are made, follow-up tasks allocated get done, participants feel that they have been listened to – even if no one agrees with them? All of these things are important but, too often, poorly-planned meetings turn into poorly-run meetings where decisions made earlier are resurrected and changed, half of the participants are switched off, and discussions take a long time to get anywhere.

Tips to make your meetings fantastic include:

- Use ground rules
- Manage participation
- Manage the timing
- Manage the energy – mental and physical
- Manage meeting presentations
- Manage yourself!

Use ground rules

Ground rules are a set of behaviours, generally agreed by a group of people who meet regularly (for example, a team or project group) that help to make meetings better.

Ground rules can be set:

- Around courtesy issues, for example:
  - o No mobile phones
  - o No side conversations
  - o Meetings start and finish on time
  - o Don't re-cap items for latecomers

- Around participation issues, for example:
  - Disagree with the argument – not the person
  - Challenges are welcomed
  - Everybody's opinion is welcomed
  - Sometimes the chairperson has to cut the discussion
  - Don't speak a second time until everybody has had a chance to speak once
  - No diversions– stick to the agenda
- Around decision-making, for example:
  - Work by consensus
  - Majority rule
  - 2/3rds majority needed to change policy
  - Chairperson will listen to debate and decide.

Talking about behaviour emphasises that how people behave at meetings is important. Agreeing ground rules means that participants who contract to a particular type of behaviour are more aware of and committed to that behaviour. It is also much easier for the chairperson to tackle unhelpful behaviour at meetings by referring to agreed ground rules.

Case Study

Maria was asked to co-ordinate her company's move from two adjacent buildings into a newly-built office. She took on the project with reluctance, knowing how emotional the subject of space allocation can be. She decided to organise regular meetings for all Heads of Department in the year before the move. At the first meeting, the group spent a considerable amount of time working out some ground rules, and talking through their implications – how the group would work, how decisions would get made, what would happen when there was conflicting requests or when consensus was not possible.

"Because the ground rules were agreed upon by the group before any major decisions had to be made, it really helped the work of the group. Sometimes I had to make tough decisions, but I knew even if a Department Head was unhappy about a decision I had made, he or she had been part of the group that established the parameters for those decisions, and it all worked out fairly well."

Manage participation

As chairperson, you don't want people to just go through the motions. You want them to be really committed to what is happening in the meeting. Giving people the opportunity to participate in a worthwhile debate is important. For you, as chairperson, the challenge is to ensure that the people with something to say are heard and that those who have the floor are making sense and contributing something worthwhile to the discussion.

Frequently, people leave meetings dissatisfied because participation was not properly managed. The chairperson may be aware of these issues but is worried about appearing rude to people who dominate or about putting the people who are not contributing on the spot.

Here are some of the common problems and ideas on how to tackle them (and remember – good ground rules can really help you here):

PROBLEM	**SOLUTION**
Meeting dominated by one or two people, who either feel passionate about the subject or love the sound of their own voice.	Say *"Before I hear from you again John, I'd like to get some other views"*, or *"John, just let me hear some other opinions before I come back to you"*.
People repeating themselves and time is getting short.	Say *"We need to finish by 12.30, so, new information only from now on"*. If somebody repeats themselves, you need to say *"Amy, we've heard that point, do you have new information to add?"*.
Discussion is going off-track or participant is rambling on.	Say *"How does that tie back to our objective of…"*.
Some participants not saying anything.	Say *"I'm going to go around the table now and ask everybody to … (give their opinion, summarise their position …)"*.
Participant speaking for the whole group *"we all think…"* or making assumptions/general statements *"it's obvious that …"*.	Say *"Anna, I'll be happy to hear from other members of the group who have an opinion on this. For the moment, let's just hear what you think"* or *"how else could we look at this issue?"*.

Manage the timing

Clearly the length of the agenda and the issues on the table will determine the length of the meeting. When organising your meetings, however, bear the following considerations in mind:

- Large meetings (six people and over) are generally best held in the morning. The time before lunch is very suitable, as participants are generally anxious to get to the staff restaurant before all the cheesecake is gone! Try to avoid the time after lunch for large meetings, as people are generally quite tired and may "coast" (or even fall asleep – especially if it's PowerPoint time!)
- Smaller meetings are OK after lunch as the smaller number generally gives people the energy to stay awake!
- Conditions being right at meetings (fresh air, lively debate, etc.) participants can generally concentrate for about 60 minutes. Build in a five-minute stretch break every hour and a 15-minute refreshment break every two hours.

QUICK TIP

Stand-up meetings – where participants stand around a flipchart or whiteboard or gather in a space where there is no meeting table/chairs – can be really effective for small, informal briefing meetings. There is a noticeably different change in the dynamic and in the energy.

Manage the energy – mental & physical

Generally, the energy at a meeting will follow a standard bell-curve shape. At the beginning, people are arriving, greeting colleagues, grabbing coffee, settling themselves, seeing who's in the room, etc. They are also mentally tuning out of the cares and busyness of the outside world and tuning in to what is happening in the meeting room. About 10 minutes before the end of a meeting, participants begin to "tune out" – they start thinking about what they have to go back to.

Energy also relates to the group dynamic – whether people are pulling together, whether personal agendas are surfacing, etc. Frequently managers make the mistake of putting the "meatiest" item (the item which is likely to generate most controversy) either first on the agenda ("get it over with") or last on the agenda ("put it off as long as possible"). It may make more sense to go for some "quick wins" and to establish a positive dynamic by discussing some easy items, making some easy decisions and then moving on to the more difficult items.

In terms of the design of the agenda, it may make sense to think of a template like the following:

- **Beginning of the Meeting** (tuning-in time)
  - Open the meeting – Formalities – Courtesies
  - Go through minutes or list of decisions from last meeting and quickly check whether tasks carried out (Make sure not to pre-empt discussions scheduled for later on the agenda)
  - Non-controversial information items
  - Easy items, likely to lead to short discussion and uncontroversial decisions
- **Middle of the Meeting** (full focus time)
  - Moderately difficult items
  - Most difficult item
  - Controversial information items
- **End of the Meeting** (when attention may be wandering)
  - Moderately easy items
  - Formalities. Next steps. Date for next meeting.

Manage meeting presentations

Be sure, as the chairperson, if you ask somebody to make a presentation, that you give them a clear objective for the presentation (for example, *"We need to make a decision about X – what do we need to know about your project?"*, or *"Can you summarise the top three lessons that we learned by tendering for that contract?"*).

Don't just ask people to present "about" something. Give the presenter an idea of the level of detail that you expect. People using PowerPoint tend to make presentations that are far too detailed. Spend some time with the person who has to present clarifying clear parameters for the presentation and clearly communicating the time available.

QUICK TIP

When asking people to present at meetings, ask them to present "The 5 key points" or "The 3 main things I learned on the training course". This helps the presenter to give a meaty, focussed, short presentation.

Manage yourself!

Generally, the person chairing the meeting has the most power at the meeting. This means that what you do and say carries more weight than other participants' behaviour. Fantastic meeting chairpersons use this power wisely and well:

- As a general rule, approach the chairing of meetings with integrity and good intention. If you do, you're more likely to have a good result than if you are trying to settle scores, play politics or further your own agenda
- Don't get emotionally hooked by issues – stick to the facts. For example, saying "You only replied yesterday" sends a very different message to "I received your reply yesterday" or "Finance couldn't be bothered to send somebody to our meeting" is very different to "Finance have decided not to be represented at our meeting"
- Don't judge the behaviour of other participants, not least, because it takes too much mental energy. For example, if a participant arrives late, assume that there is a good reason for their late arrival and carry on. Deal with the problem if it happens again. Similarly, if a participant is sending non-verbal signals that they are bored or exasperated with the proceedings, gently (and with good intention) say "Tony, is there something that you'd like to say here?"
- Treat all participants with dignity and respect, even when they have criticised you. Thank participants for their contributions,

even when you don't agree with them. If somebody makes a statement that you disagree with, you may want to say "Thank you. I don't see the issue in the same way …"

- Keep an eye on the process and on the group dynamics. Look around and be aware of what people in the room are doing and feeling. If you feel that the energy for a particular issue is very low, say "I sense that the energy in the room is very low, what can we do about that?" or "I'm getting no response to my question – what does that mean?"

FANTASTIC MEETING FOLLOW-UP

What happens after the meeting often sends a message about how much you mean business – or whether your meetings are just talking-shops.

Here are some tips to follow-up on fantastic meetings:

- Circulate minutes or decision/action-lists within 24 hours
- Evaluate your meetings.

Circulate minutes or decision/action-lists within 24 hours

If you need to write minutes, write them as soon as possible after the meeting has taken place. It's amazing how quickly information is forgotten. In any case, think carefully about whether minutes (recording the discussion) are needed or whether a list of decisions will suffice.

If decisions were made and actions need to be taken, circulate a decision list. Even if you have prepared full minutes, prepare a list of decisions and actions that need to be taken and fix this to the front of the minutes. This then becomes your working document – the basis of your agenda – for the start of the next meeting. Your list of decisions, could look something like this:

Agenda Item	Decision	By Whom?	By When?
1. New Website Design	Obtain quotes/samples from three potential designers for next meeting.	JB	15 March
2. Health & Safety	Revise company policy and circulate to Heads of Department for comment by 5 March.	AD	27 Feb'y
	Amended policy circulated to whole company by 10 March.	AD	10 March
3. Product Launch	Brainstorming session to take place at beginning of next meeting.	PD	15 March

Evaluate your meetings

How do you know whether your meetings are any good? A really simple way to find out is to ask the participants. Bearing in mind that people will rarely tell you that your meetings are a waste of time, soliciting honest and constructive feedback is an art worth developing. Throwing in *"any suggestions as to how we could improve our meetings?"* at the end of the meeting might not elicit much response. Participants will feel put on the spot, unsure of what response you are expecting and probably need to rush back to their desk.

Here are some tips for getting useful feedback about your meeting management:

- **Signal:** Let people know (in advance if possible, but certainly at the beginning of the meeting) that you will be asking for feedback. You may wish to include "How can we make our meetings more effective?" as an agenda point from time to time
- **Pay attention to how your phrase your request:** You don't only want polite positives, nor do you want a moaning session. Therefore, it is generally a good idea to ask for both positive and constructive feedback. This will help to reinforce what you are doing well. Also, having the opportunity to give positive feedback gives "permission" to people to give specific suggestions on "points for improvement" as well

- **Think through the method that you use to get feedback:** Open discussion, individual or small group feedback (groups of two or three may help less assertive/junior/newer participants to participate), written (freeform), tick-box questionnaire, marks out of 10 ...This will depend on the dynamics in your meetings – whether people may feel constrained (not just by you but by longer-serving, more senior, more dominant participants).

Here are some ways to elicit feedback:

- **Freeform:** Ask an open question and get participants to respond in writing or by discussion. The question could be very general, for example: *"How could we make these meetings more effective?"*, or *"What do we need to do to get more from our meetings?"*, or they could address a specific issue, for example, *"What can we do to make sure that tasks allocated are completed on time?"* or *"How can we ensure that everybody contributes to our meetings?"*
- **Stop, Start, Continue:** Ask participants (either individually or in small groups) what you should
  - o Stop doing (what they don't like)
  - o Start doing (what you're not doing, but could)
  - o Continue doing (what you're doing and they like)
- **More of / Less of:** Ask participants what they feel "more of" and "less of" would make for better meetings.

Remember! Asking for feedback creates an expectation that things are going to change. Only ask for feedback if you are really prepared to take it on board.

If you get feedback, listen to and respond to the feedback that you receive. Think carefully about sharing the main points (both positive and negative) with the group (so that people aren't wondering – it's not a big hidden secret). Don't respond by explaining, arguing, defending why it is not possible to put feedback ideas into action. Take time to reflect on the feedback, and come back to participants as quickly as possible with the ideas that you have decided to take on board.

TIPS FOR YOU AS A MEETING PARTICIPANT

If you're invited to attend a meeting, make sure that, as well as the obvious arrangements (time, venue, etc.), you have the following information:

- A clear objective of the meeting
- A full agenda, including timings
- Relevant working papers.

If you're not sure why you've been invited, don't just go. Talk to the chairperson and clarify what's expected from you.

If you are worried that a meeting is going to drag on, agree to attend, but let the chairperson know that you have something else on afterwards "I'll have to leave at x o'clock". Fifteen minutes before your deadline, remind the chairperson that you have to leave in 15 minutes, ask whether there is any information that is needed from you before you leave.

Other ways of getting the best from meetings as a participant include:

- At the beginning of the meeting, ensure that the meeting objective(s) is clarified with the chairperson and write it down
- If a discussion is going off topic, you may not wish to be seen to undermine the chairperson by pointing this out. A more diplomatic way of making the point is to ask *"How does what we're discussing now, relate to our objective?"*
- If you feel that there are people at the meeting who are not getting their turn, say, *"I'd love to hear what other people think about this"*
- If you are at a large meeting and find it difficult to break through the discussion to make your point: raise your hand – straight up – very slightly off the table and hold it there. A

raised hand is a very powerful signal to everybody at the table that you want to participate in the discussion.

FACILITATING FANTASTIC MEETINGS

The terms "chairing" and "facilitating" are sometimes used interchangeably, although there is a different focus to both activities. The difference in focus refers to the amount of authority used by the person running the meeting compared with the amount of freedom given to meeting participants, as illustrated in **Figure 8.1**.

FIGURE 8.1: FACILITATING FANTASTIC MEETINGS

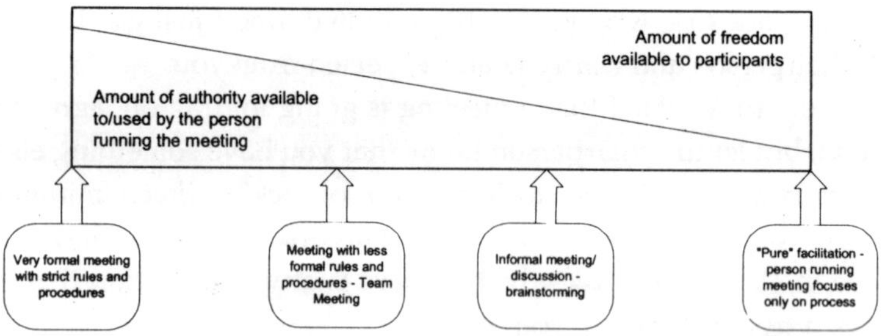

Source: Based on Tannenbaum and Schmidt's Leadership Continuum (1958).

Where meetings are chaired, the chairperson generally has high authority (people speak 'through the chair' and participants are free to participate within limits (an agenda). The person running the meeting has "content expertise" or "line authority".

In facilitated meetings, the person running the meeting (the facilitator) is the "process expert" and does not need to know about the content. The facilitator focuses on processes such as clarifying goals, ensuring equal participation, ensuring decisions are appropriately made – and not at all on the content – for example, the quality of a decision.

In reality, many managers use both styles, although some managers feel under pressure to know the answers (focus on content) rather than to ask the right questions (focus on process).

Case Study

Jane holds a very senior position in a European institution. She is intelligent, independent, quick and very logical. She works hard, tries to be fair and sets a high standard. She sees the value of organising regular meetings of her division and used to organise monthly meetings. She got disillusioned because nobody would contribute and so she looked for advice from a business coach. It turned out that Jane always had an answer ready, always had a reason, always knew better than everybody else – and she let people know. After all, she was the manager. The result was that her staff felt exposed at those meetings and felt that there was no point in contributing.

Working with her coach, Jane slowly learned to let go of having all the answers. She learned to ask questions – and listen and then to ask more questions. Her staff have responded to this new approach and now feel happy contributing ideas, discussing problems and finding solutions and taking responsibility. Jane sometimes finds it frustrating to let a discussion take place when she has the answers and could short-cut all of the discussion. However, she sees that, long-term, there is huge value in this approach.

There are many similarities between chairing fantastic meetings and facilitating fantastic meetings. The challenge for the facilitator is to take a step back from the proceedings and to see themselves as process managers, facilitating the group to come up with the right answers.

Here are some tips for facilitating fantastic meetings:

- As process is so important in facilitated sessions, ground rules are particularly appropriate, and these need to be suggested, debated and agreed by the group. The facilitator is also free to suggest ground rules that are particularly important for them.
- You are not the content expert – so don't *tell* people. Rather, *ask* powerful questions, including:
  - *"What do we want to achieve today?"* (at the start of a session)

  - *"Mary, when you say 'better' results – what exactly does that mean?"* or *"If you felt more confident dealing with customers, what would I see you doing/hear you saying and how would you feel?"* (helping to clarify the session objective)
  - *How does the group want to deal with this information?*
  - *How will this help us to achieve our goal?*
  - *If we decided to do that, what would be the implications?*
- Ensure that the organisation of the time available will lead to achieving the objective – this could mean organising people to work in pairs or small groups, obtaining input from one or more participants, finding out what people know about an issue. Keep the group focussed on achieving the goal
- Ensure the availability of a wide variety of resources – for example, flip-charts, markers, post-it notes, index cards, envelopes, postcards, magazines (to cut out pictures) ...
- Use a variety of tools, according to the objective of the meeting. Tools could include Edward de Bono's *Six Thinking Hats* (for mapping out the parameters of an issue), brainstorming (for generating ideas), force-field analysis (for evaluating ideas), SWOT analysis (for establishing current situation *versus* future possibilities).

SUMMARY

This chapter has looked at some key ideas for running fantastic meetings. The ideas are simple but challenging. They require time-pushed managers to invest time in preparing their meetings.

By investing time up-front, managers will find that:

- Their meetings are fruitful
- Objectives are achieved
- Relationships are enhanced
- Action is taken
- There is energy and commitment for the next meeting.

CHECKLIST

- ☐ Circulate an agenda and all working papers in advance.
- ☐ Write your agenda as a series of questions that will trigger participants' thinking.
- ☐ Formulate and communicate a clear objective for the meeting – or for the separate agenda points.
- ☐ Make sure the right people are invited.
- ☐ Ensure that participation at the meetings is fairly managed.
- ☐ Summarise and repeat decisions before moving on to the next agenda point, for clarity and agreement.
- ☐ Finalise and circulate minutes/ follow-up action items within 24 hours.
- ☐ Consider how you position yourself at the meeting in order to get the best result – as content manager or process manager and use appropriate tools and techniques.
- ☐ Treat all participants with respect at all times – even when you disagree with them.

REFERENCES & FURTHER READING

Barker, A. (2002). *How to Manage Meetings*, London: The Sunday Times/ Kogan Page [Clear layout and structure; pragmatic "how to do it" approach; dip in and out.]

Dunne, P. (1997). *Running Board Meetings*, London: Kogan Page [Easy to read, light-hearted and with plenty of humour – but some serious points.]

Forsyth, P. (1994) *The Meetings Pocketbook*, Melrose Press [Quick read; full of interesting ideas and tips.]

Rae, L. (1996). *Let's Have a Meeting*, McGraw-Hill.

Tannenbaum, R. and Schmidt, W. H. (1958). How to Choose a Leadership Pattern, *Harvard Business Review*, 1958, 3, pp. 95-101.

Tropman, J. E. (1996). *Making Meetings Work – Achieving High Quality Group Decisions*, Thousand Oaks, CA: Sage Publications [More in-depth; needs reading (not dipping in).]

9: MANAGING PEOPLE

Martin Farrelly

Key Learning Objectives

- ☐ Recruit and select staff effectively.
- ☐ Learn the dos and don'ts of selection interviewing.
- ☐ Manage employee performance.
- ☐ Acquire practical guidelines on conducting performance management meetings.
- ☐ Master the skills of delegation.

There are many pertinent human resource-related issues that managers and their organisations are currently grappling with. This chapter deals with the current topics of recruiting and selecting staff, managing their performance, and delegating effectively. These are issues that you are sure to have encountered and have wrestled with throughout your managerial career.

RECRUITING & SELECTING STAFF[7]

The importance of recruiting the right staff is a crucial management activity and one that deserves particular attention. This issue was highlighted in a recent IMI survey, where O'Connor (2003) found that attracting and retaining key staff was viewed as a major management challenge for organisations. There is no doubt that the quality of staff hired has a significant impact on efficiency and morale. However, managers should not be expected to recruit and select staff without being given the necessary skills. These skills are vital, not only for the selection process, but also to ensure adherence to legal obligations.

The requisition process

For good reasons, many organisations put in place a requisition process when selecting and recruiting staff. If you want to spend €100,000 on a piece of capital equipment, you will undoubtedly need to follow a process that will include many of the following: cost-benefit analysis, business justification, provision of a number of competitive quotes and a submission to the appropriate deciding group. Strangely, in organisations sometimes the hiring of an executive costing more than the €100,000 is done for no

7 Recruitment is concerned with how organisations attract competent individuals to fill job positions. Traditionally, recruitment has been viewed as the staffing function preceding selection. However, according to Schmitt and Chan (1998), separating staffing practices into recruitment and selection is artificial. They should instead be viewed as a "two-way decision process", in which both the organisation and the individual make judgements and choices.

other reason than because someone has left the organisation. Little thought is invested up-front to determine whether the hiring decision should be made. This is not to be recommended!

As in all policies, line managers need a degree of autonomy coupled with control. In **Appendix 1**, a staff requisition form is presented. In many organisations, this is used only in times of tight cost control, when all hiring authorisations must be made by the Chief Executive. In the normal course of business, this process should be used as a prompt, to encourage the hiring line manager to requisition the vacancy and to confirm whether it is within budget.

The benefits of this document are:

- To activate the human resource systems
- To request the raising of a job description
- To consider the suitability of the role for job rotation, enlargement or enrichment
- To create an advertisement – whether internal, external or both.

Once the system is activated, the flow of applicants needs to be managed on a professional basis. The use of eHR (electronic HR) solutions by many larger organisations has changed the management of the whole hiring process. It is worth bearing in mind that sometimes applicants are also potential customers or suppliers, so they need to be treated with courtesy. Project yourself into their position – how have you felt when waiting for a response to a job application?

Figure 9.1 sets out the process by which a vacancy is filled (for a more detailed overview of the selection process, see **Appendix 2**).

FIGURE 9.1: THE SELECTION PROCESS

Step 1	Vacancy identified
Step 2	Staff requisition (business justification) and job description
Step 3	Business unit head/HR/CEO review and approval
	BREAKPOINT if not approved
Step 4	Equity check
Step 5	Job posting. Media/external/internal
Step 6	Application review
Step 7	Interview(s) and selection
Step 8	Reference check
Step 9	Offer and feedback.
Step 10	Arrival day

offer declined

Step 1: Vacancy

A vacancy can arise in a department for any of the following reasons:

- Resignation / termination
- Transfer / secondment
- Planned recruitment as part of business growth
- Unplanned addition realised as a consequence of business performance
- Reorganisation – new position identified as part of a change / restructuring process.

Vacancies can be resourced on either a temporary or permanent basis. This should be decided up-front and, in the case of a temporary role, a timescale should be considered in advance.

Step 2: Staff requisition and job description

The staff requisition form is completed, setting out the business case for the position, with the job description and person specification attached.

The review of the requisition process should take place within an agreed timescale, based on a service level agreement. Any additional information that is needed should be requested at this point. Again, it is important that boundaries are clarified, for example: Do all jobs, or those under certain salary levels or grades, need to go forward for approval?

Step 3: Business unit head / HR / CEO review and approval

The job should be submitted to the appropriate party for approval before any further activity is undertaken. The requisition can be challenged at any stage – for example, business unit level or HR. All the vacancy paperwork should support the application. The process should prompt a quick turnaround.

If the decision is made to recruit, then the position is deemed open and the process commences. If the requisition is turned down, then the manager is left with the challenge of dealing with current resourcing arrangements and productivity levels.

Step 4: Equity check – the salary!

Before proceeding, the salary attached to the post on offer should be reviewed to ensure equity is maintained. Salaries are not confidential and it would be damaging to a blossoming employment relationship for a new hire to find they were being paid significantly less than their peers. Indeed, as managers, we are often faced with the challenge of an employee who, despite having longer service with the organisation, find themselves receiving less pay than a new hire as a consequence of market pressures on selection.

Step 5: Job posting

There are a variety of means to access suitable candidates.

Internal search

If you have not got an internal recruitment and selection policy, you should set about doing so. Whether your enterprise is unionised or not, this should be in place. In the normal course of events, it will provide for:

- Jobs to be advertised internally
- A clear number of days within which internal applicants can apply
- Prescribed application forms or a request for a resumé of career to date
- A decision on whether all applicants have to be interviewed – this decision should be at management's discretion
- The right to recruit externally – the company retains this right.

In the interests of fairness, a manager should be aware that one of their staff is making an application for a job elsewhere in the organisation. Finally, should you select an internal candidate, the "notice" period should not exceed one month.

External Search

If the decision is made to recruit externally, there are a multitude of ways in which this can be achieved:

- **Advertising:** Through the media, be they national newspapers, local newspapers, professional journals, etc
- **Career/ jobs fairs:** Depending on the type of role to be filled, this can be a very useful method
- **eRecruiting:** This covers all Internet-based methods of attracting potential employees to careers at your organisation. The beauty of this approach is that, with the alignment of systems, candidates, upon becoming employees, can be electronically processed and their details recorded
- **Employee referrals:** This activity was more common during the times of the Celtic Tiger, where staff received incentives for

introducing prospective employees with the incentives increasing if staff were hired

- **College placements:** Many courses provide a job placement for the student. Both parties get an opportunity to experience what each has to offer and this often leads to a link-up after graduation
- **Employment agencies:** These are a useful source of potential candidates but you must manage the relationship with the agencies by preparing clear job specifications. The best approach is to have a preferred agency and work closely with them
- **Executive search:** Reserved for very senior roles. Very focused approach, based upon a strong working relationship with the advising firm.

Simple practices make for good selection processes. Time-scales for applications and responses are extremely important. For the purpose of the process, it is important to respond within the agreed time-scale. Failure to do so may alienate a candidate irrespective of whether they are internal or external and may lessen credibility in the recruitment and selection process.

Step 6: Application review

The review of applications is undertaken after the closing date. Candidates should be advised in writing (by email or letter) of the outcome. Internal applicants should be offered feedback as to why they did not get to the interview stage. Remember that applicants may be future buyers / customers / suppliers of your business, so treat them as you would like to be treated.

Those candidates identified as suitable on the basis of a review of their application and a comparison of it with the job specification will be invited to interview.

Step 7: Interview and selection[8]

The process has now reached the point where a few applicants are to be called for interview. Candidates should be given sufficient notice of the time and date of interview, who they will meet, and a copy of the job description. If necessary, you should attach a map with directions to your premises or direct them to your website. Depending on the job level, a copy of the annual report or appropriate brochures can be issued to prospective candidates. If a candidate is travelling a distance, deal explicitly with the issue of expenses in advance.

Given the legal constraints surrounding interviews, hiring managers (in conjunction with HR) should agree the specific competencies to be explored and the roles to be performed by the interviewer. The use of competencies can root interviews, by forcing interviewers to seek out evidence of the traits sought. Some organisations use psychometric tools as part of this process. In using such tools, it must be borne in mind that these are a means to an end and not an end in itself.

There are a few basic requirements for the holding of an interview (see **Figure 9.2** for the dos and don'ts of interviewing). They should be held in a room conducive for interviews – a place with adequate space and comfort to conduct an interview, where no interruptions will occur. They should be undertaken by skilled interviewers – who are, after all, representing you and your company.

Subsequent interviews may follow. However, we will now assume that, from an identified short-list, the most suitable candidate is selected.

---

8 This chapter adopts a general approach to selection – the interviewing process, while outlined, is not accorded significant attention.

FIGURE 9.2: THE DOS & DON'TS OF INTERVIEWING

DO	DON'T
Listen and encourage.	Talk too much.
Maintain eye contact and smile.	Look bored.
Probe and explore.	Exhibit mannerisms.
Ask 'open' questions.	Use closed or confusing questions.
Keep an open mind.	Avoid stereotyping and prejudices.
Make essential notes.	Spend time writing.
Control the interview.	Interrupt the candidate.
End positively.	Rush candidate out of the door.
	Argue or criticise.

Step 8: Reference check

A reference check may be carried out to confirm some of the details discussed at interview. Where possible, contact should be made with previous employers to validate information obtained at interview. The current employer should not be approached, until a letter of offer has been issued and has been returned, signed.

Some companies, at this point, conduct a pre-employment medical examination, however this is becoming less common. Most organisations are now appointing staff without this being undertaken.

Step 9: Offer and feedback

Having agreed the salary or the salary range at Step 4, the manager or the HR professional offers the job and the attendant package to the successful candidate.

There are two possible outcomes: either (a) the candidate accepts or (b) they decline the offer.

If the candidate accepts, then:

- The hiring manager should be advised
- Feedback is offered to all unsuccessful candidates
- If the successful candidate is internal, they receive a letter amending their contract of employment and a start date is agreed. All the necessary documentation for payroll, etc., is completed.
- If the successful candidate is external, they receive a contract of employment, confirming the start date and a starter pack with staff handbook, benefits information, etc.

Depending on the type of role and level, the hiring manager may consider meeting the new employee during their notice period.

Should the candidate decline the offer, the following should happen:

- Notify the manager
- Review the panel from the interview process
- Move on to the next suitable candidate on the panel
- Make a decision to offer
- If no one outside is available or another identified candidate turns down the offer, the process needs to recommence.

Step 10: Arrival day

Make the arrival day special for the employee. The tales of new, keen employees questioning their decision on day one owing to an apathetic "*here's your desk*" attitude are too numerous.

Have the simple things ready: desk, phone, stationery supplies – they count for a lot.

Find a way to make them the focal point for their colleagues to speed up their induction. Pair them off with a "buddy", a colleague who will navigate them through the organisation in those first few critical days and weeks.

MANAGING EMPLOYEE PERFORMANCE

Performance management is a critical management tool and HR lever. From IMI research on managers, performance management is widely used by organisations and records a high satisfaction rating among managers, relative to other HR tools (Cullen *et al.*, 2003). The key task of any manager is to maximise the return of all the resources they have under their control – financial, physical or human. A coherent, aligned and consistently applied performance management system can enable the manager to deliver on this objective.

The performance management process commences as presented in **Figure 9.3**. The organisation sets out its strategy and performance objectives for the year ahead. This is then cascaded down through the structure – for example, by division and department, resulting in team goals that eventually lead to the identification and creation of individual employee goals.

FIGURE 9.3: PERFORMANCE MANAGEMENT CULTURE

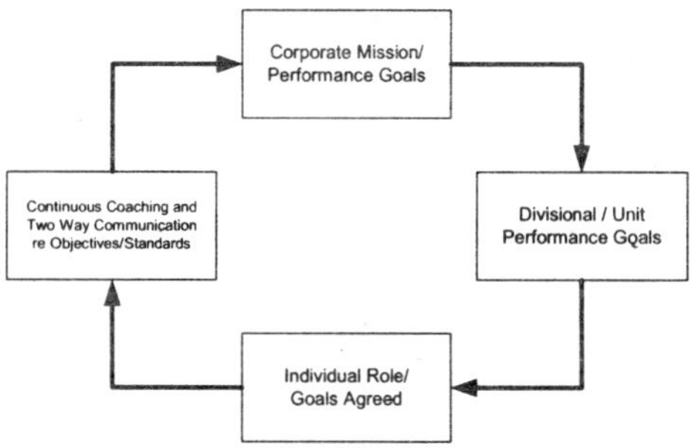

Most organisations undertake a business review and planning process that produces the performance goals for the organisation. It is essential that the linkage between organisational and individual objectives are explicit and targeted. This is to ensure that every employee feels they are contributing to the success of the enterprise.

Advantages of performance management to the employee include:

- Clarity about their role
- Clarity of their manager's expectations
- Awareness of the company's direction
- Opportunity to discuss personal development.

For the manager, the benefits of the business review and planning process include an opportunity to:

- Discuss individual performance with the employee
- Reinforce team goals and individual direction
- Place individual's performance in the team context
- Appraise the employee of changing objectives (with regular meetings).

When setting objectives, they should be linked to business priorities, should be measurable and specific, attainable and worded clearly.

Setting out the organisation's goal-setting system is straightforward. However, the application of the performance management system, as set out in **Figure 9.4**, requires a consistent approach.

FIGURE 9.4: THE PERFORMANCE MANAGEMENT MODEL

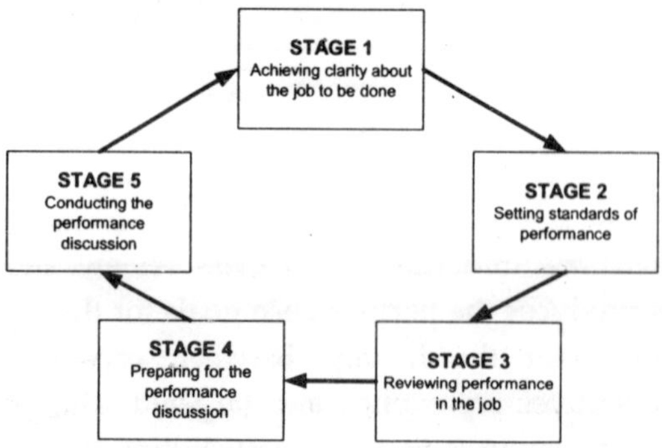

Performance management meetings

> *"If the manager must put on his judicial hat occasionally, he does it reluctantly and with understandable qualms."* (McGregor, 1957).

Performance management meetings should be held frequently with employees. This is a bone of contention in many organisations, as many managers feel that they have neither the time to conduct these reviews nor feel comfortable in doing so. Therefore, here are some practical guidelines for the running of these meetings:

- Provide an interruption-free, neutral location
- Ensure that both parties are prepared
- Bring all of the relevant documents to the meeting
- Create the necessary atmosphere
- Allow sufficient time for discussion
- Listen and talk in proportion to your physical attributes – you have two ears but only one mouth!

To aid the employee through the discussion, you should have an opening, middle and end.

In the opening phase, we confirm:

- Why are we here? Establish the purpose
- What do we want to deliver? Agree the process.

The middle phase includes the review of performance on the year just completed, on the basis of agreed goals that may, due to business demands, have been adjusted and recorded during the year. The discussion can then move onto the identification and agreement of the performance goals for the year ahead. In some systems, the middle phase can also include a discussion about the individual employee's development plan.

In closing the meeting, you should be concerned with summarising the inputs of the meeting and seeking to ensure agreement on the outputs. Finally, confirmation of the discussion should be reflected in writing.

During the process, the employee should be encouraged to talk as much as possible. This can be achieved by:

- Asking open questions
- Asking supplementary probing questions
- Checking understanding and summarising the position
- Displaying positive body language
- Aiding team members to find solutions.

In an effort to manage this flow, I suggest that managers adopt the following approach at such meetings by using a coaching process (see **Figure 9.3** earlier):

- Open the meeting
- Listen to the other person's views
- Offer your view
- Identify areas of disagreement and resolve
- Plan action and close.

There is no magic formula for creating a performance management system for your organisation. However, there are two simple propositions on which performance management is built (Armstrong and Baron, 1998):

- When people (individuals and teams) know and understand what is expected of them, and have taken part in forming these expectations, they will use their best endeavours to meet them
- The capacity to meet expectations depends on the levels of capability that can be achieved by individuals and teams, the level of support they are given by management and the processes, systems and resources made available to them by the organisation.

DELEGATION

Delegation is a very close relation of performance management, which we have just discussed. When managers agree the department's objectives and the objectives of those reporting to them, this presents a unique opportunity for managers to pinpoint the activities that are essential but could possibly be completed by someone else. A major benefit of delegation for employees, assuming they have the skills to undertake the tasks, is that they can avail of a strong learning opportunity.

If we accept that management is getting things done through others, then the concept of delegation is already embedded. If management is getting things done through others, it can be compared with doing things yourself – if you are doing it yourself, you are not managing (see **Figure 9.5**).

FIGURE 9.5: THE THEORY OF MANAGEMENT

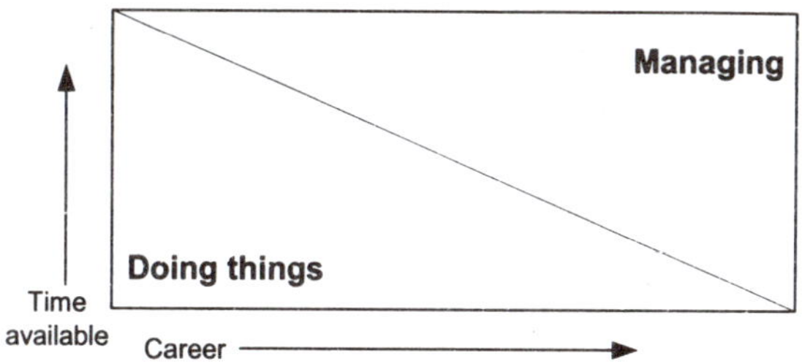

Source: Adapted from Ashridge (2001b, p.5).

As managers, starting out in your career, you spent significantly more time doing things. Upon progression, however, you started to spend more time managing. As the progression curve straightens, a greater proportion of time is spent managing and less time is spent doing. Nice in theory, however the reality is best conveyed in **Figure 9.6**.

FIGURE 9.6: THE REALITY OF MANAGEMENT

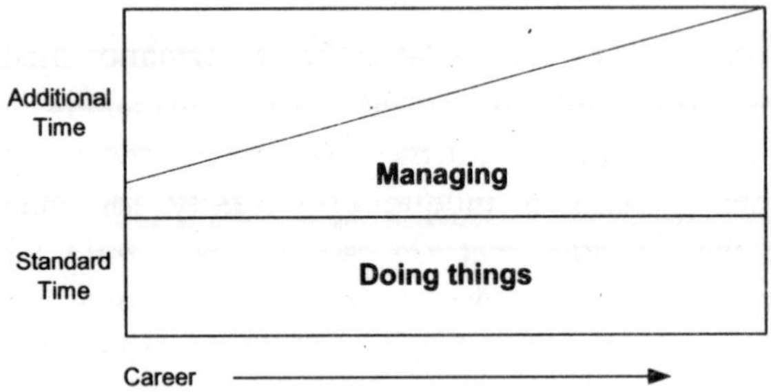

Source: Adapted from Ashridge (2001b, p.6)

Here, the "Additional Time" section reflects the fact that many managers continue to "do" and manage only after the end of the normal day.

How do we avoid this? The key is to use delegation as a lever – a crucial one for managers. It can provide wonderful opportunities, albeit tempered with dangers and traps.

Benefits of effective delegation

These include:

- Frees the manager to devote more time to important tasks
- Decisions can be made closer to the front line and usually quicker
- Your reports will enjoy their newly-acquired autonomy and will grow and develop.

With such possibilities, why would a manager not delegate tasks to capable employees? Failing to delegate creates a vicious circle, as staff:

- Do not have the authority or information to make a decision
- Lack self-confidence
- Are afraid of criticism.

Finally, to avoid all of the above, they delegate upwards back to the manager.

On this basis, you end up doing those jobs that do not directly support your objectives. By delegating, recognise that more responsibility may come your way by giving it away. Coach your employees, but with specific aims:

- Agree goals
- Secure commitment
- Coach, counsel and develop
- Energise.

Common comments from managers on delegation

In my experience, many managers fail to delegate, making excuses such as *'it is easier to do it myself'* or *'I've delegated before and the job wasn't done to my satisfaction'*. However, as a manager, you need to learn how to delegate *effectively*. By failing to delegate, you may be snatching a potential learning opportunity from an employee and creating an additional workload for yourself. What you gain in the short-term, by doing the task yourself, you may lose in the long-term, as the employee will be unable to conduct the task in the future.

Personally, as a manager I have undertaken tasks myself in situations where it would have been more efficient for one of my employees to do so. We have all been there. However, for the future, it is important that you identify situations where you must put your delegation skills to good use.

FINALLY, HR IS NOT JUST FOR THE HR DEPARTMENT!

People are a key source of competitive advantage for any organisation. Formulating and implementing a culture in your organisation that nurtures employees and their performance is key to creating advantage for your organisation. Admittedly, in an environment where cost-cutting is the order of the day, this can be difficult. However, the HR issues managers are facing are no longer issues that managers can attempt to avoid or automatically re-direct to the "HR Manager". Instead, they feature in the roles of managers from various functions, spanning across all management positions, levels and organisations. So the next time you have to deal with a "HR issue", first consider whether you can deal with it effectively yourself as a manager or whether it really requires the help of the HR department. Remember, every manager has a "HR aspect" to their jobs. It's part and parcel of the very essence of being a manager!

REFERENCES & FURTHER READING

Armstrong, M. and Baron, A. (1998). *Performance Management: The New Realities,* London: Institute of Personnel and Development.

Ashridge (2001a). *Performance Management – Learning Guide, UK.*

Ashridge (2001b). *Delegation – Learning Guide, UK.*

Brown, C. L. (1997). *Essential Delegation Skills,* Aldershot, Hampshire: Gower.

Cullen, J., Mangan, J. and Dwyer, G. (2003). *Management Tools and Techniques, A Study in the Irish Context,* Dublin: Irish Management Institute.

McGregor, D. (1957). An Uneasy Look at Performance Appraisals: *Harvard Business Review.* May-June, and reprinted again in September/October, 1972, p. 135.

O'Connor, M. (2003). *Top Challenges for Managers,* Dublin: Irish Management Institute.

Schmitt, N. and Chan, D. (1998). *Personnel Selection: A Theoretical Approach,* Thousand Oaks, CA: Sage Publications.

Appendix 1: Recruitment Requisition Form

Department: ______________________________

Job Title: ______________________________

Reports To: ______________________________

Cost Centre: ______________________________

Position:	Permanent	Temporary (state reason)	Contract (fixed term) Date from ________ to ________

(A) If a new position, has the position been budgeted for? Yes No

(B) If replacement, date of leaving: ______________________________

Requirements of position: (see attached job and person specification)

____

____

Business case for recruitment:

____

____

Conditions

Salary Range: ________________

Company Car: Yes No

For Human Resources Use Only

Media to be used:	internal	external	
If external use:	agency	newspaper	website

Requested by:	________________	Date: ________
Approved by Department Head:	________________	Date: ________
Approved by Managing Director:	________________	Date ________
Approved by HR Director:	________________	Date: ________

Recruiter assigned: ______________________________

Date process commenced: ______________________________

Date process concluded (offer issued): ______________________________

Name of person appointed: ______________________________

Appendix 2: The Selection Process

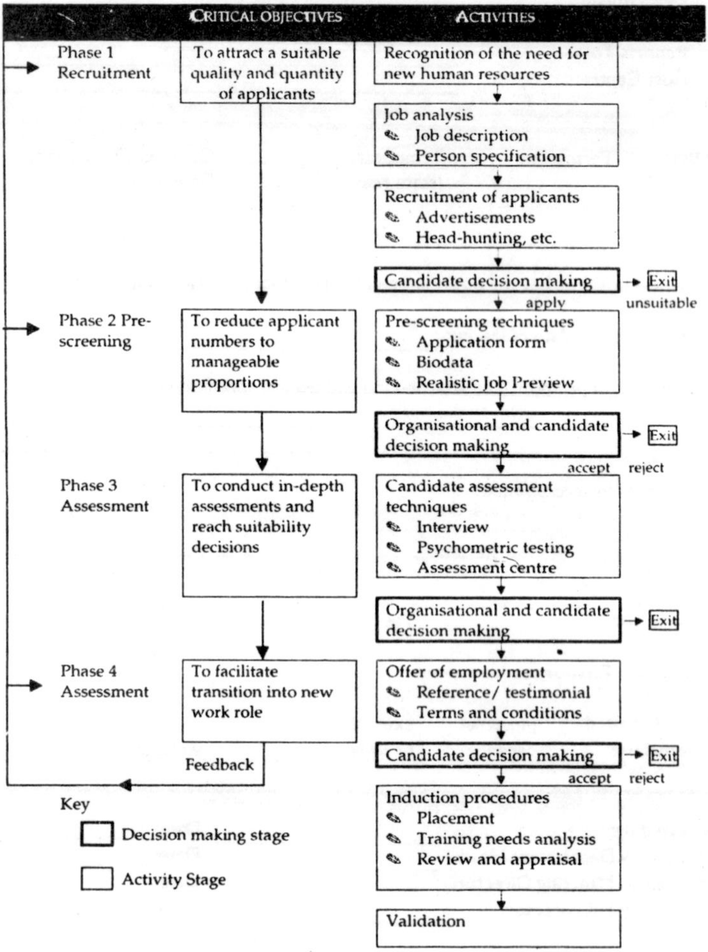

10: MANAGING THE CUSTOMER

Siobhan McAleer

Key Learning Objectives

- ☐ Describe customer relationship management.
- ☐ Develop a strategy for customer management.
- ☐ Identify and segment your customers.
- ☐ Understand what drives customer satisfaction, retention and loyalty.
- ☐ Implement a customer management strategy.

The breadth of choice of suppliers available and depth of products on offer means that the customers are in the driving seat: deciding how (mobile commerce), where and when they want to buy from you. They are managing you!

We are living in an over-communicated world and your offer has to have distinct and different value to customers. This is the starting point of any customer relationship. Today's companies must attract customers with strong customer value propositions, keep them by delivering superior value and manage the company and customer interface effectively.

The term "customer relationship management" (CRM) has been hijacked and equated with a technology-driven solution to manage customers. In this chapter, we will define customer relationship marketing and technology's role, and also put it into the overall context of marketing in the company. We will also look at customers in the context of the business to the consumer market (B2C) and the business to business market (B2B). This will also include services ... as all businesses are now in the service business.

The ability of a company to manage customers is vital. It is a function of their organisational culture and values and how far they sustain the view of "the customer comes first." If you want to know where your future profits will come from ... look to the source of your cashflow, your customer.

The success of your customer plan is dependent on everyone in the organisation. The notion of customer centricity, as defined by Adam Smith ("*consumption is the sole purpose of production*") or Drucker ("*the purpose of business is to create a customer*"), is even more relevant in today's highly competitive environment. The paradigm has shifted. Products come and go. The unit of value today is the customer relationship.

DEFINING CUSTOMER RELATIONSHIP MANAGEMENT

Customer relationship management (CRM) is a critical subject for all businesses and companies have made significant investments in new systems, strategies and channels for managing their customers – often with disappointing results, due to a lack of understanding of what customer management is, how it can deliver value and to a lack of leadership in driving the strategy through the business.

There are many definitions for CRM. The lack of a single agreed and generally accepted definition is one of the key problems in this area. I suggest as a preferred definition:

> *"Customer Relationship Management is the strategic process of selecting the customers a firm can most profitably serve and shaping the interactions between the company and these customers. The goal is to optimise the current and future value of the customer for the company as well as satisfaction for the customer."* (Reinartz, INSEAD, 2002)

Other definitions such as *"one-to-one marketing"* and *"customer intimacy"* highlight the segmentation of the customer-base to the level of a single unique customer.

Customer relationship management is based on deep customer knowledge. Information is the engine that drives the process and the ability of the company to act on the information to make a difference to how the customer is treated.

Drivers in Managing the Individual Customer Relationship

The driving force behind the growth in CRM comes from the understanding that it is more profitable to seek growth from existing customers than it is from new customers. Retention costs less than acquisition and a customer in their sixth year of doing business with a company is seven times more profitable to that company than a customer in their first year.

Research by Reichheld of Bain & Co in the 1990s also examined the cost of customer defections, in industries as varied as credit cards and industrial laundries, and found that reducing customer defections by even 5% can boost profitability by as much as 85%. While more recent research has questioned some of the findings, it is undisputed that loyalty pays. The customer is no longer seen as an exploitable source of income but as a long-term asset.

Figure 10.1: Why Customers are More Profitable over Time

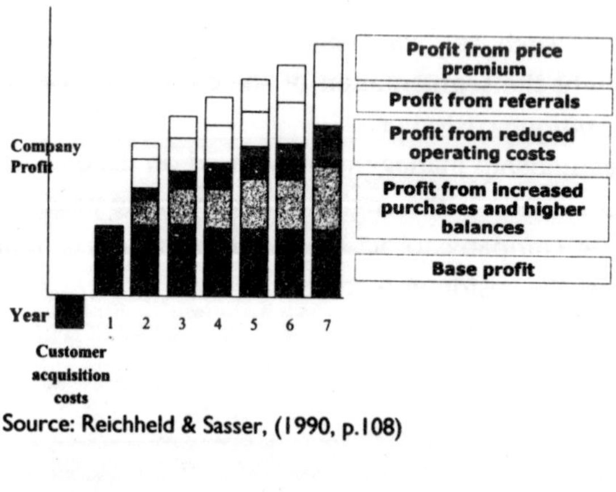

Source: Reichheld & Sasser, (1990, p.108)

In B2B marketing, companies have long realised the value of looking after their most important customers. They have adopted many of the theories and practices of relationship marketing as formerly much of the consumer marketing practices were not relevant to their businesses. The organisation of the sales function into Major Account Management is one of the most widespread manifestations of the applicability of relationship marketing to B2B companies. The use of sales force automation, which originated in the 1980s, has allowed everyone in the company to have the same view of the customer. This allows for increased effectiveness – better customer targeting as well as sales force efficiencies. Improvements in data storage and data-mining techniques means that sales force automation has progressed into additional company-wide functionality, to the point that most large-scale Enterprise Resource Planning (ERP) systems now incorporate a CRM component.

In consumer businesses, managing customer relationships to the level of the individual has been an extension of database and direct marketing. The improvements in technology – the volume and speed of data storage and the ability to interrogate and understand customer information – has meant that companies with large customer-bases on the one hand and with detailed customer information on the other are able to harness technology to make sense of the data in a more cost-effective way.

Consumer companies now have the ability to connect with each customer on an individual level. In direct marketing, the connection with the customer is a monologue – one way – while CRM allows a dialogue with the customer. Firms can use the answers from this dialogue to acquire new customers intelligently, provide better service and support, customise offerings more precisely to customer preferences, cross-sell, close deals faster and provide on-going value to satisfy and retain profitable customers.

IS CRM FOR EVERYONE?

While the logic of identifying and managing the relationship with those customers that you can best and most profitably serve is unquestionable for all businesses, the degree with which it is applied to the level of the individual customer is dependent on several factors. In B2B markets, there are generally fewer customers and it is easier to identify the most profitable than in a consumer business served through an intermediary, the retailer. Those companies that are rich in customer data, such as banks, airlines and supermarkets, have the customer information on which to build knowledge – and hence strategies – to differentiate their offering on an individual level.

Before embarking on a one-to-one relationship strategy, companies should also ask whether the customer wants to have a relationship with them. One of the cornerstones of relationship marketing is that there must be sound reasons on both sides of the relationship.

THE ROLE OF TECHNOLOGY

Increasingly, companies have the choice of connecting with customers through multiple channels, direct sales forces and self-serving technologies such as the Internet and call centres. This can make managing the relationship more complex, as contact information is coming into the company from multiple sources, although the use of technology can enable the co-ordination of these multiple contact points. Technology is the enabler that has brought the personal service of the corner-shop to multi-site multi-customer businesses.

However, in using technology, less is often more and companies should take an incremental approach if they decide to enable their customer plans by acquiring CRM software. There are many pessimistic voices that quote the failure and disappointing results that companies have achieved by implementing CRM software packages. Most research has found that it is not the technology that has been at fault, but the lack of a customer-centric business philosophy and the pre-existence of non-customer-friendly business processes.

Employee motivation and commitment, as well as top management leadership, are the next cornerstones of relationship marketing. A failure in change management has been the major cause (some 70% +) for failure. This echoes the need for a "customer first" ethos and practice before any investment in technology.

However, in the adoption of any new management tool, there is always a steep learning curve. The lessons learned from companies that have had disappointing results should serve as a base for future progress. In a comprehensive hindsight view of previous adoptions of a CRM strategy using technology, Rigby *et al.* (2002) caution against the "four perils of CRM":

- Implementing a CRM strategy before creating a customer strategy
- Rolling out CRM before changing your organisation to match
- Assuming that more technology is better
- Stalking, and not wooing, your customers.

Implementing a CRM strategy before creating a customer strategy

Ask yourself these questions:

- How much must our value proposition change to earn greater customer loyalty?
- How much customisation is appropriate and profitable for our strategy?
- What is the potential value of increasing the loyalty of our customers in each segment?
- How much time / money can we allocate to CRM right now?
- If we believe in customer relationships, why are we taking steps towards a CRM programme today? What can we do next week to build customer relationships without spending on technology?

Rolling out CRM before changing your organisation to match

A customer-focused organisation is the foundation stone. Job descriptions, performance measures, compensation and training programmes have to be restructured prior to implementing any technology. If one of the key aims is to have a common view of the customer across the organisation, the organisation must be aware that it needs a common view!

Assuming that more technology is better

CRM does not have to be technology-intensive. Customer relationships can be managed just as well by motivating employees to be more aware of customer needs.

Technology can give deeper insights and allow the company to realise opportunities that it could never have achieved without technology, such as managing its logistics and supply chain more efficiently. However, the implementation of CRM technology requires a thorough analysis of customer strategy. In addition, it can be implemented incrementally, with learning achieved *en route.*

Stalking, and not wooing, your customers

Relationships are two-way streets. If you fail to build relationships with customers who want relationships with you, you'll lose them to competitors. Try to build relationships with disinterested customers and you will be perceived as a stalker.

Such shortcomings are not new. Instead of CRM, substitute the word "marketing" and it's easy to see why adding technology does not create an immediate panacea. Superimposing technology on weak manual processes, and in the context of a poor culture that does not value the customer, will not create successful customer relationships. Therefore, we must look at customer management in the broader context of marketing within the company.

DEVELOPING A CUSTOMER STRATEGY

Developing a CRM strategy requires being clear about the following simple, but strategic, issues:

- Who is your target customer?
- What value are you providing them?
- Who are your most valuable customers now, and into the future?
- How can you best develop a relationship with these customers?

A good customer management strategy should also address those whom the business will not serve – non-customers. Information on, and about, the customer, whether from market research, customer intelligence or internal data forms the foundation of this strategy.

Who is your customer?

The starting point of developing a customer strategy is to determine the target market and build from there.

In practice, a business cannot be all things to all customers. Successful companies segment the market of all available customers into more specific groups or segments of customers for which their offering has greater appeal and offers the best profit potential. As markets become more diverse and dynamic, Levitt's proclamation some 20 years ago has become all the more valid:

> "*If you're not thinking segments, you're not marketing.*" (Levitt)

SEGMENTATION OF B2B CUSTOMERS

Allied Irish Bank (GB) adopted a clear segmentation strategy in the UK. Given the size and scale of the large UK banks and clearing houses, AIB decided to pursue a strategy of targeting the smaller business user. It focused their resources and built knowledge and deeper relationships with this sector so effectively that, from 1994 to 2003, the Forum of Private Businesses has awarded AIB the accolade of being the "Best Business Bank" in the UK.

Traditional bases of business segmentation are outlined in **Figure 10.2.**

Figure 10.2: Traditional Bases of Business Segmentation

Traditional Segmentation Bases	Some Examples
Demographics	Industry type, company size or location.
Operating variables	User/non-user status. Customer capabilities.
Purchasing approaches	Purchasing criteria – quality, service or price seekers? Purchasing function organisation – decentralised or centralised? Nature of existing relationship – already strong or the most desirable companies?
Situational factors	Specific applications – focus on certain applications rather than all applications. Size of order.
Personal characteristics	Focus on companies with similar values to ourselves. Risk-takers or risk-avoiders?

Demographics – industry, customer size and geography – are the traditional methods of segmenting business markets. Increasingly, as in consumer segmentation, many companies believe that understanding a customer's purchasing approaches, buying behaviour and the benefits that they are seeking are more effective means of segmenting the market. Segmenting even deeper on the basis of the customer's application, capabilities, business priorities, usage situations and contribution to profitability give a more detailed understanding of how customer requirements and preferences may vary.

We will look at purchasing approaches or buying behaviour and contribution to profitability in more detail. While it is important for you to decide how you are going to segment the market, it is worth considering first how customers decide they are going to segment you.

Purchasing approaches or buying behaviour

In practice, B2B companies commonly select from three purchasing orientations:

- Buying
- Procurement
- Supply chain management.

In a buying orientation, the focus is on minimising the price paid in a given transaction.

In a procurement orientation, the company looks deeper at the concept of value (benefits *versus* cost) and strives to reduce the total cost of ownership. The offering here often comprises a bundling of products and services into an overall solution.

In a supply-chain management orientation, the aim is to seek to obtain the greatest value relative to price from a close working relationship with a supplier. The continuum of relationship that the customer wants can go from a transaction sale to the deepest commitment that goes beyond supply chain management to "enterprise" sales. An "enterprise" commitment goes beyond both the product and the sales force. Here, the customer is looking for an extraordinary level of value creation. They are seeking ways in which the supplier can leverage any or all of the supplier's corporate assets to contribute to the customer's success. For example, an insurance broker could look for the placement of an underwriter from the insurance company, or for them to develop new risk management systems. Such a relationship can go as far as outsourcing certain processes.

Kraljic's (1983) purchasing model (see **Figure 10.3**), and the variations developed over the last decades, have been used by companies to assist in the selection of the most appropriate purchasing strategy for different types of products, optimising the trade-off between cost and risk. Companies assess their purchases on the basis of their impact on their overall financial results, on the one hand, and the level of supply risk, on the other hand.

The impact on financial risk is determined by factors such as:

- Direct cost of the product purchased
- Percentage of total costs in the end product
- Indirect cost of purchasing.

The supply risk can be determined by:

- Number of suppliers
- Availability of alternatives
- Stability of the potential supplier
- Costs of switching to an alternative.

By plotting their purchases along these two dimensions into a matrix, a company can decide how to segment you, the supplier!

FIGURE 10.3: THE PURCHASING MODEL

High **IMPACT ON FINANCIAL RESULT**	**LEVERAGE PRODUCTS** **alternative suppliers** ***Let suppliers compete***	**STRATEGIC PRODUCTS** **difficult to switch suppliers** ***Engage in partnerships***
Low	**ROUTINE PRODUCTS** **widely available diverse or complex to manage** ***Systems contracting & EDI***	**BOTTLENECK PRODUCTS** **monopolistic market or high entry barriers** ***Secure supply & develop other options***
	Low **SUPPLY RISK**	**High**

Source: Adapted from *Key Management Models* (2003, p.117).

Looking at the model, we can see:

- **Strategic products** (for example, new technology) have the greatest impact on the bottom line as they are often hard to get.

As the supply risk is high, a partnership approach is recommended. The supplier seeks to lower the costs through early supplier involvement, co-development and co-design

- **Leverage products** (for example, raw materials) represents a high percentage of the impact that purchasing has on the company's financial result. However, there are many suppliers whom the buying company can leverage off each other. Leverage products require central contracts with general terms and conditions
- **Bottleneck products** (for example, essential spare parts) where disruption of supply would have serious consequences for the company, the company must secure supply or be protected against the lack of it. This usually leads to extra inventory, hedging and or supplier contracts with major penalties for breach of contract
- **Routine products** (for example, office furniture and stationery) where the company will seek to reduce the number of suppliers and will set up systems to streamline purchases, such as EDI (Electronic Data Interchange) or automatic call-offs. Many companies are seeking to use e-commerce to manage company-wide contracts across multi-sites to ensure maximum efficiency of purchasing and that all parts of the business benefit from company-wide price agreements.

Understanding a company's buying orientation, how the buyer perceives the value of your product or service and the supply risk they encounter, should help to determine which customers a company wants to work with and on what basis the relationship will develop – how they can create and deliver value to those customers.

Contribution to profitability

The maxim that 20% of your customers provide 80% of the profit has also become commonplace, but nonetheless critical.

In practice, companies often have difficulty assessing the true profitability of a customer due to their accounting systems, which are often product- or business unit-focused rather than organised on a customer basis. The availability of such data is the basis of a relationship strategy as it is imperative to understand the costs of serving the customer before allocating them major customer status. They may be big in volume terms but not necessarily profitable.

The use of customer profitability as a means of segmenting customers also brings further practical issues. The term *Customer Lifetime Value* is in vogue. Effectively, it means assessing the value of the customer over "their lifetime" relationship with you rather than viewing each sale as a single transaction. The concept is appealing, since its main benefit lies in focusing others in the business, who perhaps do not have a customer-facing role, to appreciate the importance of the customer.

SEGMENTATION OF CONSUMER MARKETS

Similar to business markets, there is no single way to segment a consumer market. Companies use multiple methods and continue to segment deeper and deeper into the market to identify an attractive market segment. The main methods are:

- **By geography:** From nations, states, regions, counties, cities or neighbourhoods
- **By demographics:** Age, sex, gender, family size, family life cycle, income, occupation, education, religion, ethnic community or nationality
- **By psychographics:** Based on social class, lifestyle or personality characteristics
- **By behavioural characteristics:** Dividing buyers into groups based on their knowledge, attitudes, uses or responses to a product.

Many marketers have found that segmenting the market using behavioural characteristics is the best starting point. They look at:

- **Occasions:** When do customers get the idea to buy, make their purchase or use the purchase – for example, mobile phone network operators are promoting the use of camera phones for work purposes, such as fashion buyers at a suppliers sending back ideas to colleagues, or architects and surveyors using the camera on site
- **Benefits sought:** Identifying the main benefits that they seek from the product class – for example, toothpaste, the kinds of people who look for each benefit and the brands that deliver each benefit. Research into segmentation of the toothpaste market found four benefit segments – economic, medicinal, cosmetic and taste
- **User status:** Non-users, ex-users, potential users, first-time users and regular users
- **Usage rate**: Light, medium and heavy users. Heavy users are often a small percentage of the total market, but account for a high percentage of the total buying (80/20 rule again). Loyalty programmes by supermarkets and airlines have been a response to identifying heavy or frequent users in order to gain their repeat business. Other loyalty schemes include attempting to build a relationship with the customer through clubs, newsletters, samples and gift catalogues. The effectiveness of loyalty schemes and segmentation by loyalty is limited by how people buy. Most customers will use various brands and will choose from a range of preferred brands, as well as buying opportunistically
- **Buyer-readiness stage:** Consumers go through various stages before the purchase – from awareness to knowledge, liking, preference, conviction and, finally, purchase.

The Buying Decision-Maker

B2B markets

Once the target segment and the companies within the segment are identified, the next step is to identify the decision-maker(s) in the buying process, and beyond that their professional and personal objectives.

Case Study

For example, a provider of intelligent navigation and personalisation technology to the mobile phone industry, *Changing Worlds*, identified that their customers were not the design engineers of the mobile network operators, as might have been expected, but the "revenue responsible" marketing department. *Changing Worlds*' application allowed the end-customer – the mobile phone user – to access content on their phone in a user-friendly manner personalised with their preferences, such as sports results and news services. This drove revenue to the mobile phone network provider and increased the ARPU (average revenue per user – a key metric for mobile operators). As a result of targeting the user within the company who gained the most value from their product (the marketing department), *Changing Worlds* were able to gain access to the technical specialists and get product approval. They were then able to piggyback on the success of this customer to access the networks' sister companies throughout Europe, as they had a credible reference point in a leading European market.

Often there are *several participants* who influence the buying process – called the buying centre or unit. Typically three parties can be involved in a buying process assuming at least one, if not several, of the following roles:

- **Users:** Members of the organisation who will use the product or service. They often initiate the purchase process and help to define specifications
- **Influencers:** Affect the buying decision. They often define the specifications and provide information on evaluating alternatives. Technical people can have the most influence here

- **Buyers:** Have formal authority to select the supplier and arrange the terms of the purchase. Their main role is to select vendors and to negotiate the deal
- **Deciders:** Have formal or informal power to select, or approve, the final suppliers. In routine buying, the buyers are often the deciders or, at least, the approvers
- **Gatekeepers:** Control the flow of information to others. Often this is the buyer who may deny the supplier access to others involved in the decision-making process
- **Approver:** Has the power to say "Yes" or "No". Often, this is a technical person with specific, and often unquestioned, product knowledge.

As the relationship between a buyer and supplier develops, the depth and breadth of contact between them grows.

The major challenge for the marketer is to establish:

- Who is part of the decision?
- What decisions do they influence?
- What is their relative degree of influence?
- What evaluation criteria each participant uses?
- What are their professional and personal motivations?

Since the answers to these questions have significant implications for your marketing strategy, you should ask yourself :

- **Your value proposition:** Does your offering meet the needs of each member of the buying unit?
- **Your account management capabilities:** Are they proficient in identifying the unit, uncovering each role's requirements and developing contacts and the appropriate relationship with them?

Mapping the different decision-makers through the various stages of the buying process is a key tool in managing the range of contacts and in identifying any gaps and strongholds.

B2C markets

Increasingly, females are the decision-maker in most domestic purchases – in the US, research has found that women make, or influence, 80% of all products or services purchased.

You may also be surprised to learn that 67% of all car purchases are determined by the children – not the parents. Tweens (8 to 14 year-olds) are an increasingly powerful and smart consumer group, which in 2003 alone spent, and influenced, an astounding US$1.88 trillion.

It is also important to consider that the buying decision-maker may change after the initial purchase is made. This is important for products where the purchase is reconsidered – for example, mobile phone providers and banks. Sky Television found that, while the male in the household made the initial decision to subscribe to Sky, it was the female who decided whether to renew the subscription! Thus, the marketing communications objectives for acquiring the customer and those for retaining the customer will be different.

Customer Satisfaction, Retention & Loyalty

Critical for medium to long-term success is developing and building customer satisfaction and, thereby, retaining the customer as long as possible through winning their loyalty.

How do you satisfy customers?

The starting point is to consider customer value. Exploring the process of value creation gives firms a better grasp of the ups and downs of customer satisfaction.

Customers choose the company that gives them most value. Customers are, in the main, value-maximisers, with a *caveat* that their propensity to seek value may be diluted by the costs of searching (time or information availability) and their income levels. Value is determined by the "perceived benefits " they get from the company minus the cost or "perceived sacrifice" (see **Figure 10.4**).

FIGURE 10.4: THE COMPONENTS OF CUSTOMER VALUE

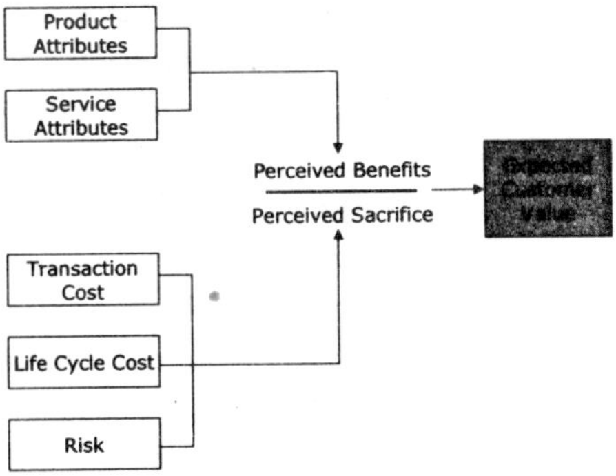

Source: Naumann (1995, p.103).

Although buyers do not always exhibit rational behaviour (by choosing the company that offers the best value), **Figure 10.4** nonetheless offers useful insights into assessing the total customer cost and value of their own and competing offerings.

A seller who finds that a competitor delivers greater value has two choices:

- The seller can try to increase customer value by strengthening or augmenting the product, service, personnel or image benefits of the offer. This includes building the company's brand to create emotional ties
- The seller can also decrease the total customer cost by reducing its price, simplifying the order and delivery process, absorbing some buyer risk by offering a warranty or examining the customer's total cost of ownership.

Managing expectations

Customer satisfaction with a purchase is dependent on the product's performance relative to their expectations. If the performance falls short of expectations, then the customer will be dissatisfied. However, if performance matches expectations, then the customer is satisfied. If performance exceeds expectations, then the customer will be highly satisfied or delighted.

Expectations are formed by the buyer's past experiences, the opinions of friends and opinion-makers (increasingly, consumer information sites on the Internet) and the company and their competitors' information and promises.

Expectation management is key. Too low and you fail to attract new customers, too high and customers may be dissatisfied. The key is to underpromise and overdeliver.

You meet or exceed customers' expectations by managing the customer experience. The important dimensions of this experience are easily remembered by the acronym **TREAT.** A company should endeavour to ensure that it can exceed customers expectations through:

- **Total responsiveness:** Prompt service, immediate response, individualised attention and quick complaint resolution
- **Reliability:** Product does what it is supposed to do and the company is there when it is needed
- **Empathy:** Taking time to really understand the customer's situation and engages in joint problem-solving
- **Assurances:** Knowledge of the employees and the ability to convey trust
- **Tangibles:** The outward appearance of the company, its employees, communications and any physical contact point the customer has with the company.

Why even satisfied customers defect

However, is customer satisfaction enough to ensure retention and long term loyalty? It has long been managerial wisdom that the effort and cost required to boost customer satisfaction from, say, a

4 to a 5 in a 1 to 5 scale is not worth the return and that more impact can be made by concentrating on those customers who scored 2 or 3. Research by Xerox shattered this conventional wisdom, which found that totally-satisfied customers (those that scored 5) were six times more likely to repurchase in the next 18 months than those that scored 4. This further reinforces the argument that exceeding and delighting are the only routes to customer loyalty. Delighted customers are also likely to act as evangelists and advocates for the company and its products, creating positive word of mouth.

Limitations of customer satisfaction surveys

As a tool for measuring the value a company delivers to its customers, satisfaction surveys are imperfect. As a tool for predicting repurchase intention, they are also highly imperfect.

Satisfaction surveys have several problems:

- Satisfaction scores have become an end in themselves
- The scores are meaningless unless they are translated into loyalty and profits
- They are often poorly designed and conceived
- Most often, they ignore the differences between different customer segments – the aggregate score will include both profitable and unprofitable customers. For example, a bank's branch manager might receive many complaints about the lines at the counter but the most profitable customers do most of their business on the phone, Internet or at ATMs. Investing in more counter-staff may inflate satisfaction ratings, but actually deflate profits, by increasing service levels and increasing costs in an area their best customers don't care about.

In short, customer satisfaction surveys should be designed robustly, tested carefully and interpreted with caution. The good news is that research shows that, asking a customer whether they are satisfied, makes them more satisfied (but don't ask too often)!

Other methods of tracking customer satisfaction are complaint and suggestion schemes, ghost shopping and customer defection analysis.

A recent development has been the use of Customer Journey Mapping, which enables organisations to understand how their customers use various channels and touch-points to interact with the organisation and the potential barriers and obstacles they encounter in attempting to complete a transaction successfully and satisfactorily.

How to build customer relationships and loyalty

Exceptional customer service ("delighted" customers) is the basis for building a customer relationship, as discussed previously.

Other methods include:

- Loyalty schemes
- Structural ties
- Brand-building.

Companies can give enhanced benefits of loyalty such as financial or social benefits – discounts for repeat purchases or other rewards for loyalty. Typical examples include loyalty cards or frequent flyer awards. However, experience has shown that the latter incentives are more about customer retention than long-term loyalty and that their effects will only last until there is a better offer available. If all competitors offer the same schemes, then such "customer loyalty" programmes become the cost of doing business rather than a differentiator. Experience has also shown that the customers can become more loyal to the scheme than to the brand.

Through enhanced benefits, companies may build structural ties with their customers that can make it difficult or costly for them to defect. These can take the form of corporate hospitality through to bundling of products, sharing equipment, knowledge and expertise. **Figure 10.5** presents the range of tools a company can employ.

FIGURE 10.5: LEVELS OF RETENTION STRATEGIES

Foundation: Excellent Quality and Value	
1. Financial Bonds	Volume and Frequency Rewards Stable Pricing Bundling and Cross Selling
2. Social Bonds	Continuous Relationships Personal Relationships Social Bonds Among Customers
3. Customisation Bonds	Customer Intimacy Mass Customisation Anticipation / Innovation
4. Structural Bonds	Shared Processes and Equipment Joint Investments Integrated Information Systems

Source: Zeithaml and Bitner (2003).

Brand-building can create an emotional connection with the customer and improve the customer's perception of value. In business brands, this connection can be related to a feeling of reduced risk and the brand is a mark of trust and continuity. Companies have long realised the value of building brands, but the renewed enthusiasm has come from the experience that, in many product categories, building strong brands creates loyal customers.

Strong brands have also been shown to endure. Those that were number 1 in many categories in 1923, such as Coca-Cola in soft drinks, Wrigley's in chewing gum and Gillette in razors are still number 1 today!

Increasingly, companies are ensuring that the brand values that they espouse are reflected in the behaviour of their employees. This is especially important in service businesses, where the employees are in direct contact with the customers and "the moments of truth" occur – the customer's experience at every touch-point, and at every stage of the relationship from initial contact to the handling of any service issues.

Employees are motivated by different issues and companies must seek to understand and build in their employees values in building a coherent and integrated brand communication programme. The external brand promise set by every aspect of the external communications must be consistent with the service delivery. A clear strategy, excellent internal communications, as well as aligned business processes and motivated employees are the final cornerstones of building enduring customer relationships (see www.corptools.com for more information)

Implementation of a Customer Management Strategy

"A company is either customer focused from top to bottom, or it is simply not customer focused ... to become genuinely customer focused you have to be prepared to change your culture, processes, systems and organisation." (George Cox, Chief Executive, Unisys Ltd, 1995)

Figure 10.6: The Components of Customer Relationship Management

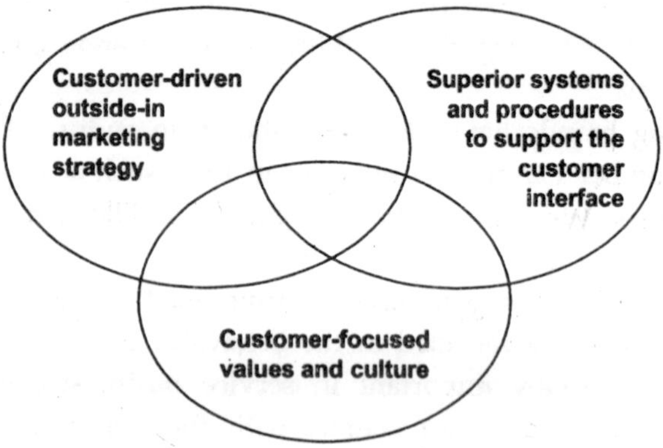

Source: Have *et al.* (2003, p.63).

Effective customer relationship strategies (**Figure 10.6**) require the commitment, enthusiasm and conviction of a company's employees. Indeed, companies such as Virgin and Southwest Airlines believe that looking after the employees should be the priority, as a contented motivated employee will lead to contented customers. The employees will define the "moment of truth" with the customer.

The importance of delivering customer value and satisfaction is not a new concept, but it continues to pose a serious challenge to many companies. The failure of many technology-enabled customer management strategies and customer service strategies has been attributed to lack of change management ... changing the culture of the company from an inward-oriented culture to an externally customer- or market-focused organisation.

Faith is easier than conversion but, if the company does not have a culture that values customers, and does not translate those values into effective processes and systems, the starting point for conversion is effective leadership. This leadership has to come from senior management and not just the marketing department. If, as David Packard from Hewlett Packard says,

"... marketing is too important to leave to the marketing people",

then customer centricity, the key component of marketing strategy, has to be the guiding philosophy in the business. While not everyone in the company is involved in marketing, they are involved in the process of going to market (Piercy, 1997) with the goal of delivering value to the customer.

CONCLUSION

In an environment where products and services are quickly replicated and cost savings can have a bottom limit, building enduring customer relationships is a key success factor for organisations. The logic is simple but the implementation can be more challenging. This rapid walk-through of managing customer relationships illustrates that customer relationship-building is not a destination, rather it is a journey.

CHECKLIST

- ☐ Put the customer at the heart of the business, understanding the importance of your employees in delivering the customer strategy.
- ☐ Segment, segment, segment your market, down to the level of one, if appropriate and profitable.
- ☐ Understand what causes satisfaction and dissatisfaction in each segment.
- ☐ Understand what drives loyalty in your business.
- ☐ Don't assume that more technology is better for supporting your customer management plans. Ensure you have the right culture to support any introduction of new systems and processes first.
- ☐ Use expert help when implementing technology. Use people who understand the business and the customer, not just the technology.
- ☐ Measure satisfaction using various methods including measuring your brand
- ☐ Cultivate good word-of-mouth recommendations from evangelists and advocates.
- ☐ Map your customer's experiences as they "travel" through your company ... walk in their shoes!

REFERENCES & FURTHER READING

Barletta, M. (2003). *Marketing to Women: How to Understand, Reach & Increase Your Share of the World's Largest Market Segment*, Chicago: Dearborn Trade Publishing.

Coyles, S. and Gokey, T. C. (2002). Customer Retention is Not Enough, *Mc Kinsey Quarterly*, 2002, Number 2.

Doyle, P. (2002). *Marketing Management and Strategy*, London: FT Prentice Hall

Have, S. ten, Have, W. ten and Stevens, F. (2003). *Key Management Models*, London: FT Prentice Hall.

Hooley, G., Saunders, J. and Piercy, N. (2004). *Marketing Strategy & Competitive Positioning*, London: FT Prentice Hall.

Jones, T. O. and Sasser, E. J., Jr. (1995). Why Satisfied Customers Defect, *Harvard Business Review*, November / December.

Kaljic, P. (1983). Purchasing Must Become Supply Management, *Harvard Business Review*, September / October, pp.109-118.

Kotler, P., Armstrong, G., Saunders, J. and Wong, V. (2001). *Principles of Marketing*, Englewood Cliffs, NJ: Prentice Hall.

Lindstrom, M. and Seybold, P. (2003). *Brandchild: Remarkable Insights into the Minds of Today's Global Kids and Their Relationships with Brands*, London: Kogan Page.

Naumann, E. (1995). *Creating Customer Value: The Path to Sustainable Competitive Advantage*, Cincinnati, OH: Thomson Executive Press.

Naumann, E. and Jackson, D. W. (1999). One More Time: How Do You Satisfy Customers?, *Business Horizons*, May / June.

Piercy, N.F. (1997). *Market-Led Strategic Change: Transforming the Process of Going To Market*, Second edition, Oxford: Butterworth:Heinemann.

Qci Report (2001). State of the Nation II, 2002: How Companies are Creating and Destroying Value Through Customer Management (written by Neil Woodcock, Michael Starkey, Professor Merlin Stone, Paul Weston and John Ozimek).

Reichheld, F. F. and Sasser, W. E. (1990). Zero Defections: Quality Comes to Services, *Harvard Business Review*, September / October.

Rigby, D. K., Reichheld, F. F. and Schefter, P. (2002). Avoid the Four Perils of CRM, *Harvard Business Review*, February.

Zeithaml, V. A. and Bitner, M. J. (2003). *Services Marketing: Integrating Customer Focus across the Firm*, New York: McGraw-Hill.

Websites

www.corptools.com
www.crmdaily.com
www.crmforum.com
www.crmguru.com

PART 3

MANAGING COMMUNICATIONS

11: PRESENTATION & COMMUNICATION SKILLS

Lynda Byron

Key Learning Objectives

- ☐ Understand the dynamics of making brilliant presentations.
- ☐ Know the five key stages in preparing presentations.
- ☐ Maximise the delivery of your presentations.
- ☐ Develop awareness of your own habits when making presentations.

When you're asked to make a presentation, what is your first reaction? Are you thrilled, excited and delighted to be asked? Or are you panicked, scared witless and wondering how you're going to get out of it? Maybe, you're a mixture of the two. Many managers, when asked to make an important presentation, go through phases. They start off by being thrilled, excited and delighted to be asked, followed by a lot of hard work, putting together the material, followed by ... *"Oh my God! This is going to be a disaster, I can't stop shaking, why me? They'll hate me, they'll be bored. I'm not interesting. This stuff is awful..."* ... followed by a sleepless night or two and then finally, on the day itself, shakiness, fear and the resolve never to agree to do this again.

But it doesn't have to be like this. Imagine enjoying your presentations. What would that feel like? You stand up in front of your audience, the board, the senior management team, whoever, and relax. You connect with the audience, make them smile, their faces show real interest in what you're saying. You deliver your message firmly and clearly and even answer questions concisely and with authority. Afterwards, you sit down knowing it went well and they were with you every inch of the way.

This is possible every time. You just need to know how.

There are two main parts of every presentation. One is the preparation, the other is the delivery. If you prepare well, the delivery is actually quite easy.

PREPARATION

There are five phases to the preparation:

- Setting a goal
- Getting to know your audience
- Making it memorable
- Persuading your audience
- Topping and tailing your presentation.

SET A GOAL

First, you need to know what message you want to get across during your presentation. What do you want to achieve? You need to know precisely what your goal is. It must be achievable and useful.

I remember many years ago making a sales presentation without thinking through the goal. It went well. The audience were each representing their companies and were interested all the way through the presentation. I thought I had them. However, I didn't sell anything. This surprised me. After thinking about it for a long time afterwards, I realised the thrust of my presentation was wrong. What I was selling could only be sold face-to-face with one company at a time. I needed to use the presentation to get in front of the buyers on a one-to-one basis. The purpose of my presentation was all wrong.

So I changed it and tried again, this time with a different group. Second time around, I changed my goal to selling appointments. The structure of the presentation was the same. The content was largely the same. But the focus was different. The interesting thing was that one simple change meant the presentation now worked. I got lots of phone calls after the presentation and got to meet the buyers face-to-face and sold a large amount. All I changed was the goal.

The first vital element of preparing a good presentation is to set a focused goal. In setting your goal, consider what you are trying to achieve, what you want your audience to be thinking and feeling as they leave the presentation and what action you want them to take as a result.

KNOW YOUR AUDIENCE

In order to make a brilliant presentation, you need to connect with your audience. This means connecting with their hearts, as well as their minds. All too often, presenters concentrate on facts and figures to persuade their audiences. This is simply not enough. The more you know about and understand the people you will be talking to, the easier it is to really connect with them.

So, think about who they are:

- What level are they at in the organisation?
- What educational backgrounds do they have?
- Are they all male, or all female, or a mixture of both?
- What functional areas do they work in?
- What interests them?
- What are they measured on?
- How do they feel about the topic you are about to talk to them about?
- How much do they know about the subject?

If you answer these questions well, and have set your goal clearly, you are half-way to preparing for a superb presentation. What you are really doing here is finding the gap between what your audience already know (or feel) about the topic and where you want to bring them – your goal. All you have to do during your presentation is close that gap. You would be amazed at how many competent presenters don't do this and wonder why their audience just isn't persuaded.

Next, you need to identify three or four key messages to give your audience, which will close that gap and help you reach your goal.

MAKE IT MEMORABLE

There is simply no point going to the trouble of making a presentation, if your audience doesn't remember anything you said afterwards. Once you have identified your three or four core messages, you need to find ways to get them across in a memorable way.

One way to do this is to consider the ways we take in information. We all work on three communications channels:

- Visual
- Hearing
- Feeling.

However, most of us have one we prefer.

Those who prefer taking in messages in a visual format love pictures, diagrams, charts, graphs and photographs. They love to see the message, not just hear it. This doesn't, however, mean reading lots of text on a PowerPoint slide. Very short bullet points work well, coupled with a picture that depicts the main message.

Those who prefer using the hearing channel are more interested in actually hearing the message. They love stories and pay close attention to the tone of voice used during the delivery of the stories. You can connect with the hearing channel when you use sounds or music and can help their recall by associating a message with a particular sound or piece of music.

Those who prefer the feeling channel, on the other hand, love the element of touch. This can be emotional or physical. They like to really feel how the message will affect them or others or hold something in their hands. They also like a lot of audience participation. You can grab them by giving very real, personal examples which they can feel, allowing them to get involved in a discussion or actually trying out your ideas or products, there and then.

There is a fourth way of connecting: auditory/digital. Some people simply prefer the facts and figures, the details, the data.

Slides with the concise details of your message will be a winner with people who prefer this way of taking in information.

The secret to brilliant presenting is to work on all three channels and adding the necessary facts and figures for those with a preference for auditory/digital. This way, you will grab the attention of everyone in your audience and let them have the message in four different ways which will both help them to be persuaded and help them to remember your key messages.

THE ART OF PERSUASION

Most presentations are persuasive in one way or another. We are usually trying to sell something to others. It may be your company, a product or service, it could be an idea, or even the fact that your team have worked well over the past quarter.

One model that works well in persuasive presentations and is easy to use is the four-step persuasion model (**Figure 11.1**).

FIGURE 11.1: THE FOUR-STEP PERSUASION MODEL

Step 1 **Create Dissatisfaction in the *status quo***	This is where you connect with your audience, outlining what they may be unhappy with at the moment.
Step 2 **Paint a bright new future**	You need to think of a future your audience would like and which is attainable by using whatever it is you're selling.
Step 3 **Set out practical easy steps**	Show them just how easy it is to attain their bright new future. Explain the first step. This should be easy for them to do.
Step 4 **Reduce the risk**	There is risk in anything new. Any change brings up uncertainty. It is important that you work out what this particular audience will find risky and deal with it here.

To take a simple example, imagine for a moment that you are in middle management in your organisation. A member of your staff has suggested that an on-site canteen would be a good idea. You've thought this through and agree. However, you can't make the decision yourself, you have to bring it to the senior management team. You are aware that there may be some resistance from within this group. The MD has said that, if you can persuade them, you've got it. She lets you have 10 minutes at the next management meeting to make your case. The four step influencing model works well here.

Before going to the model though, you must have completed the first two parts of the preparation – setting your goal and analysing the audience.

Set the goal

Your overall goal is that you want agreement for the canteen. However, it is unlikely you will get this in a 10-minute slot at a management meeting, especially when you know that you have some people in the audience who are hostile towards the idea. So what you are really looking for from this short presentation is agreement, in principle, for you to look further into the issue and bring back an in-depth report at a later meeting. This is much easier for them to say "Yes" to, and you will have got them to make a small commitment towards your goal, which puts you at an advantage.

Know your audience

There are six senior managers:

- The MD who has a reputation for caring for her staff
- The Production Manager, who recently came from a tough manufacturing environment where there were no facilities. He thinks the MD is a bit soft and wouldn't give the staff anything extra. He is measured on productivity and just wants everyone to work harder

- The Financial Controller, whose main concern at the moment is cost-cutting
- The IT Manager, who loves technology of any sort, gadgets are her hobby
- The Sales Manager, who is always on the road, has a team of 12 salespeople to contend with and seems to spend his life up to his neck in expenses
- The Human Resources Manager who is worried about absenteeism and has the Production Manager on his back regularly about the drop in productivity.

Looking at the diverse group above, you can guess that two people will be reasonably supportive – that is the MD and the HR Manager, but only if you show them that the canteen will help them with their agendas of caring for the staff, helping them to work more productively and reducing absenteeism. The Financial Controller will be okay, once it doesn't cost money. The Sales Manager will be happy if it can help him with the burden of expenses – maybe the salespeople could eat in the canteen when they're in the area instead of in local pubs and restaurants – this would also keep the Financial Controller happy as it will help to keep the costs down. The Production Manager's main concern is productivity so he must see that the canteen can help staff to work harder. The overall thrust also of a group like this is also higher profitability.

These give us a few themes to work with:

- The canteen will show we are caring for staff and thus helping to reduce absenteeism
- It will lead to higher productivity
- It may lead to cost savings, or at least, not costing much more and any costs will be outweighed by gains in profitability.

Slotting these themes into the model, we get the following:

Step 1 **Create dissatisfaction in the *status quo***	We have a lot of absenteeism due to sickness, colds etc. The staff are unhappy with having to go looking for somewhere decent to have lunch in the local area. Sales reps, in particular, submit high expenses from eating in local pubs and restaurants.
Step 2 **Paint a bright new future**	Wouldn't it be great if our staff had a place to go where they could get a hot meal, and a good place to sit down and chat over lunch? People would be back to work quicker as they wouldn't have to contend with all the traffic Staff can be more productive, if they are happy and well fed. At the end of the day, providing staff with wholesome, nutritious food will make them more productive and cause less absenteeism due to sickness. This will make our company more profitable. *Some photos of good canteens could be used here (with shiny, high-tech equipment to appeal to the IT Manager).*
Step 3 **Set out practical easy steps**	We have the space – on the second floor There is already a kitchen there, which just has to be extended. I can do up a spec and get three competitive tenders for the work. I'll also look into options for staffing the canteen and running costs. We can discuss it again in a month's time when I have got this information. If we act quickly, we could have it ready in time for the Christmas party!
Step 4 **Reducing the risk**	The cost savings over a few years could be quite considerable – sales reps eating here more often, a place to bring clients for meetings, huge cost savings on Christmas parties and other functions The biggest advantage cost saving, however, is in higher productivity and reducing absenteeism.

This presentation will need to be made using photographs of canteens, with happy workers (which will appeal to both the visual and feeling people). It will need some statistics on the relationship between absenteeism, productivity and cared for staff for the digital/auditory preferences and a story about another company that successfully did this to appeal to anyone who has a preference for hearing.

Topping and tailing your presentation

Any good presentation must open with a bang. This is to make sure you grab the attention of the audience. Opening with a bang means saying something that the audience will connect with. It must surprise them, shock them, or simply interest them. It could be an interesting fact they don't know or a statistic that surprises them – for example, *"I'm going to show you how you can save €80,000 over the next six months"*. This will appeal to most business audiences. It must, however, link closely with your presentation. You can't open with this line and then make a presentation about an idea that will just cost them money.

For the canteen presentation, you could open with *"Would you like to reduce absenteeism, increase productivity and have more motivated staff?"*. This line will appeal to the entire group as it hits all their wants and needs.

The end of your presentation is also a key element. Most of us have poor memories. We have to take in a lot of information each day. We remember very little of it. We will remember the most interesting pieces, and the most recent things, we heard. Therefore, you must aim to make some interesting points during the presentation and finish with these main points in the last 30 seconds. *"So, by putting a canteen here on-site, we will increase profits for the company by reducing absenteeism, increasing productivity and ensuring a healthy, more motivated staff. What I need is an agreement to look into this further and come back to next month's meeting with some options"*. That is the message you are sending them away with and the one they'll remember most.

DELIVERY

If you've put the time and effort into the preparation as outlined above, you are 80% there. When you are well-prepared, and know that you have put together a strong presentation that is focused on your particular audience, it will be much easier to present.

The main areas to watch out for during delivery are:

- Eye contact
- Body language
- Voice tone
- Annoying habits.

Eye contact

During a presentation, you need to get good eye contact with the members of your audience for two reasons.

The first is to get information from them. You will be able to tell how your message is going down by watching people's eyes. You can tell whether they're interested, whether they understand or whether their energy is low. You need this information, so that you can adjust your presentation as you go along. There is no point in continuing if your audience has switched off and are not listening. If this happens, you need to be flexible. Either cut your presentation short or change tack. Work with them, not against them. A good presentation is a two-way process. You present, they react, and you react to their reactions.

The other reason is to show them respect. Often, presenters avoid eye contact with their audience because they're nervous. The problem with this is that your audience doesn't know this. They may believe you're not looking at them because you don't feel they're important enough. You should get eye contact randomly with different members of your audience and for long enough to have individual "conversations" with them, probably for about 20 seconds at a time. This will be sufficient for you to connect with them, for them to realise you respect them and for you to get the information you need to make your presentation a success.

Body language

A large part of your message will be conveyed through your body language. This should be as natural as possible.

Nervousness can make our bodies quite rigid. This is the effect of the adrenaline running through your blood stream. Shaking out your arms and legs before a presentation (obviously, not in front of the audience!) is a good way to eliminate this problem. Your arms and legs will then feel relaxed and energised and your movements will appear more natural as a result.

Use your hands to help you describe things – this is what you do when you're talking in a relaxed fashion to a group of friends – why not when presenting?

Voice tone

A good presenter needs to sound credible, confident and warm. The best way to ensure these qualities in your voice is to warm up your voice in advance. Simply spending five minutes "humming" on your way to the presentation will do this for you. You can do this in the car, the shower or walking down the corridor.

Other problems with the voice come from speaking in a monotone, which is more likely to happen when we're nervous. Deep breathing exercises can help to relieve this, by reducing the constriction in your throat. Try breathing out for twice as long as you breathe in – if you breathe in for a count of three, breathe out for a count of six. Do this for about five minutes and you will start to feel calmer. Make sure, however, that when you breathe in, your stomach expands and when you breathe out, your stomach flattens, like inflating a balloon.

Annoying habits

We all have them. However, most of us aren't aware of them.

We use particular words too regularly, like "actually", "basically", "you know like", "okay" and lots more.

Most of us are guilty of other habits too, clicking pens, fiddling with paper, clearing our throats or even pacing up and down all through the presentation.

The problem with any of these is that they can distract your audience from your message. Become aware of your annoying habits by asking a trusted colleague or friend and gradually break them.

SUMMARY

If you prepare well for a presentation, it will be much easier to deliver. The key elements in preparation are:

- Setting a realistic goal
- Analysing your audience
- Making it memorable
- Persuading your audience to your way of thinking
- Topping and tailing your presentation.

When this is done, the main areas to focus on during the delivery are:

- Maintaining eye contact with all of your audience
- Making sure your body language and voice tone match your message
- Becoming aware of, and breaking, any annoying habits you may have.

REFERENCES & FURTHER READING

Byron, L. (1999). *Being Successful … in Presentations*, Dublin: Blackhall Publishing.

James, T. and Shephard, D. (2001). *Presenting Magically – Transforming Your Stage Presence with NLP*, London: Crown House Publishing.

Walters, L. (1993). *Secrets of Successful Speakers – How You can Motivate, Captivate and Persuade*, London: McGraw-Hill.

Westcott, J. and Landau, J. H. (1997). *A Picture's Worth 1,000 Words – A Workbook for Visual Communications*, San Diego, CA: Pfeiffer Co.

12: INTERNAL COMMUNICATIONS

Tim Wray

Key Learning Objectives

- ☐ Reframe your thinking on internal communications.
- ☐ Learn how to create a culture that welcomes open communication.
- ☐ Appreciate the importance of leadership clarity in communications.
- ☐ Understand the need to align communications strategy with overall organisational strategy.
- ☐ Develop an awareness of the desired outcomes of the chosen communications media.

The experience of most companies in today's marketplace is one of fierce competition and turbulent change, played out on a global stage. The entry ticket to the game involves delivering efficiency and productivity, combined with world class levels of customer service and quality. Creating a competitive edge that can deliver sustainable business success requires companies to innovate constantly, finding new ways to meet and exceed customer expectations. To have any chance of success, organisations need to fire the imagination and creativity of their people and generate higher levels of motivation and commitment than ever before. The core process that drives employee engagement is internal communication.

However, the problem for many organisations is that traditional approaches to internal communications are failing to deliver results. Organisations have set up whole departments to look after internal communications and invested significantly in all forms of communication media. Yet, in many cases, the impact on satisfaction ratings of internal communication is negligible. Why is this and how can we address the problem?

To begin, we need a fundamental shift in how we think about communications in an organisation. Traditionally, internal communications has been thought of as a functional activity. The internal communications department is responsible for developing and implementing processes and systems for communicating messages and gathering feedback. As a result, when we think about how to improve internal communications, our focus inevitably falls on improving the quality and reach of the intranet, the effectiveness of team briefings, the professionalism of the staff newspaper and so on.

However, internal communications is more like the bloodstream of the organisation and our challenge is to unblock the arteries! If we think about what blocks the flow of communication within an organisation, we come up with a multi-faceted answer. Yes, there is a need for professional internal communications media, but there are much more powerful and significant issues to be considered.

First, what is the degree of strategic clarity within the organisation? Does the top team have a coherent and shared understanding of where they wish to take the organisation and why? Have they communicated this throughout the organisation, such that it provides a framework for decision-making at all levels?

Second, what is the state of well-being of relationships within the organisation? Do people trust each other, or is the communication process characterised by suspicion and scepticism? Remember trust works both ways. Do leaders trust employees enough to share the way forward with them and do employees trust the leaders of the business sufficiently to tell them what they really think, to tell them what is really going on in the business?

Third, do the leaders of the organisation, through their own actions, demonstrate that communication is a priority? Do they encourage healthy debate and discussion of activity? Do they prioritise communication events in their calendar?

The point is that an organisation can have superb communications media but, if the top team is unsure of the way forward, you cannot expect the troops to exude confidence in, and commitment to, the future of the organisation. Senior managers may hold regular briefings with employees but, if there is no trust, you cannot expect people to engage in the dialogue. And, if the boss continually postpones the weekly team meeting because of other pressing priorities, you cannot expect line managers to do anything different with their own people.

The challenge for organisations is not to put in place more or better internal communications media, but to develop a communicating culture. As a result, the role of the internal communication professional moves away from media magnate and much more towards consultant and coach. The old maxim says that *"actions speak louder than words"*. In organisations, management has concentrated on the words, while employees have concentrated on the actions. Employees judge the integrity of what senior management says on the basis of the decisions senior managers take and the activities they prioritise. Employees will accept the invitation to speak their mind only when the senior team demonstrates in practice that they are ready to accept, and even welcome, diversity of opinion. The job of internal communications becomes one of creating and facilitating opportunities for dialogue at all levels of the organisation and acting as a coach to senior management in terms of their communications capability.

So, if we accept that the challenge of organisational communications is much broader than the traditional focus on media, can we develop and refine this perspective, to allow us to create effective internal communications?

THE STRATEGIC CONTEXT

The starting point for an effective internal communications strategy is to ensure that it is embedded in the business strategy of the firm.

Strategy is about ensuring you are "doing the right thing" as opposed to the operational focus of "doing things right". Too often, internal communication is reduced to "tick box" exercises focusing on the delivery of inputs – newsletters, team briefings, the number of people accessing the company intranet, and so on. This misses the point completely. The real question is what are the outputs? What have people understood, how do people feel about the business, what are people doing that is different as a result of the investment in the communication process?

Strategy implies setting a direction and making decisions. Strategic decisions and investments have a medium- to long-term timeframe and are not easily reversed – there is a sense of crossing the Rubicon. How do we translate this idea into the communications arena? An effective communications strategy will first identify core themes – for example, cost reduction, customer service, innovation – and then set about finding ways and opportunities to constantly reinforce them.

In essence, a communications strategy is about setting the agenda, dictating what issues and priorities are at the forefront of people's minds and providing them with a framework, a context, within which they can evolve strategy and plans at all levels of the organisation. Thought about in this way, it is clear that the communications strategy needs to be embedded in the overall business strategy.

Two words are important in this context: *integration* and *consistency*. Integration refers to the need to ensure that all communications are aligned to the business strategy. Our focus here is primarily on internal communications. However, it is almost impossible to think about internal audiences and channels of communication in isolation from external ones, given the considerable overlap in terms of impact. Consider the employee who, as is often the case, is also a shareholder in the business and a customer. It's likely that this individual, as a shareholder, will receive communications from the investor relations department, as a customer from the marketing department and as an employee from internal communications. An added dimension is the external media. The old maxim is *"never believe what you read in the papers"*, but most employees seem to follow the principle of *only* believing what they read in the papers! Try convincing an employee that the story they read in the morning paper is not to be believed. The danger in all of this is that employees receive conflicting messages about the issues and priorities for the business. One solution to this is a structural one – bringing all dimensions of corporate communications under one department, and putting in place an integrated communications plan, with consistent themes that underpin all communications activity, both internal and external.

The second key word is consistency – ensuring that the communication themes are reinforced every time a communication event takes place. A great example of integration and consistency in communications is Ryanair, the low cost airline. The company's business strategy is based on a low-cost model that permeates every aspect of its operations. The alignment of the organisation behind this strategy is enabled by a communications strategy that informs the behaviour and attitudes of employees. This is achieved by constantly reinforcing key themes, including the value proposition to customers, the no-frills approach to customer service and the need to be constantly focused on finding ways to drive down the costs of the business. These messages are constantly reinforced, and in a consistent manner, through internal channels, the company's approach to marketing and in media appearances by the CEO.

Clampitt *et al.* (2000) have identified five typical approaches to internal communication:

- **Spray and pray:** This approach is based on showering employees with all kinds of information and hoping they will sort out the significant from the insignificant. The assumption is that more equals better
- **Tell and sell:** Here, the approach is more focused, concentrating on some key messages that address core organisational issues. Managers communicate the messages and then try to sell employees on the wisdom of their approach. Large amounts of time spent packaging the message and little time spent in real dialogue with employees are the telltale signs of this approach
- **Underscore and explore:** The key difference here is that, while managers again focus on a small number of key issues, these are explored in a structured dialogue with employees. Although this approach involves a much greater level of engagement with employees in strategic conversation and debate within the organisation, managers still set the agenda, an important tool in the formulation of a strategic approach to communications
- **Identify and reply:** This approach hands the initiative in the communications process to employees, who set the agenda by raising issues of concern, to which managers respond
- **Withhold and uphold:** A favourite of many! Managers withhold information until necessary; when confronted by

rumours, they uphold the party line. Secrecy and control are often the implicit values of those who embrace this approach.

The two approaches most consistent with strategic internal communications are "tell and sell" and "underscore and explore" because they both involve managers in setting the agenda – identifying a small number of core themes or messages that are consistently reinforced using both internal and external media. As a general rule, Clampitt *et al.* (2000) identify "underscore and explore" as the most effective approach, a view I support for reasons we will explore later in this chapter.

So how do we identify those key themes? Roger D'Aprix (1996) suggests that one should ask the two key parties – the leadership and the employee audience – some pointed questions.

Individual leaders need to be asked:

- What market forces are driving this organisation's strategy?
- What briefly is that strategy? How are we responding to the marketplace?
- What are the main obstacles to our success in implementing our strategy?
- What is our vision for the business?
- Do we have a set of company values that guide our behaviour in running the business? What are they and why are they important?
- In clear and simple terms, what do you see as the critical success factors for the business? What do these factors say about what our priorities should be?
- What does success look like? What are the vital measures (market share, profitability, stock price, and so on) that tell us whether we are winning or losing?
- As you look into the future, what worries you most? Where are the company's vulnerabilities?
- What do you want employees to understand better about the company and their jobs?

Employees in focus groups will be asked a different set of questions:

- Where do you now go to get information about the company and your job? Why there?
- Among all of those varied sources, which ones do you find most useful, which do you most trust?
- Which do you find least useful?
- Can you say what is missing from your communication experience? Why is it important to you?
- What is the impact of poor communication on your ability to do your job?
- What suggestions or ideas do you have to address some of these issues?

Answers to these two sets of questions begin to shape the nature of the leader's communication task.

Setting objectives

Once the themes of the communications strategy have been identified the next challenge is to formulate specific objectives. These typically fall into four categories:

- What do you want people to **think**? What are the core messages that people need to know and understand about the strategic direction of the organisation, its market, how the company is performing, etc.?
- What do you want people to **feel**? Most organisations would like their employees to be proud of working for the company, and to be confident and excited about its future
- What do you want people to **do**? If communication does not influence what people actually do – how they behave towards customers – the wisdom of investing in communications must be questioned
- The final category of objective focuses on communications **process**: How many people use the intranet, what do people think about the staff newspaper, are team meetings held regularly, and so on?

It's important to note that, when we measure what people think, feel or do, we are focusing on the outputs of the communications process. Too often, internal communications objectives and measurement systems are focused only on the communications process itself, which represents the input side of the equation. A focus on *inputs* will tell you something about the efficiency of what you are doing. A focus on *outputs* will tell you more about the effectiveness of what you are doing.

Communicating the message

Organisations first have to make sure they are communicating the right thing by connecting the communication strategy to their business strategy. Then, they need to make sure they do things right – they must have efficient and effective communication processes in place.

Ask any internal communications manager about methods of communication and they will throw up all the usual suspects, from staff newspapers and intranets to focus groups and team briefings. However, what is crucial to understand is that all communication media – particularly in an internal context – are not born equal! Many managers expend lots of their creative energy trying to come up with the new, next big thing in internal communications, striving to find that extra something that will win the attention of staff and get the message heard. But that is to miss the point. What is important is not doing something new but understanding the potential and limitations of media already familiar to us.

In the same way that advertisers communicate their message using a mix of print and broadcast media, too often the advice to senior management is to plough considerable resources – people, money and time – into the creation of slick, professional communication campaigns to deliver their message. Yet frustration mounts as the impact of such campaigns appears to be constantly undermined by the power of the grapevine.

The grapevine is that continuous organisational conversation, a subversive, informal process, that runs parallel to the formal communications process but that seems infinitely more powerful in shaping peoples' understanding and interpretation of what is going on around them than the channels used by professional communicators. How can this be? Understanding why the grapevine is so potent a form of communication will help us design communication processes that have some chance of succeeding in delivering the communications strategy.

There are two key issues:

- First, the difference between rich and lean forms of communication
- Second, how to best leverage the power of rich forms of communication.

Daft and Lengel (1986) have defined a continuum for communications media ranging from "rich" to "lean" media. Information richness is the "ability of information to change understanding within a time interval". Different communication channels vary in their ability to process rich information, and therefore in their capacity to shape and influence the thinking of people within an organisation. Communication channels that can overcome the different perspectives held by various groups of employees, and create a common understanding of an issue in a reasonable timeframe are considered rich. Those channels that take a long time to enable understanding and that cannot bridge the gap between the differing views of people, are lean channels of communication.

Channels of communication

Channels of communication typically used in organisations, such as newsletters, e-mails, intranets, memos and notices are "lean" media, suited to the communication of simple and well-understood messages and data. The richness of the media increases as one moves from impersonal written communication, to the staff newspaper, to video, to various forms of face-to-face communication. The last is by far the richest medium, providing multiple cues and immediate feedback.

Direct contact allows individuals to exchange views and to disagree, which allows subjective as well as objective information to surface and to be processed. Through discussion, a greater shared understanding can be established and uncertainty reduced. Face-to-face communication can involve both informal direct contacts between individuals and more formal team meetings and workshops.

Before moving onto the second critical point – how to best leverage the power of rich forms of communication – it is important to reflect on the media currently in use in most organisations. Think about your own organisation. How do you communicate with your employees? What communication media do you most rely on to get your message across? In most organisations, 90% of the effort and resource goes into the creation and distribution of communications "product" – newsletters, videos, intranets, etc. – all lean forms of communication. At best, the CEO or other senior managers may conduct a presentation, followed by a questions and answers session that represents a token move towards the rich end of the continuum. While this may represent a form of face-to-face communication, too often it is just as planned, controlled and, dare I say it, contrived an event as the CEO's column in the staff newspaper.

Why do we do it? Why do so many organisations pour so much time, money and effort, into the production of lean forms of communication?

First, there is the pragmatic reason. It is easier to prove that some effort has been put into the communications process, when you can point to tangible products. This is the "tick box" mentality towards communication, the need to be seen to do something.

The second reason is fear. Many managers prefer to remain in the comfort zone that is the article in the staff newspaper or the carefully crafted and prepared presentation, to direct contact, conversation and debate with staff. The problem is that there is an inverse relationship between control and impact. The more one seeks to plan and control the communication process, the less impact it appears to have.

Leveraging the power of rich forms of communication

This brings us to the second issue. Moore (1996) has observed that as organisations focus their energies on those communications initiatives that can deliver real impact, it is likely that there will be a decrease in the number of newsletters, brochures, videos, etc. that are produced and a much greater emphasis on the quality of face-to-face communication between individuals and groups.

From the employees' perspective, communication is not a thing, it is an interaction between people. A successful communications programme is not necessarily one that wins awards for the quality and professionalism of its products but rather one that strengthens relationships, which are a pre-requisite for influencing the thinking and changing the behaviour of people throughout the business.

According to Aranson (1995), three key factors influence the acceptance or rejection of a message:

- The source of the communication (who says it)
- The nature of the communication (what he or she says)
- The characteristics of the audience (to whom he or she says it).

Here, we are focusing on the source of the communication. A wealth of research (which Aranson goes into in some detail) exists to prove that a credible communicator more readily influences us. Credibility rests primarily on the expert knowledge and trustworthiness of the communicator. Intuitively, we know that it makes sense to be influenced by someone who is trustworthy and who knows what he or she is talking about.

When an individual is faced with a message that runs counter to their own personal beliefs, they will experience a degree of dissonance. As human beings, how we view ourselves – our self-concept – is vitally important. We like to consider ourselves as basically good, honest, sensible and wise. When our actions or beliefs threaten this self-concept, we respond by seeking ways to justify ourselves and so restore a sense of well-being.

This process of self-justification has been encapsulated in Leon Festinger's (1957) theory of cognitive dissonance: the state of tension that occurs when we are faced with contradictions in our experience. When this occurs, we are motivated to correct the situation by modifying either our behaviour or attitudes. The theory of cognitive dissonance does not picture human beings as rational, rather as rationalising – that is, we will seek retrospectively to justify ourselves. Argyris (1994) describes this as a deeply defensive strategy designed to avoid vulnerability, risk, embarrassment, and the appearance of incompetence. The best and easiest ways to reduce dissonance are to reject or distort the message or to denigrate the communicator. However, the more credible (expert and trustworthy) the source of the communication, the more difficult this becomes and the more likely that the message will be accepted.

The power of the grapevine

The best example of this is the grapevine. As has been said already, acceptance of the message is heavily dependent on the credibility of the communicator. A crucial factor in establishing credibility, particularly in a time of change, is trust.

Aranson (1995) points out a number of ways that the perceived trustworthiness of a communicator can be increased. The attractiveness or likeability of the communicator increases trust. We are influenced by people we like because we seek to please them by agreeing with the points they make. However, there is a limit to our agreeability on this basis. A more powerful force is at work when the audience believes that there is no overt attempt taking place to persuade or influence them. According to Brehm's (1997) theory of reactance, when our sense of freedom is threatened, we attempt to restore it. The media employed in most corporate communications are clearly identified by employees as attempts to persuade them of something that runs counter to their own beliefs. As Aranson (1995) points out, warning people in advance that you are going to try and persuade them is guaranteed to prompt a defensive response.

In contrast, the grapevine involves communication between individuals who usually enjoy high mutual trust, and in the absence of any suspicion of persuasion. So the challenge becomes clear. How do we create communication processes that are primarily informal, and involve communicators who enjoy high levels of trust and, at least from the perspective of the listener, know what they are talking about?

Front-line managers – key communicators

Time and time again, across all sectors, research points to front-line managers as the key communicators. They are the immediate managers for the majority of employees and enjoy a high level of trust and credibility. Communication has the best chance of changing the attitudes and behaviour of employees if it comes from the most desired and credible source (Larkin, 1994).

This is supported by Klein (1994), who suggests that, in an era of empowerment, the significance of the organisational hierarchy should not be overlooked. Such structures are viewed as legitimate, and communications coming from those in authority carry weight. People expect to hear important, officially-sanctioned information from their immediate line manager. Moving down through the levels of the organisation hierarchy, the role of the front-line manager as the last communications link to employees is crucial. Front-line managers are in frequent contact with employees and can engage in constant, informal face-to-face communication. Klein concludes that, by keeping front-line managers informed about the rationale and progress of change, it is very likely that lower levels are also well informed.

The pivotal role of the front-line manager or supervisor can also be viewed from a more negative perspective. Lindo (1996) points out that, as organisations continue to thin out the ranks of middle management, they increase the responsibility on supervisors for communication and interpretation of corporate plans. As the individuals giving direction to the workforce, supervisors can be a tremendous aid to communication or they can become an obstacle. According to Lindo, supervisors can "effectively stop every organisational and strategic plan management announces". Supervisors provide the vital communication link to the front line. For an organisation to implement successful change, supervisors must forge a strong, two-way communication link with the people that work for them. In this way, supervisors are the formal and informal integrators of management initiatives as they affect the organisation's people, systems, policies and procedures.

Larkin (1994) takes up this point with reference to the "Pelz effect", so called because it was first discovered by Donald Pelz at the University of Michigan in 1952. Pelz discovered that employees' satisfaction with their line manager was primarily dependent, not on the leadership style of an individual manager, but on the degree of the manager's perceived power in the organisational hierarchy. If their manager has upward influence, subordinates express high satisfaction. Critically, from a communications perspective, further work by Roberts and O'Reilly (Larkin, 1994, p.15) associated working for a powerful manager with increased trust, increased belief in the accuracy of information provided by the manager and an increased desire for communication. According to Larkin, the power of front-line managers, and consequently their ability to influence employee behaviour, is enhanced when they are treated as privileged senders and receivers of information.

Communication that seeks to put the CEO or senior managers in face-to-face contact with employees can undermine the position and credibility of the front-line manager. For example, sitting front-line managers down in the same room as their subordinates to get a presentation from senior management has the consequence of undermining their position and authority with other employees. They are no longer privileged receivers of information, now they only know the same as everyone else. Larkin argues that, while this may reflect a desire to demonstrate democracy and equality, it dramatically reduces the potential impact of the message.

What are the consequences of this for the communications programme? First, target front-line managers as privileged receivers of information within the organisation. Establish direct two-way communication between senior management and front-line managers. Ensure that they have a clear understanding of the message and rely on them to communicate with front-line employees. Avoid other forms of communication that involve senior management communicating directly with the front line.

While communications between employees and their immediate line manager at times will occur in a formal context such as a team briefing, most of the time. they will take place informally, one-to-one, and usually prompted by the employee. The key to successful communication is to ensure that front-line managers are equipped to meet the challenge of satisfying these casual enquiries. It is exactly at these moments that opinions are formed.

The critical importance of such interactions between employees and their immediate line manager also raises the issue of the manager's personal communication style. The communication skills set for managers will include good listening, the ability to facilitate discussion, and a willingness to invite, welcome and handle debate and sometimes conflict, as an inevitable expression of more open and complete communication.

Pulling it all together

So, does what we have discussed so far spell the end of the staff newspaper? Not quite. What is important is that we know what the staff newspaper can achieve and what are its limitations and that we use it as a media in an appropriate way.

Quirke (1996) has applied the notion of rich and lean communication channels to the process of change in organisations, developing the concept of the "communications escalator". The escalator represents different levels of engagement by employees in the change process (**Figure 12.1**).

FIGURE 12.1: THE COMMUNICATIONS ESCALATOR

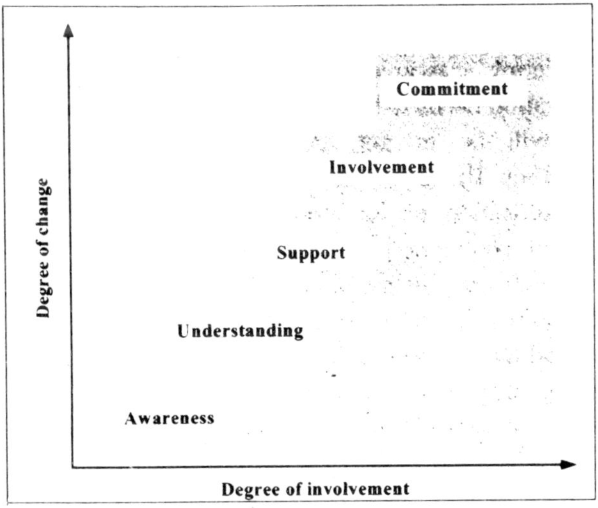

Source: Quirke (1996, p.125).

In an organisation undergoing change, it is not necessary to have all employees on the same level of the escalator at the same time. Those directly affected by changes need to be actively involved in and committed to the change taking place In contrast, other staff in the organisation need only be aware of what is happening and how this affects the company's overall position. The communication requirements of the two groups are not the same. As Daft and Lengel have pointed out, different communication channels achieve different communication objectives. The more the organisation needs an employee to move up the communications escalator, the greater the requirement to use rich channels of communication.

On the bottom step of Quirke's escalator, the focus is on communicating a general awareness of the issues to the mass audience within an organisation. This is likely to be achieved using tools such as the in-house newspaper, bulletins and video.

These media are arms length and involve limited interaction and feedback. The measure of effectiveness is the penetration rate of the message.

Moving up the escalator shifts the focus of the communication from creating awareness to ensuring understanding. Communication needs to be more interactive and face-to-face. The objective will be to get feedback in order to check for understanding. The target audience is still broadly defined and the communication media employed will include roadshows, management conferences and the use of videoconferencing or satellite broadcasts. The meetings will typically take the form of a presentation from a senior manager, often the CEO, followed by a question and answer session.

Securing support for the proposed changes involves gaining acceptance of the rationale for change. The communication focuses on education rather than presentation. This may involve inputs from outside the organisation, and a review of the changing dynamics of the business. The numbers involved will be limited, and sessions will typically be less formal with the expectation of continual interaction rather than set piece presentations and question and answer sessions. As Quirke (1996, p.126) says:

> *"... at the top end of the escalator, the focus is more on management willingness to listen, and do less talking".*

Another key distinction is that, as the focus of the communication turns towards the creation of involvement and commitment, the quality of relationships between communicators (generally management) and employees becomes increasingly important.

Project group meetings, team meetings, and informal conversations between participants in the change programme are all used to tease out the issues involved in the implementation of change. The communication becomes more of a process, involving dialogue rather than the mere dissemination of information. The aim is to share thinking, pool experience and expertise, evaluate possible solutions and to define the best means of implementation.

The communications escalator suggests that media such as newspapers, video, noticeboards and even briefings may be useful tools for creating awareness and understanding, but a communications plan designed to actively engage people in the change process needs to concentrate on richer communications channels. In other words, a mismatch exists between what organisations want from their people and the communication channels and strategies being used to achieve this.

Many organisations motivated by a genuine desire to improve communication fall into the trap of thinking that more means better. So, employees are subjected to special editions of the newspaper, glitzy roadshows, costly video productions, etc. The simplistic view that more is better does not stand up to scrutiny, nor does it take into account an understanding of the behavioural and cognitive dynamics surrounding the process of persuasion.

Quirke's analysis suggests that the media typically used within organisations at least have a use and application in creating awareness and understanding of change. However, Larkin (1994) takes a harsher and more radical view. He suggests that all the research available shows that communication only works when it is face-to-face, through front-line managers and relates directly to the local work area.

SUMMARY

The objective of this chapter has been to provide some principles to guide you as you think about internal communications rather than off-the-shelf solutions.

In summary, the key points are:

- We need to change our thinking about internal communications. Instead of focusing on media, we need to concentrate our efforts on the creation of a communicating culture within the organisation

- A communicating culture involves much more than communications media does. Even more important is the behaviour of leaders, their own clarity in terms of the future direction of the business and whether they are trusted by employees
- The internal communications strategy must be aligned to the business strategy. This will generally involve focusing on a small number of key issues and exploring them in a structured dialogue with staff
- Our focus should be more on *outputs* – what do people think, feel and do as a result of the communications strategy – rather than *inputs* such as team briefings, staff newspapers and so on
- In most organisations, the most credible communicator is the front-line manager. The aim of any communication process should be to support the line manager in developing strong, positive relationships with staff that enable real, open and honest dialogue to take place. Front-line managers should be made privileged receivers of information
- Other, more traditional and formal methods of communication have a role to play. For example, the staff newspaper can be effective in creating awareness about issues. However, we need to understand the limitations of certain media and use them appropriately.

References & Further Reading

Aranson, E. (1995). *The Social Animal (Seventh Edition)*, New York: W. H. Freeman and Company.

Argyris, C. (1994). Good Communication That Blocks Learning, *Harvard Business Review*, Vol. 72, No. 4, July / August.

Brehm, J. W. (1997). A Theory of Psychological Reactance, in Staw, B. M., *Psychological Foundations of Organisational Behaviour*, Santa Monica, CA: Goodyear.

Clampitt, P. G., DeKoch, R. J. and Cashman, T. (2000). A Strategy for Communicating about Uncertainty, *Academy of Management Executive*, Vol. 14, No.4.

D'Aprix, R. (1996). *Communicating for Change*, San Francisco, CA: Jossey-Bass Publishers.

Daft, R. L. and Lengel, R. H. (1986). Organizational Information Requirements, Media Richness and Structural Design, *Management Science*, Vol. 32, No. 5, May.

Festinger, L. (1957). *A Theory of Cognitive Dissonance*, Stanford, CA: Stanford University Press.

Klein, S. M. (1994). Communications Strategies for Successful Organizational Change, *Industrial Management*, Vol. 36, Issue 1, January / February.

Larkin, T. J. and Larkin, S. (1994). *Communicating Change: Winning Employee Support for New Business Goals*, New York: McGraw-Hill.

Lindo, D. K. (1996). Are You An Obstacle Course or A Key Resource?, *Supervision*, Vol. 57, No. 10, October.

Moore, T. (1996). Building Credibility in a Time of Change, *Communication World*, Vol. 13, No. 7, September.

Quirke, B. (1996). *Communicating Corporate Change*, London: McGraw-Hill.

13: ASSERTIVENESS

Lynda Byron

Key Learning Objectives

- ☐ Understand the importance of being assertive.
- ☐ Learn the three building blocks of assertive behaviour.
- ☐ Develop tactics for being assertive.
- ☐ Know how to deal with bullying.

Assertiveness has had a lot of bad press over the years. Images of assertive people strutting around the office, demanding their rights and not taking "No" for an answer hasn't helped. This image, of course, has nothing to do with real assertive behaviour, it's simply someone who has got out of hand.

Assertiveness is not what you are, but what you do. It's about behaviours. It's also about rights – not about always demanding your rights but being aware of them and trying to find a way of getting what you're entitled to without upsetting others. This can be a difficult balance to achieve but very satisfying when you do.

First, let's look at the two extremes:

(a) You have lots of ideas of what could be done but no one listens to you. You wish you could stand up to others when it is important and you know you're right. You would love to be able to speak up at meetings and really get your point across – you often leave meetings without giving your opinion or mentioning your good idea. You sometimes feel intimidated by hostile or angry colleagues or customers or even your boss. You don't seem to get noticed by others. Even when it was your idea, someone else gets the credit. Presentations and interviews make you squirm.

(b) Your staff avoid asking you questions about a task they're doing. You have a tendency to shout and walk away during conversations. Your staff and colleagues do what you tell them out of fear, rather than because they want to. You make a scene on a regular basis. You find it difficult to influence others. Conversations you're involved in often get heated. Others may describe you as difficult or pushy.

Can you identify with either of the above scenarios? These are both a little extreme but if you can see yourself in either of them, even when they're watered down a bit, then you may need to look at your work behaviour as you're probably not fulfilling your potential as a manager.

WHY BE ASSERTIVE?

We have to be a bit careful about categorising people. If you behave predominantly like our example (a) above, it doesn't mean you're a passive person, it just means that you have a tendency to display passive behaviours. The same goes for type (b) above. This describes aggressive behaviours – it doesn't mean you're an aggressive person. We can all behave passively, aggressively or even assertively at different times. In business, it is usually preferable to behave assertively most of the time. But there are times when each of the other behaviour types are appropriate too.

When you behave assertively regularly, you will achieve more and build good relationships with others in the process. As a manager, if you are perceived as being pushy, you are likely to get your colleagues' backs up. They may go along with you in the short-term but could let you down in the long run or agree with you at the meeting and then not carry out their part of the bargain. Managers who get their own way all the time, often do so out of fear. They have a tendency not to listen to others and, therefore, can make horrendous mistakes because they base decisions on only half the facts. If, on the other hand, you give in too easily and just go along with other people's ideas without giving your opinions, you can be seen as a pushover and not taken seriously. This can be stressful for you, as you can resent their pushiness afterwards and go home feeling used. Also, either of these behaviours can lead to you not being respected or taken seriously as a manager. There are no downsides to assertive behaviour. So it makes good business and personal sense to develop these behaviours as fully as possible.

There are three fundamental building blocks to assertive behaviour (**Figure 13.1**). If you work successfully on these three areas, you will begin to notice a shift in the way other people perceive you, in your ability to influence others and in your own feelings about yourself.

FIGURE 13.1: THE BUILDING BLOCKS OF ASSERTIVE BEHAVIOUR

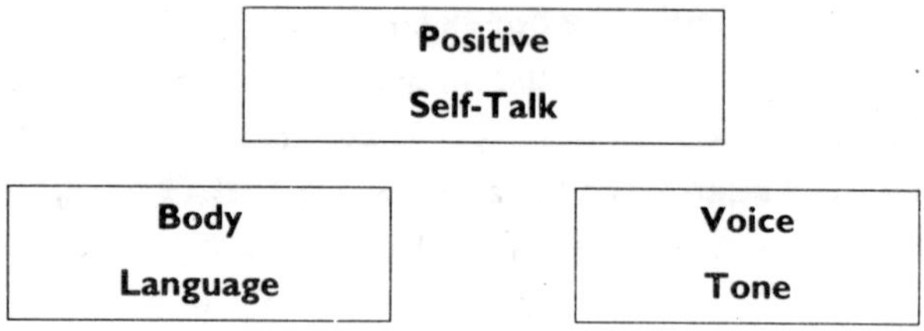

Positive self-talk

We talk ourselves into not being able to do things all the time – for example, *"I'll never be able to persuade them of this ..."*, *"Last time I tried this, it was a disaster ..."*, *"The only way to get through to this crowd is to show them who's boss ..."*, *"I'm no good at getting my point across at meetings ..."*. If you can make a shift from this negative self-talk to more positive phrases, you can make a dramatic difference to your performance as a manager.

Try thinking of the negative things you say to yourself. Work on it for a few days, making a note of them as they come up. What do you say regularly that puts yourself, or others, down? How could you say it more positively? Then try saying it each time you think the negative thought and see what happens.

For instance, you may have a habit of saying to yourself, *"I'm no good at getting my point across at meetings ..."*. One way to change this is to say, *"I'm not good at getting my point across at meetings yet, but I'm learning"*, or *"I think I know where I'm going wrong so next time I'll see if I can do it better"*, or *"Last time I tried X and it didn't work so well, next time I'll try Y"*.

Body language

Body language and voice tone form a large part of the message you communicate so it's worth paying a lot of attention to how you use both of these.

Notice your own body language while you're speaking. Do you stand still while you're relaxed and talking to a friend or do you move your hands, arms and feet? Try describing a huge building, a tiny speck or a spiral staircase without moving your hands. Pick a common phrase like "It's a beautiful day, isn't it?" Try saying it in lots of different ways, using different body gestures, facial expressions and voice tones and see how it comes across differently. The more natural you look, the better. This makes you more believable and credible as a communicator.

Facial expressions are also important as a means of communicating a message. When you're having a conversation with a friend or colleague, and they're doing the talking, you watch their face while listening to them. You do this, because you get a lot of information from their facial expressions. Others do the same when they're listening to you. They're watching your face to get a large part of the message. If you're smiling, they will take one meaning; if you're scowling, they will get another. Sometimes our faces go blank when we're nervous. This can make others believe that you're not interested in what you're saying yourself and it may be harder for them to take your message on board. It may also let them see that you're unsure of yourself. If you're scowling, they may find you intimidating. Again, you may be scowling because you're nervous. Your facial expressions can so easily be misconstrued by other people.

Be careful how you stand, sit and walk. Try standing in an aggressive stance and notice how it feels. Feet about 18 inches apart, shoulders forward, face like a thug, and hands on hips. You will probably feel invincible, confident and strong. Now try standing in a passive pose. Feet together, head down, rounded shoulders, slouch and wring your hands. If you find this difficult, close your eyes for a second and focus all your attention on a point about a foot above your head, like you're dangling on a piece of string like a puppet. How does this feel? Most people report that this posture makes them feel weak and vulnerable.

Now, for an assertive posture, place your feet hip distance apart, relax your shoulders, and smile pleasantly. Focus all your attention to a position about an inch below your belly-button. You will notice how much stronger and more "grounded" you feel.

You will have the confidence and strength of the first position but without the aggression.

The important thing to notice here is how you feel. There is a strong link between our physiology and our brains. If our posture says one thing, it is likely that our feelings go along with it. We can make ourselves stronger simply by changing our posture. We can also make ourselves less aggressive by doing the same.

Eye contact

There are two reasons why you should work on getting good eye contact with others. First, you need to get information from them. If you look at their eyes throughout a conversation, you will know how the other person is feeling about the different issues you're talking about. Watch their face as you try to explain a complicated or complex area and you will know whether they understand you. If they understand you clearly, you will see them smiling and nodding; if they are lost, they are likely to have quizzical looks on their faces. This is useful information. Make the most of it.

The second reason to make eye contact with your audience is to show that you're interested in them and not afraid of them. This will help you to build a good relationship with them. Remember, people buy people. If you want them to buy what you're selling, they must buy you first. They need to like and respect you. The best way to get people to like you is to show you're interested in them. You do this mainly through eye contact. Don't just glance at them. You need to hold the eye contact long enough to actually connect with them, but not too long so as to stare at them which could be misconstrued as intimidation.

Using your voice

Your voice is one of your most persuasive features. It can say so much about you and your commitment to what you're saying. It can also show whether you are scared, pushy or being reasonable. Listen to the way people use their voices on television programmes. Who sounds most assertive and why? What are they doing to make them sound that way? What pitch, speed, volume, etc. are they using? Start really listening to people's voice tones when they talk to you. Think of someone you know who behaves assertively. Listen to their tone. Listen to how they ask for things to be done. Listen to how they say "No". Then, try listening out for people behaving passively and aggressively and see what the differences are.

Usually, an assertive tone is calm, clear and firm but warm and friendly at the same time. Practise by talking into a tape recorder. Use some phrases that you'd like to say assertively. Try them different ways and see which sounds best to you.

Be aware of the tone at the end of your sentences. Take a sentence like "I'd really like you to have this finished by tomorrow". Say this sentence and let your voice tone rise while you say the last three words "finished by tomorrow" and you will notice it will sound like a question. Try it again, this time letting the tone flatten off for the last three words. This time it sounds more like a statement. Now try it once again, but with your tone falling at the end. This time, it may sound more like an order.

You can play around with the voice tone in a number of ways. But always ensure your voice tone is congruent with your body language and your words, so you're not giving two different messages.

SAYING "NO"

Saying no is one of the toughest things to do if you tend to behave passively. Human beings, by our very nature, like to please others so our natural reaction is to say "Yes", either to make the other person happy or simply because it's easier as it avoids confrontation. The problem is we often regret saying "Yes" very shortly afterwards and it can cause us a great deal of stress due to resentment, anger with ourselves and, in some cases, the added workload of the extra job or task.

There are two techniques, which when used in conjunction with the three building blocks of assertive behaviour, tend to work very well:

- The positive-negative-positive sandwich
- The "broken record".

Positive-negative-positive sandwich

What you have to do here is to sandwich the "No" between two positive statements so it doesn't sound so negative or blunt.

For instance, your superior asks you to take on an extra task at the last minute, that must be completed this evening and would mean you working late again. Maybe you have been asked to do this regularly and you feel that, if only your superior would organise themselves better, it wouldn't be necessary. Although, in the past, you have always given in and done it, you've decided this time that you will say "No".

The first thing you need to do is to work on some positive self-talk. Be clear in your mind that you are going to say "No" and that you will succeed without giving in.

Next, work on the sandwich. One way of doing this is:

- "I'd love to be able to help" (positive)
- "Unfortunately, I have other plans for this evening" (negative)
- "If you need a hand finishing it off in the morning, I could work with you on it at 9 o'clock" (positive).

This sounds like you really would like to be helpful, however you just can't do it and, in addition, you're offering an alternative. You're also saying "No" politely.

You must be very careful with your body language and voice tone. If you sound too apologetic, or look as if you might cave in if they argue, you will give them an opportunity to try and persuade you. Your voice must sound definite and firm. Make absolutely certain your voice doesn't trail off at the end or, worse, let the tone go up at the end. This can make it sound like a question. You need it to sound more like a statement. You also need to maintain good eye contact and keep a pleasant facial expression throughout the encounter. Break the eye contact at the end. If you continue looking at them, they may see this as looking for approval for what you've just said. If they do continue to try to influence you, you can then use the second technique.

The "broken record"

This is where you firmly repeat the core of what you want to say until they get the message. "I'm sorry, I have other plans".

These two techniques work well either used together or separately and in any situation you can think of.

But beware. The techniques alone won't help much. The three building blocks (**Figure 13.1**) will do much more.

Dealing with a Bully

One reason managers like to become more assertive is to help themselves when they are faced with a bully. It doesn't matter what level you are working at in the organisation, it is possible for you to become the victim of a bully. If the person at the top is a bully, then the culture in the entire organisation can be one of bullying.

Why do people bully?

It is useful to be aware of why bullies behave the way they do. Bullies are usually weak. They often feel threatened and inadequate and suffer from low self-esteem. They choose their targets carefully. Often their target is a person who they see as a threat to their position, an efficient, capable person or someone who is popular, while they themselves find it hard to get on with people.

Certain events can trigger bullying:

- The bully's previous target leaves
- You become the centre of attention by getting recognition for good work, which causes the bully to be jealous

- An obvious display of affection, respect or trust by others, particularly if the bully doesn't get too many of these can lead you to become a victim.
- Also, if you refuse to obey an order, stand up for another victim or even expose their incompetence in some way, often unwittingly, this can lead to you being bullied.

What is bullying?

A bully's behaviour can be displayed in many different ways. It is often vindictive, humiliating and cruel behaviour, like making nasty comments or starting vicious rumours about you when you have no way of even knowing what is being said about you, still less of refuting it.

This behaviour is often carried out behind closed doors, when there is no chance of a witness. Unfair behaviour by a boss, like withholding resources, information, support or equipment, giving consistently unfair performance reviews and rewards or interfering in your work, can be bullying. You can be passed over for promotion, your boss can take the credit for your good ideas or work and they can also change your targets to ones that can't be achieved. Often, if a bully believes you to be a threat to their position, they will stop at nothing to get rid of you.

Bullying behaviour is persistent and can result, over time, in chronic stress. The victim can eventually lose all self-belief, suffer ill-health and mental distress.

Tackling a bully

If you have become the victim of a bully, or even suspect that someone is trying to bully you, your first line of defence is assertive behaviour. If you behave assertively, it will show the bully that you will not be pushed around, that you can and will say "No" to their demands and that you are prepared to stand up for yourself. They will also get the strong message that you will only respond to reasonable behaviour on their part.

Above all, stand firm. If you are being verbally abused, tell the bully firmly that you will not tolerate personal remarks. Remember to use assertive body language and voice tone.

Whatever happens, remain confident in your own judgement and ability. Bullies thrive on weakening their victims so that they no longer believe in themselves. Positive self-belief is essential. Say your positive sentence over again in your head. Don't let them win the mind war.

If you are given unclear instructions or objectives, ask for written clarification. This may help you to understand what is being asked of you but also may be useful later on. Check your previous performance appraisal reports to see how you were rated before. Check with trusted colleagues that your performance hasn't slipped. Hold onto copies of all correspondence, including memos and emails and take notes of every meeting you have with the bully. Avoid being alone with the bully, even in a work situation. It is harder for them to intimidate you if you have a witness.

If you find this is not enough, then you will have to take your case to someone else. In order for this to be successful, you will need evidence. Make a note of every incident, however silly or small. Write down the date, place, time, and name of any witnesses. Also try noting down how the incident made you feel. This can be a great help in getting others to understand the situation from your point of view. Writing a diary like this can be therapeutic in itself, since you feel you are now taking some firm action. You will need to take this journal of events to someone in authority, whoever is the right person in your organisation. It may be senior management, a trade-union representative, or the HR manager. Check your staff procedures handbook if you have one.

SUMMARY

There are good personal and business reasons for behaving assertively most of the time.

The three basic building blocks (**Figure 13.1**) are:

- Positive self-talk
- Assertive body language
- Voice tone.

These should become part of your regular behaviour (see **Appendix 1** for a comparison of passive, assertive and aggressive behaviours).

Some extra techniques may be used when you need to say "No". These are the "positive-negative-positive sandwich" and the "broken record". But both must be used in conjunction with the three basic building blocks or they won't be effective.

Bullying is quite common and it is easy to become a victim. The strongest weapon you have in your armoury against a bully is assertive behaviour. If you need more help, document everything and bring it to the appropriate person in your organisation.

REFERENCES & FURTHER READING

Adams, A. and Crawford, N. (2000). *Bullying at Work – How to Confront and Overcome it*, London: Virago.

Back, K. and Back, K. (1999). *Assertiveness at Work – A Practical Guide to Handling Awkward Situations*, London: McGraw-Hill.

Bishop, S. (2000). *Develop Your Assertiveness*, London: Kogan Page.

Graves, D. (2002). *Fighting Back – Overcoming Bullying in the Work Place*, London: McGraw-Hill.

Lindenfield, G. (2001). *Assert Yourself – Simple Steps to Getting What you Want*, London: Thorsons.

Appendix 1: A Comparison of Passive, Aggressive & Assertive Behaviours

Some Behaviours to look out for	Passive	Aggressive	Assertive
Body language	Minimal eye contact. Taking up very little space. Wringing hands. Not easily noticed. Shoulders slumped. Fidgeting. Worried or uncertain facial expressions. Walking unsteadily or nervously.	Excessive eye contact. In other people's space. Finger-wagging and pointing. Feet wide apart when standing, shoulders back, chest puffed out, sometimes hands on hips, head up straight, often leaning forward. Angry or sneering facial expressions. Walking quickly and heavily.	Just the right amount of eye contact. Taking up own personal space. Standing confidently. Steady on feet. Relaxed gestures. Smiling or pleasant facial expressions. Walking steadily and firmly.
Voice tone	Quiet, sometimes squeaky or shaky voice. Doesn't always finish sentences. Hesitant, questioning tone. Uses phrases like *"I just want to..", "I think that maybe".*	Loud, obtrusive voice. Defiant, harsh tone. Telling rather than asking. Uses phrases like *"You'd better, or else", "I want ...", "Why the hell not?".*	Firm, moderate, neutral voice. Asking rather than telling. Calm, pleasant tone. Uses phrases like *"I would like", "We can work out how to do this together".*

Some Behaviours to look out for	Passive	Aggressive	Assertive
Actions	Often says "Yes" when meaning "No". Avoids conflict. Bottles things up. Puts others' needs first. Doesn't express feelings. Apologises excessively.	Quick to blame others. Criticises the person, not the behaviour. Uses sarcasm, ridicule, criticism. Makes requests sound like orders.	Listens to understand. Treats others with respect. Explains or states needs and wants. Solution-centred. Straight but not abrupt. Persists nicely.
Advantages	You avoid confrontation.	You achieve a short-term victory.	You achieve results. People like and respect you. Your confidence and self-esteem remain strong. You build good relationships. You suffer less stress.
Disadvantages	You're not taken seriously. Your viewpoint can be ignored. You don't achieve your potential. You suffer stress. People don't respect you.	You lose in the long-term. It irritates people. People avoid you. You dis-empower staff as you stop them using initiative.	There are no downsides to assertive behaviour.

14: INFLUENCING OTHERS

Jill Stamp

Key Learning Objectives

- ☐ Recognise the importance of influencing as a key skill for effective management.
- ☐ Understand how to use "Push" and "Pull" energy.
- ☐ Be able to use a range of influencing methods.
- ☐ Know what skills will increase your effectiveness.
- ☐ Be aware of the impact of your influencing style on relationships with others.
- ☐ Understand the psychology of influence.
- ☐ Know how to influence with integrity.

This chapter looks at influencing and why it is an important skill for managers. The process of influencing is examined in terms of the methods used to influence other people, the skills managers need to be influential and the impact of influencing on relationships with others. Finally, the psychology of influence is considered, looking at the six human drives that people can appeal to in order to influence others.

INFLUENCING

"Let no man imagine that he has no influence. Whoever he may be, and wherever he may be placed, the man who thinks becomes a light and a power." Henry George (1839-1897)

Some years ago, Guinness was conducting focus group research with Guinness drinkers. Most people were chatting away about the various beer products and advertising campaigns. One man, however, didn't get involved at all. Finally, he announced to the group, *"I eat what I like. I drink what I like. I buy what I like. Advertising has no effect on me!"*. So the researcher inquired, *"Why do you drink Guinness?"*. To which he replied, *"Because it's good for me"*, unconsciously repeating Guinness' long-time advertising catchphrase.

We all like to think that we make up our own minds, have our own opinions and are not easily swayed by other people. While the extent to which this is true depends in part on your personality, you are influenced by other people in all kinds of ways. Equally, you affect other people around you all the time, sometimes consciously and sometimes unconsciously.

Influencing is simply having an effect on other people. This may be "getting your way", persuading people to do something, having your ideas accepted, creating interest or increasing motivation. Most of the time, we don't analyse exactly what it is we are doing when we try to influence others, it is simply something we do to achieve an end.

Influencing others is, however, a complex process and a skill that can be developed and enhanced. This chapter picks apart the various factors involved in influencing others so you can maximise your level of influence when and where you need it.

Why does influencing matter?

Think about all the people you depend upon in your role as a manager to get your job done – among them your boss, senior management, the board of directors, your team, colleagues, other departments, key customers, and outside contractors. You must be able to get these people to assist you, co-operate with you or provide you with information or resources in order to fulfil your role and yet, in most cases, you do not have direct control over them. It is your interpersonal skills, namely your ability to influence others, that you must employ in order to get your job as a manager done effectively. If you are good at influencing others, you will get things done more quickly and easily, find less resistance, encounter less stress and tend to achieve your goals while maintaining good relationships with people.

CASE STUDY

Sarah works as a business analyst in a large private sector organisation.

"My role is essentially to provide the link between the client and the IT department. I find this quite stressful at times because I need certain information on time from the client otherwise the developers will be held up in their work and at the same time I have to try to get the developers to produce the system to meet the client's deadlines and yet none of them work for me. I get on pretty well with most of them, but at times when the IT people are very busy I don't seem to be able to get them to realise how urgent it is."

Even with your direct reports, influencing is a fundamental skill. Organisations today tend to be flatter and the style of management is much less authoritarian, and so traditional approaches of relying on your formal authority will simply not wash with most people. That is why the ability to influence other people is now, more than ever, a critical part of being a manager.

Case Study

Philip has been in a managerial position in the bank for the past 22 years and has noticed that he has had to adapt his style to the changing environment.

"The culture of the bank has changed a lot over the years and even though there is still a hierarchy it's now less about being 'the boss' and more about using my own personal skills to get things done. I find that people will no longer accept simply being told what to do by their boss. The good managers in the bank are the ones who know how to handle people well."

The Influencing Process

Managers need to be aware of three main aspects of the influencing process:

- The methods of influencing
- The skills required to apply these methods
- The impact on the target audience.

Methods of influencing

If you wanted to persuade a friend to train to do a marathon with you, how would you do this? You might try to get her excited by asking her to imagine how incredible it would feel to cross the finishing line after 26 miles. You might describe the benefits in terms of how much fitter and healthier she would be and how much weight she would lose in the process. You might listen to any concerns she had about the training regime and try to make things as easy as possible for her such as suggesting joining a running club and making it fun and sociable.

If you were in a meeting to decide departmental budget priorities for the next quarter, you might try to convince others of your viewpoint by giving some logical reasons for your preferred choices. You might join forces with others who hold similar views, and perhaps concede on some of the aspects you feel less strongly about, in order to get your key points accepted.

Clearly, we use different strategies in different situations in order to get what we want.

To be an effective influencer, you need to have a range of different ways of influencing people at your disposal. The various methods of influencing can be broadly categorised into whether they are using "Push" or "Pull" energy (Vengel, 2000).

Using "push" energy

In a situation where one person tries to influence another, there is a certain energy involved. "Push" energy is direct and assertive. It can involve putting forward ideas and suggestions, arguing your case, stating your needs, exerting your authority or putting pressure on the other person. Push behaviour has a one-way feel to it. The focus is on your own needs. For this reason, it is sometimes also called "moving against" others rather than "moving with" them.

It can be very effective, in that you are clear about what you want and are being direct in your approach to getting it. Presenting a logical argument, for example, is one of the most common ways managers try to influence others.

There are often situations where it is necessary to use a direct approach. If someone on the factory floor is about to put their hand near a dangerous machine without wearing protective equipment, telling them to stop is the imperative, not explaining why this is a desirable action and hearing their views on it!

There is, however, a potential danger with push energy. If you feel pushed, your natural inclination can be either to push back or to pull away altogether. This is often what happens in negotiations. Each side reacts to the other's demands by arguing their own case even more forcefully. For this reason, managers are generally more effective if they use "pull" methods in conjunction with the more direct push methods.

EXERCISE

Try this experiment with a friend. Get them to put their two palms against yours. Then push against their hands and see what happens. Most people will automatically push back against you.

Using "pull" energy

"I would rather try to persuade a man to go along, because once I have persuaded him, he will stick. If I scare him, he will stay just as long as he is scared, and then he is gone." (Dwight D. Eisenhower, 1890-1969)

"Pull" energy is more involving and inclusive, with a greater focus on the other person and their needs. It is a carrot rather than stick approach and is more about getting the person to want to do what you want rather than making them do so. You are "moving with" the other person.

It can include listening to the other person, understanding how complying with your wishes may be of benefit to them, inspiring them, finding common ground or looking for a win-win situation. For example, if someone strongly disagrees with you about an issue and you ask for their views and are genuinely interested in their concerns, you may find the wind being taken out of their sails somewhat and they may be more prepared to give a little ground.

Sometimes, managers feel that it is push methods of influence that get you ahead but Bill Clinton is an excellent example of how influential pull energy can be. During a visit to Ireland, Clinton addressed the audience by saying "I know you probably think I'm just here for the Irish vote ..." and immediately reduced the cynicism of the audience by addressing the very issue that might have made them resistant to what he had to say.

If you start by meeting your audience where they are, you will find it much easier to take them where you want to go. Lancing the boil early is particularly important when the audience is potentially hostile. The most influential managers address difficult issues and bring them out into the open rather than allowing them to get in the way of what they are trying to achieve.

POINT TO PONDER

The most important word in the whole of the English language is your own name. Switched-on managers use this to their advantage.

I watched the Managing Partner of a law firm at a formal dinner, where he knew no-one, quickly become the focal point in the conversation because he remembered everyone's name and used it.

His secret? He wrote down their names on a napkin!

He became the most influential person there not because he pushed his views, but because he made the effort to make everyone feel important and involved.

People generally feel better about being convinced to act in a certain way by pull, rather than push, methods. Pull methods can help gain commitment, break down resistance and maintain and even enhance good relationships between people. Since they are a less direct approach, they may not always be effective on their own. You might therefore be more effective persuading your team to put in extra hours in the run up to an important conference by getting them excited about the conference (pull) as well as explaining the necessity for this extra work (push).

FIGURE 14.1: METHODS OF INFLUENCING: PUSH BEHAVIOUR

Proposing	Putting forward ideas and suggestions.
Rational reasoning	Using logical arguments, reasons or facts in support of your position or to refute another's position. It is important to bear in mind that, while logic and facts are often valued in business, individuals frequently make decisions based more on their hearts and their "gut instinct".
Legitimising	Using the fact that a request is consistent with organisational policies, practices or a requirement of the role. Upward appeals – using the approval or claimed authority of higher management – is a common form of legitimising. Rather than taking ownership, managers sometimes hide behind this approach, particularly when it is something they are not comfortable with themselves. If over-used, this approach tends not to engender respect in the long-term.
Expertise	Using special knowledge or experience. For example, asserting your authority as the technical expert or the one who has been working on the project the longest.
Authority	Using status or formal position. This tends to be a more directive approach.
Pressure	Using forceful approaches such as demands, intimidation or aggression. This can lead the person being influenced to feel they have been coerced or bullied into compliance.
Sanctions	A form of pressure, this is threatening a penalty or negative consequence for not complying. For example, *"If you don't start coming in on time, I am going to have to issue a formal warning"*. This approach works on the basis of fear.
Bargaining	Promising either explicitly or implicitly that the person will be rewarded or get something in return for acting a certain way. It can also include reminding the person of a favour yet to be repaid.
Personal appeal	Asking someone to do something out of friendship or loyalty.
Coalition	Persuading the target that because others are in agreement or acting a certain way, they should too. Coalition tactics rely on social pressure.

FIGURE 14.2: METHODS OF INFLUENCING: PULL BEHAVIOUR

WIIFM	One of the strongest motivating factors for a person to do something is when they will benefit from doing so. This approach appeals to "*What's In It For Me*" factor for the other person.
Friendliness	Getting the person to think favourably of you because you are more likely to respond to people you like. The term with a slightly more manipulative connotation, ingratiation, is about putting the target in a good mood or getting them to think positively about you before making a request.
Inspirational appeals	Using emotion to arouse enthusiasm or foster commitment. It often involves appealing to the person's basic values or ideals. The power of inspirational influence is that people tend to feel good about what you want them to do. Richard Branson is a classic example of someone who uses the inspirational style.
Involving	Soliciting the views and opinions of others, listening to them and being responsive to their ideas and questions. Participation is often used if you want commitment to a decision because, when a person is involved in decision-making, they are more likely to identify with the decision and accept it.
Understanding	Trying to see things from the other person's perspective. This can involve clarifying, summarising, paraphrasing to test understanding and reflecting back opinions or feelings to communicate interest and understanding.
Finding common ground	Finding and communicating areas of agreement – common views, goals, values or interests.
Personal disclosure	Being honest and open, including admitting mistakes or a lack of knowledge and revealing intentions, motives or feelings. This engenders trust and openness and tends to break down barriers. It also makes it more likely that the other side will reciprocate in kind.

The skills of influencing

When it comes to influencing, it is one thing to know about the various methods, it is another to know *how* to use them in the most effective way. While this is linked to skills in other chapters such as assertiveness and general communication skills, two additional factors are:

- Adapting your approach to the audience and the situation
- Planning your approach.

Being adaptable

Most managers choose a style of influencing based on what they are most comfortable with. A range of factors such as their basic personality type, values, upbringing, previous experiences in their working life, attitudes, confidence and their previous role models will affect what they are most comfortable using. Yet the most effective managers use different methods to influence people depending on the situation, what they are trying to achieve and most importantly who they are trying to influence.

While we have all heard of "Treat others as you would like them to treat you", the most effective strategy is to "Treat others as *they* would like to be treated". You may be most comfortable giving a member of your team the logical reasons why you need them to stay late at work one evening, but they might respond best to hearing that you really appreciate their hard work and extra effort. This means that, to influence others most effectively, you need to make a switch from influencing others the way you are most comfortable doing so, to the way which will be most effective *with that particular person or audience*.

Planning your approach

As busy people, managers often don't spend enough time planning their interpersonal interactions in a strategic way but simply think on their feet. Even just stopping for a moment to think about who you are trying to influence, and how best to do it, will pay dividends.

So, rather than simply jumping in, take a moment to consider two fundamental factors:

- Your goal
- The other person.

First, be clear in your mind about what exactly you want. While this sounds obvious, we often try to persuade others when we have only a general idea of what we want, rather than knowing *exactly* what we are asking them to do. Your goal should be positive – for example, *"I want all our meetings to end on time"* rather than *"I don't want us to waste so much time in meetings"*. It should also be specific – for example, *"I want all meetings to be a maximum of 30 minutes"* as opposed to *"I want our meetings to be shorter"*.

Second, the more you have thought about the other person and seen things from their perspective, the better position you will be in to tailor your approach to make sure it pushes the other person's "hot buttons".

The questions you might ask about the target audience are:

- What is their mindset? What is important to them?
- What is going on in their organisation, department, role or life that may affect the situation?
- What barriers might there be or what objections might they have?
- How could you overcome these? What could you do to make it easier for the person to go along with you?
- Put yourself in the other person's shoes – how would you respond? Why?
- What ways of being influenced has worked with them before? What do they respond best to?
- In what ways does the person need you?

Case Study

I worked with a woman recently promoted to sales director of a large organisation and observed her intended opening speech for a three-day sales conference – her first public event in her new role. It was a professional, competent presentation displaying her extensive knowledge and experience.

After coaching her on how her audience would be feeling, she realised the staff, all of whom would be making their own presentations, were likely to be a little apprehensive and unsure what to expect of the next few days. It became clear that her aim was not to establish her own credibility and authority, but to encourage the audience to feel at ease and look forward to an interesting and valuable few days ahead.

Having put herself in her audience's shoes, she completely changed her speech and the conference was a great success.

One key factor to take into consideration is personality type. I don't mean that you need to give everyone you want to influence a psychological assessment, but simply being observant about the way people like to do things will make your attempts to influence them much more effective. For example, if you are an extrovert who bounces into your boss's office full of enthusiasm about an idea and feel frustrated when your boss doesn't share your enthusiasm, you may need to change your approach, not your idea. If your boss is a more introverted person who likes to reflect on things and have all the information before deciding, you are more likely to have your idea accepted if you put it in writing in a detailed, systematic way before discussing it with her.

Quick Tip!

If trying to argue a point, do not bombard the person with all your arguments at once. If you do this, the most important points may be lost and you are providing ammunition for the person to counter-argue. If they can find a flaw in one of your arguments, you have lost some ground. Stick to your strongest arguments and have the others as back-up.

The impact on the target audience

Some influencing situations are a once-off. If you are trying to buy a new car, then your objective is to get the best possible deal and you are probably not too concerned with your relationship with the salesperson in the future. However, many of your dealings as a manager are with people you work with or come into contact with on an ongoing basis and with whom it is important to maintain, and even strengthen, relationships.

So, when you consider how best to influence others in your role as a manager, it is imperative to consider the impact that the *way* you influence someone has on your relationship with them. Two types of influencing – manipulation and coercion – have a somewhat negative connotation. Manipulation suggests a deceitful approach and coercion implies a perception that a level of force was used.

If you get your way by putting a colleague on the spot in a meeting where they feel they can't say "No", how do you think they feel afterwards? If you coerce a junior member of staff into taking on an unpopular piece of work, they are less likely to give it 100% commitment and are more likely to give up if they meet difficulties.

Coercing, pressuring or manipulating someone into agreeing to something, will probably achieve compliance but there may be a pay-off for this in the longer term. As a manager, the end does not always justify the means. So, in deciding what method is best to use, influencing with integrity is about weighing up the effectiveness and the impact of the approach.

THE PSYCHOLOGY OF INFLUENCE

Think of a person to whom you pay attention when they express an opinion in a meeting. What is it about that person that makes you likely to be influenced by them more so than by the others present? Perhaps you respect that person, like them or believe that they know what they are talking about. Among your friends, think of the person you are most likely to do a favour for. It may be that you know they would do the same for you or that they have gone out of their way for you in the past.

There is no doubt that certain kinds of people influence us more than others. Social psychologist Robert Cialdini (2002) found the reason for this is that people are best influenced by appealing to a limited number of deeply rooted human drives and needs. A skilled manager can utilise these principles in order to increase his or her effectiveness.

The six fundamental principles of persuasion Cialdini identified are:

- Liking
- Authority
- Consistency
- Reciprocity
- Social proof
- Scarcity.

The principle of liking

This principle relates to the fact that people are most likely to be influenced by those they like. This is the basis of the highly successful concept of the "Tupperware party". It is also the essence of networking in organisations.

While there are many ways to encourage people to like you, Cialdini identifies two major factors that stand out from the rest:

- Similarities
- Praise.

We tend to like people who are similar to us. Similarities create bonds between people. Just think about the feeling you get when you meet a person for the first time and you really "click". Very often, this connection is based on mutual similarity: a love of travel, your children being the same age or supporting the same football team. Finding common ground moves you from a "ritualised" level of communication where you communicate on a small-talk level, to a deeper, more intimate level.

For managers wishing to increase their influence, finding common ground with people, particularly early on in the relationship, is a very useful skill. While this is easy enough with people you get along with, managers who are good at this find connections with all kinds of people. Often, very senior managers tell me they had been so driven and task-focused early on in their careers that, at times, they neglected relationships. They now realise that, if they had made a little more time for this, it would have made their lives much easier and they would actually have achieved just as much, if not more.

In Cialdini's words, the second factor, praise, "charms and disarms". It is a rare person who isn't pleased to receive genuine praise, yet it is often under-used by managers. Again, it is easier to praise a hard-working, motivated member of staff but praise can also help repair damaged relationships or improve difficult ones. You may not personally like someone, or may find them difficult to get on with, but you will nearly always find something to sincerely respect or admire about them if you look for it. It may be their dedication to their customers, their technical knowledge or their commitment to their team. If sincere, communicating this to the person can have a powerful impact on the relationship.

The principle of authority

The "white coat syndrome" is what I call the unquestioning acceptance of the opinions of doctors, clergy, lawyers and other such figures of authority or expertise. Although it is lessening, the tendency for people to defer to experts is still quite strong.

While it seems obvious, the mistake some managers make is assuming others know their expertise. This is in no way advocating becoming boastful about one's achievements but, done in an appropriate way, establishing your expertise or experience in a particular area can make your ability to persuade others much more effective. For example, in a meeting, a point might be raised by saying, *"I have some experience in this area, may I make a suggestion?"*.

The principle of consistency

Once people have made a choice or taken a stand, they tend to be motivated to behave consistently with that commitment. Use of this principle is sometimes referred to as the "foot-in-the-door" technique. Even a small, seemingly insignificant commitment can have a strong psychological effect on future behaviour.

Have you ever wondered what happens to petitions? In many cases, nothing. The purpose of a petition is often to get signers to make a small commitment – their signature. Having made such a commitment, they are likely to be more willing to act in accordance with this in the future.

Furthermore, commitments that are spoken out loud, written down or made public are more likely to be complied with in the future. So, if your colleague agrees in a meeting that she will commit certain resources to your project, getting her to summarise the outcome of the meeting in an email to you will increase her likelihood of her following through on this commitment. One factor to be wary of is that the initial commitment should be voluntary. If people feel coerced into the initial commitment, they are much less likely to honour it or may feel resentful about doing so.

The principle of reciprocity

There are societal norms that obligate people to repay what they have received. Free samples of food in supermarkets, test-drives of new cars, free trials in gyms, a shop assistant spending a long time helping you can all make us feel indebted.

The "door-in-the-face" technique works on reciprocation. If you ask for something far beyond what you really want, when you come back with a much more "reasonable" offer, it is more likely to be accepted. Having been seen to "concede" from your original position, the other person may feel obligated to move from their initial position in response.

This technique also works on a psychological phenomenon called the "contrast effect". When I worked as a student in a clothes store in the US, staff were trained to use this. When someone went to pay for a purchase, they were asked if they would like a pair of socks to go with the outfit. Having just spent perhaps 100 dollars, five dollars for a pair of socks seemed an insignificant expenditure in comparison.

We also have a natural human tendency to treat people the way they treat us. If we show trust, co-operation, friendliness or respect to others, we are more likely to elicit it in return. So, if a manager needs to use resources belonging to other teams at times, she should be co-operative with that team when they are looking for assistance.

The principle of social proof

This relates to the fact that, although people like to think of themselves as independent thinkers who make up their own minds, humans rely heavily on people around them for cues as how to behave, think or feel.

If you stop in the middle of a busy street and stare up at the top of a building, chances are others will do the same. If you rope some friends in and do it together, you will have even more of an effect. In one study, people were found to be more likely to donate to charity when shown a list of their neighbours who had already done so.

The implication of this for managers is that peer power can be extremely powerful.

The principle of scarcity

Every year, there seems to be a "must have" toy for Christmas and stressed parents are seen chasing around every toy shop trying to track down this elusive toy. Why? It's not only the fact that it is popular and trendy, it is the very fact that it is so difficult to get that enhances its allure. You need only think of restaurants, night-clubs or golf clubs that are "impossible to get into" and therein lies the answer – items and opportunities that are less available to us become more desirable.

Information that is exclusive is also more persuasive. In one study cited by Cialdini, buyers more than doubled their orders of foreign beef when told that there was likely to be a scarcity of it in the near future due to weather conditions abroad. When buyers were told this information came from exclusive sources in the national weather service, orders increased by more than 600%.

Managers can use this information to their benefit when influencing others by highlighting any limited time frame, limited supply, one-of-a-kind opportunities and exclusivity of information. How much more likely is your boss to sign off on a budget you are trying to get for new equipment if he hears that the prices may be about to increase?

The six principles in practice

While I have outlined the six principles separately, in practice it makes sense to use them in conjunction with each other for greatest effect.

One of the most powerful openings to a talk I have heard was at a conference on depression where the speaker stood up, waited for silence and then explained to the audience of counsellors and therapists that he was an engineer with no knowledge of psychology or counselling. His brother had killed himself, as a result of depression. He felt his brother's death could have been prevented and so decided to study to become a therapist. He went on to explain that, with the techniques he had developed for depression, he could now cure most of his clients within three weeks. At that moment, you could have heard a pin drop. Not only had he created incredible rapport with the audience through this personal disclosure (principle of liking), he had also established his credibility as a therapist (principle of authority) and got his audience eager to hear how they too could use these techniques (WIIFM).

SUMMARY

Good influencers tend to be comfortable using a range of influencing methods and know how best to utilise the advantages of both push and pull energy. Being good at influencing requires a level of adaptability, in order to influence your target audience in a way that will be most effective for that particular audience in that situation. The skills of influencing can be increased through an increased sensitivity to what works with different people in different situations, including the psychological factors that exist when interacting with others. By being aware of the impact your style of influencing can have on others, you will also ensure that you succeed in influencing with integrity.

CHECKLIST

Do:

- ☐ Use a combination of both push and pull energy.
- ☐ Become familiar with a range of methods, so that you can adapt your approach to the situation and the target person or audience.
- ☐ Plan your approach whenever possible.
- ☐ Consider the long-term impact on the other person.
- ☐ Appeal to the six psychological principles of persuasion in order to increase your influence.
- ☐ Influence with integrity.

Don't:

- ☐ Use undue force or coerce people.
- ☐ Be deceitful or manipulate people.

REFERENCES & FURTHER READING

Cialdini, R. B. (2000). *Influence: Science and Persuasion,* New York: William Morrow.

Cialdini, R. B. (2002). Harnessing the Science of Persuasion, *Harvard Business Review,* October.

Fisher, R., Ury, W., and Patton, B. (1997). *Getting to Yes,* London: Hutchinson.

Vengel, A. (2000). *The Influence Edge: How to Persuade Others to Help You Achieve Your Goals,* San Francisco, CA: Berrett-Koehler.

15: GATHERING BUSINESS INFORMATION

John Cullen

Key Learning Objectives

- ☐ Understand how to make tactical choices about your potential information needs.
- ☐ Know how to develop personal, departmental/functional and organisational competitive and strategic intelligence systems.
- ☐ Know how to use traditional and non-traditional information resources for gathering information.

It is something of a given that having timely, accurate and useful information on hand is central to making informed management decisions. The advent of the Information Age has led to the rise of new phenomena, such as evidence-based decision-making and knowledge management. A growing corpus of research, texts and journals on the management of information is testament to the fact that the availability of much more information, and of tools and systems to organise it, has led to confusion, information overload and well-publicised deficits in the "attention economy".

Many of the introductory guides to gathering information begin with explanations of how to use the Internet or library services. Although this chapter will examine some of these sources, it is not concerned with categorising the plethora of technologies available to help managers sort and analyse information, or with explaining the intricacies of the Dewey Decimal System. Instead, it aims to provide a succinct guide to some of the more practical methods for gathering information for managerial purposes. It is written with an understanding of the time restraints on managers, and with a view to cutting through some of the barriers to information-gathering that managers often face.

UNDERSTANDING YOUR MANAGERIAL INFORMATION NEEDS

To start with, the information needs of managers are distinct from other professional groupings in terms of their *range*. Scientists, accountants and lawyers have specialised types of information that they need to continually access, but the information needs of managers reflect the role of the manager. A manager of a functional department, for example, needs management information in the "classic" sense of the term: statistics and metrics on how their operation is running.

Because of the diverse nature of their role, managers need to be able to source explanatory literature on legal issues and information systems, as well as guides on organisational behaviour and motivation, industrial relations guidelines, political and policy developments that affect the running of services, environmental regulations and basically any other type of information you can think of.

It is important to understand the best sources for each type of information. For example, I would urge anyone who doubts the information-access problem-solving abilities of public library staff to eavesdrop on the types of request that they constantly receive. You'll be surprised at how the vast majority of times they get results, even with some of the most obscure requests.

Don't focus on the particular document where you think the information you need "lives": focus on the data relevant to your particular question. If you need to source a particular piece of legislation, see the British and Irish Legal Information Website. Textbooks, research articles and guides to various areas of management expertise are best sourced through libraries. Perhaps one of the trickiest pieces of information to source is that which the manager only half-recalls having seen in a newspaper article "somewhere" recently. If the newspaper's own search engine doesn't deliver results, the best tip is one that I offer several times throughout this chapter: ask a librarian!

Turning to information-gathering tactics, it is important to recognise that education systems encourage us to "hoard" information in order that it can be used in the future. Managers need to gather information in a different way, particularly as they simply don't have the time to assimilate all the information that comes their way. A simple way to manage information overload is to cut it off at the source.

In **Chapter 1**, in dealing with time management, Tom McConalogue argues that life was simpler when we only had a limited number of choices to make. A large part of combating the overload of "useless" and "might-be-useful" information is through simplification. Adopt a "slash-and-burn" approach to spam, email and junk mail – indeed to all documents that impinge on your creative space. It is very easy to get snowed under with paper. Ideally, the only items on your desk should be your phone, computer, diary and whatever document it is you are currently working on. The reality is that this is quite difficult to achieve.

A well-known suggestion for keeping your desk clear is to handle each piece of paper that comes your way only once. Perhaps more practical is the "three green dots" approach, which involves marking the top right-hand corner of each document with a green pen each time you handle it. As the number of dots grow, an unconscious pressure to deal with the issue connected to the document develops.

Since the emergence of the knowledge society, information systems have become key corporate resources to the extent that it can often be said that managers work for their information, rather than it working for managers. Evaluate the amount of time you spend maintaining your database, versus the amount of information "value" it gives you.

Libraries have been dealing with the numerous problems caused by the growth of documents, books and journals that they need to store, and dwindling amounts of storage space for years. This has lead to "access" to documents, being prioritised over "holdings". This means that a librarian may not have all the items they need readily in stock at any particular time but, if they need particular items, they know where to get it. If you work in a large organisation that has a need to store a lot of paper documents, the services of a professional corporate archivist are recommended.

Another way of managing the huge amount of information that comes your way is to look at your existing staff and other resources and find ways to make them "information resources".

A key way of saving time when gathering information, whether it be for personal, study or corporate reasons, is to fully understand your own information requests. Spending time defining your own information needs is better than wasting time on wild goose information chases. As mentioned already, assuming that a particular book or report can meet whatever information need you have can often be a pointless waste of time. Stop and think about the data you need, if it exists, and where it might be. Once you've refined these questions, and if you're still unsure as to where it might be published, then you're in a position to conduct an Internet search or ask a librarian.

How often have you known that a senior manager or a board member might possibly want information on something that is soon likely to appear on the radar (such as a legal or cost issue relative to your function)? Rather than rushing off immediately to find this data, wouldn't your position be better served by *asking yourself* about what their motivations might be, what might have sparked this request and how they would like the answer framed?

INFORMATION OR KNOWLEDGE?

We have been repeatedly told that we are living in an information society/knowledge economy where creating, managing and using organisational wisdom are key to creating competitive advantage. No sooner was the role of information prioritised, than it appeared to be superseded by the emerging discipline of knowledge management. This lead to an increased interest in how firms used their knowledge resources with the aim of improving their competitive position. Knowledge management has been tainted with the brush of faddism, but the key messages it unearthed about organisational knowledge-gathering remain valid.

Definitions of *knowledge* and *information* are usually quite similar; the main difference is that information is commonly referred to within definitions of knowledge. For example, the Oxford English Dictionary definition of knowledge is:

> *"Facts, information and skills acquired by a person through experience or education: the theoretical or practical understanding of a subject."*

What is interesting is that the concept of *learning* is commonly used in these definitions. A mistake made by many information-hunters is that they seek pieces of information, data and facts; their search for information would be greatly enhanced if they didn't think about gathering information, but instead focussed on gathering *learning*. Adopting a mindset that seeks to optimise opportunities for learning has obvious advantages for learning. This means accepting that information and knowledge comes in a variety of different forms. Two of the better known of these forms are:

- **Explicit Knowledge:** Knowledge that is known, codified and transmittable
- **Tacit Knowledge:** The *"personal, context-specific, and therefore hard to formalise and communicate"* (Takeuchi and Nonaka, 1995).

In one UK organisation, a senior manager has developed a collection of the "stories", "fables" and "myths" that exist within his organisation and this has helped to develop a unique picture of how his staff members view his organisation.

Another famous example of highly valuable organisational information-gathering was offered by Takeuchi and Nonaka (1995):

> *"A major problem at the Osaka-based company in developing an automatic home bread-making machine in the late 1980s centred on how to mechanise the dough-kneading process, which is essentially tacit knowledge possessed by master bakers. Dough kneaded by a master baker and by a machine were x-rayed and compared, but no meaningful insights were obtained. Ikoko Tanaka, head of software development, knew that the area's best bread came from the Osaka International Hotel. To capture the tacit knowledge of kneading skill, she and several engineers volunteered to apprentice themselves to the hotel's head baker. Making the same delicious bread as the head baker's was not easy. No one could explain why. One day, however, she noticed that the baker was not only stretching, but also 'twisting' the dough,*

which turned out to be the secret for making tasty bread. Thus she socialized the head baker's tacit knowledge through observation, imitation and practice."

THE HUMAN ELEMENT

Many managers make the mistake of assuming that information and knowledge exists separately from the people in their organisation. They feel that official reports and minutes of meetings are the sole repositories of all that the organisation knows. Experience has taught us differently. Every organisation, and every organisational sub-unit, records its own history in the memories of its staff members and customers. The lessons that they learn about success become encoded in their own cultures.

Recent advances in knowledge management theory supports this. One of the classic papers on knowledge management is *"Knowledge Sharing Is a Human Behaviour"* (Ives, Torrey and Gordon, 2000). It emphasises that organisational structure, culture, environment and HR strategies are key to ensuring that knowledge-sharing behaviours, which have direct economic benefits to an organisation, are encouraged.

Creating and maintaining a culture that encourages the sharing of knowledge is time-consuming, but there are several tactics that can help managers get to information that is truly valuable. One of the more popular ways of doing this, as is practised by several Irish companies, is to put a monetary value on organisational "micro-innovations", such as a monthly cash prize for a staff member who comes up with the most original and practical cost-cutting idea, for example. Several larger firms have specific awards that reward contributions to their organisational knowledge base.

In the non-commercial sector, where finances are often restricted, it can often prove difficult to financially reward employees' knowledge-sharing behaviour. One entertaining mechanism employed by an Irish not-for-profit organisation was the "live information newsletter", where one member of staff did a 15-minute presentation on a Monday morning on all the organisational "news" and need-to-know information for staff. Information was provided in bullet points by other staff members the previous week as material for the newsletter. Although this may appear frivolous, the "live newsletter" actually saved the organisation time and resources. The knowledge manager did not have to spend time putting together a lengthy report and staff members did not have to waste time reading it; instead, they could identify quickly those issues directly relevant to their own role and discuss these following the meeting.

Another valuable organisational information-seeking tactic is the use of the exit interview to obtain information about the organisation. Exit interviews are traditionally used to unearth the reasons why employees voluntarily leave organisations, but, as Findlay (2003) points out, they are also invaluable opportunities for gathering explicit and tacit information about aspects of an organisation's culture that are usually very difficult to access.

DEVELOPING YOUR PERSONAL COMPETITIVE INTELLIGENCE SYSTEM

Competitive (or competitor) intelligence is information on your competitors' strategic intentions. Kotler *et al.* (2001) report how competitive intelligence (CI) is part of industry culture in some Asian countries, and how several organisations in the West have specific offices set up specifically to collect and disseminate information on rivals. In the US, CI has become a profession in its own right, with college training courses and a well-established *Society of Competitive Intelligence Professionals*.

CI professionals obtain information on competitors in a number of ethical ways, which usually involve analysing information from public sources, such as websites, trade publications and published accounts. Unethical CI strays into the area of illegal corporate espionage

There are two methods by which managers can create their own CI information gathering systems that do not involve contracting external CI agencies. The first of these was outlined by Harvey B. Mackay in his famous *Harvard Business Review* article *"The CEO Hits the Road (and Other Sales Tales)"* (1990). Mackay begins by telling how, as a young salesman, he solicited the help of an older, more experienced colleague, who took him out of his cold-calling routine:

> *"We went back to the parking lot, got into his car, and, to my amazement, drove to our arch-competitor's plant. We parked 50 yards away from the shipping department and waited until the trucks began to exit to make the day's deliveries. The rest of the day, we followed those trucks. By the end of the day, we had a good idea of our competition's local customer base, obtained in record time and at no cost. It was my first lesson in the kind of streetwise salesmanship that you don't learn at a desk or studying the phone book."*

Mackay makes a number of salient points here, not least of which is the usefulness of sales staff in gathering CI. Perhaps more importantly is his assertion that relevant business information is context-specific, and that the best competitive intelligence can be garnered through actively listening to your customers: a blunt conversation with a customer will clarify exactly where you stand in relation to competitors and the reasons why you hold that position.

Another method of developing an internal CI system is to adopt a "framing mentality" towards all published sources that contain information on your industry or your competitors in the printed trade or general media. Framing methodologies emerged from research conducted in the area of the sociology of the media, with the aim of answering how media organisations influence the consumers of their products. Media framing involves identifying isolated facts found in disparate and fragmented sources and organising and analysing them in a way that creates knowledge that is pertinent to any given organisational situation. A mixture of quantitative and qualitative analytical methods can than be applied to the news sources to ascertain the intentions and levels of threat posed by the competitor. Quantitative methodologies are useful when attempting to garner hard information about particular aspects of, or to scope specific trends in a sector, but qualitative analytical approaches can unearth information about competitors which are normally more difficult to obtain.

For example, scanning relevant newspaper appointment sections for positions in your sector and collecting information inside the frames of salary, expected qualifications and levels of experience can create a picture of the talent base that your competitors are trying to develop. A qualitative review of notices for recent key appointments can enable you to "frame" information about competitors potential clients, leads and targets in a particular area and the company's strategic intentions with regard to new clients.

Many organisations already have formal or informal structures in place which could support media framing in that they collect newspaper cuttings on their industry or regularly scan or read trade publications.

ARE YOU AFRAID OF LIBRARIANS?

"Thank God for librarians! Of course, it should have come as no surprise that the librarians were leading the charge. Most people think of them as all mousy and quiet and telling everyone to 'SHHHHHH!' I'm convinced that "shush" is just the sound of the steam coming out of their ears as they sit there plotting the revolution!" (Michael Moore, *Stupid White Men*, 2002)

It's understandable that many people use the Internet as a first port-of-call when seeking information. It does amaze me, however, that they give up or assume that information is unavailable when it can't be easily found through a search engine. There are very few websites that will give away for free information that someone has invested time and money in developing. However, some of the better Irish research sites of use to businesses and managers are Government agencies (www.oasis.gov.ie) or sites that make up-to-date social and economic data available such as the sites of the Central Statistics Office (www.cso.ie) or the Department of Finance (www.finance.gov.ie). The problem with relying solely on using the Internet, as any avid web searcher will tell you, is one of authenticity.

Much has been written in the library practitioner and research journals about the persistent image problem that libraries have. I've met many third level students who make their first visit to their college library only days before their exams out of fear for the library environment! Much of this fear is due to images of rule-bound spaces, punitive fines for overdue items, complicated classification systems and stern-faced librarians "shushing" boisterous children. A visit to any library will quickly do away with this prejudice.

The central tip to getting the information you need using a library is *use the library staff*. They are trained to understand complex information queries and are experienced in helping users find what they need. If the resource you're looking for is not available in the library, most times they'll know where else you might try or they'll be able to order it for you. Public libraries, in particular, have excellent systems in place. Dublin Public Libraries, for example, have a dedicated business library service as part of their Central Library, located in the Ilac Centre. They have extensive up-to-date information files on several management issues and a range of information sources on companies operating in Ireland.

The second best thing about using public library services is that they're free, in contrast to online information services, which can be expensive.

But the best thing about libraries is the people. Talking to a trained information professional about your particular information need is much more satisfying and immediate than spending hours typing variations of search terms into a Internet engine and scanning irrelevant sites for information that turns out to be unavailable.

The factors that put most people off using a library, be it public or academic, such as coming to terms with catalogues and classification systems can be by-passed simply by asking before you begin your search. Knowing why an item gets a specific shelf mark is the librarian's job; you just need to be pointed towards it. The library profession had spent centuries organising and arranging vast amounts of information before the advent of information technology and it is perhaps the best point of human contact for anyone beginning an information search.

Bear in mind also that there are a range of libraries that meet the needs of distinct user groups. Most of professional organisations have libraries dedicated to their members' needs; academic libraries have perhaps the biggest collection and inter-lending system in the country, and some have commercial business information services. The Irish Management Institute's library service has one of the best collections of management learning resources in the country. The website of the Library Council of Ireland contains links to many of the library services available in Ireland. An overview of the IMI's library service is available at www.imi.ie/library.

CHECKLIST

Do:

- ☐ Create your own information systems – Use the trade and national media as a source of competitive intelligence.
- ☐ Get to know staff in your local or organisational library.
- ☐ Gather "learning".
- ☐ Understand your own goals for gathering specific information.

Don't:

- ☐ Assume that information is only valid if published elsewhere.
- ☐ Believe that you have to outsource information gathering and research.
- ☐ Concentrate on data sources.
- ☐ Treat information as an end in itself.

REFERENCES & FURTHER READING

Cullen, J. (2003). A Rounded Picture: Using Media Framing as a Tool for Competitive Intelligence and Business Research, *Business Information Review,* 20 (2), pp. 88-94.

Findlay, J. (2003). 'Cockroaches of Human Resource Practice'? Exit Interviews and Knowledge Management, *Business Information Review* 20 (3), pp. 127- 35.

Ives, W., Torrey, B. and Gordon, C. (2000). Knowledge Sharing is a Human Behaviour, in Morey, D, Maybury, M. and Thuraisingham, B. [eds], *Knowledge Management: Classic and Contemporary Works,* Cambridge, MA: The MIT Press, pp. 99-129.

Kotler, P., Armstrong, G., Saunders, J. and Wong, V. (2001). *Principles of Marketing,* 3rd European ed., London: FT Prentice Hall.

Mackay, H.B. (1990). The CEO Hits the Road (and Other Sales Tales), *Harvard Business Review,* March-April, pp. 32-42.

Takeuchi, H. and Nonaka, I. (1995). *The Knowledge Creating Company: How Japanese Companies Create the Dynamics of Innovation,* New York: Oxford University Press.

Websites

Department of Finance	www.finance.gov.ie
Economic and Social Research Institute	www.esri.ie
Economist	www.economist.co.uk
Forfás	www.forfas.ie
Industrial Development Authority	www.ida.ie
Irish Library Council (links to the websites of various types of libraries in Ireland)	www.librarycouncil.ie
Irish Management Institute	www.imi.ie
RTE - 'Onbusiness'	www.onbusiness.ie
Sunday Business Post	www.thepost.ie

16: BUSINESS WRITING

Mary Condren

Key Learning Objectives

- ☐ Distinguish between academic and business writing.
- ☐ Know the difference between a logical and psychological layout.
- ☐ Acknowledge the difference between your point of view (the writer) and the point of view of your reader.
- ☐ Learn the five stages of report writing.

After years of teaching writing in business, scientific, academic, and technical environments, I have discovered one common myth: people think that there is some magic trick to writing. Furthermore, everyone (except them) knows what it is. Guilty and embarrassed, business course participants on the first day will admit:

"It takes me four or five drafts before I'm finished. What I am doing wrong? How can I get it right first time?"

GOOD BUSINESS WRITING

Well, here's the secret. Few self-respecting professional writers would drop anything in the post, shoot anything off in an email, or publish anything under their own name, without first having drafted and crafted their work, often to the point of tedium.

Okay. Business writers are under pressure. Clients and bosses are waiting. Time is of the essence. Nevertheless, the principle is the same. Writing is a craft; business writing can be managed: good business writing comes from drafting, crafting, and then shafting everything in your document that is not essential. Only when you have arrived at the essence of your main message will you be ready to launch your product on the world.

Whenever senior management contact me to provide an in-company course on business writing for their staff, they invariably say:

"All I need is enough information to tell me what to do, but they insist on telling me everything they know. How can I get them to come to the point?"

Fresh out of college or business school, inexperienced writers sometimes forget that bosses may have spouses, children, elderly parents, golf clubs or other personal commitments. They hired you to condense, interpret, and present the facts enabling them to make intelligent decisions. Don't overwhelm them. Size matters!

I am constantly amazed at how much time goes into developing a product, gathering information, or collating research compared to how little time is allocated to doing justice to all that hard work.

A rushed, convoluted but unclear memo or email may be sent to 1,000 employees. Emails, faxes, and phone calls follow in quick succession seeking clarification. Amendments and revisions can clarify your original aim, and sweet talk can salvage bruised relationships, but ultimately, you waste time and energy. Spending more time on the email in the first place, making sure that it achieved its purpose, quickly and easily, would have been more time and cost effective.

Likewise with report writing: your report might contain major implications, be brilliantly researched and desperately needed, but your efforts will come to nothing if your key points are subtle, buried, or presented in such a way that your key readers can't immediately grasp their importance. Your job is to see that they do.

You will need to know the difference between:

- Academic and business writing
- A logical and psychological layout
- Your point of view (the writer) and the point of view of your reader.

Then, you will need to divide the work into five stages (it's good for mental health).

Academic *versus* business style

Academic	**Business**
Designed to be read many times: Impossible to read quickly.	Reveals full meaning on a single reading. Can be read quickly, at various levels.
Convoluted: often designed to impress.	Clear: designed to express.
Unfamiliar words.	Familiar words.
Colourful tone.	Plain language.
Variety expected.	Consistency expected.
Long, complex sentences.	Short clear sentences.
Convoluted paragraphs.	Clear paragraphs.
Avoids repetition.	Reinforces message.
Avoids emphatic markers.	Uses bold, underlining, italics and Large Text.
Imagery and symbolism.	Numbers and charts.
Visual aids inappropriate (except historical photographs).	Visual aids essential: Colours, tabs, covers, section breaks, bullets, headings.

Academic / logical *versus* business / psychological structure

Academic/ Logical	**Business/ Psychological**
Triangular: Narrow intricate argument to broad detail.	Inverted Triangle: Broad detail (main findings) to narrow technical or financial information.
Designed to make one THINK.	Designed to make one ACT.
Persuades through argument/rhetoric.	Persuades through facts.
Caters for one level of readership.	Must cater for several levels: senior management, local management, technical or other operatives.

Your point of view and your reader's

Questions writers should ask:

- What do I want to do/ achieve?
- Why do I want to do it?
- Who are my readers and how much do they know about the topic?
- How am I going to go about the task?

Questions readers will ask:

- Why should I read this?
- What are the facts?
- What methods did they use?
- What do the findings mean?
- Do I need to act on them?
- Does the author respect my intelligence and/or time?

The five stages of writing

These stages are not absolute – everyone thinks and writes differently – but they usually work.

- **Pre-Writing:** Taking the writer's point of view
- **Drafting:** Free-writing: getting the words onto paper
- **Crafting:** Re-writing — the macro approach to editing
- **Shafting:** Power-writing — the micro approach to editing
- **Pre-sending:** visual image, layout, and presentation

If you are a logical linear thinker, take the point of view of the reader early on. If not, leave it until stage three. These days, word processing allows us the flexibility to chop and change, thereby maximising everyone's particular strengths.

FIGURE 16.1: THE FIVE STAGES OF WRITING

	Stage	Point of View	Presentation
1	**Pre-writing:** Gather your information, brainstorm, ask generating questions, write your core sentence, decide what structure you will follow and choose your referencing system (where appropriate).	**Writer:** Take the point of view of the writer.	Don't even think about it!
2	**Drafting:** You will write this after you have completed your preliminary research.	**Writer:** Keep focussed on your own point of view.	Forget it!
3	**Crafting:** Add the title and draft an Executive Summary. Take a macro view of the report, ignoring style and technicalities for the moment. Focus here on producing an appropriate structure that best highlights and presents your work.	**Writer/ Reader** Start thinking about your reader. What will they see first?	Start planning!
4	**Shafting:** Start micro-editing. Make your writing verb-centred, active rather than passive; eliminate redundancy, clichés, and verbosity. This is the version you show to your friends/editing partners/willing spouse/concerned colleagues. They will pick up things that you can no longer see, as you are so close to the text. Offer to return the favour, and don't take their criticisms personally.	**Reader:** Consider your reader: How can I impress them? Look out for style, technique, layout, spelling mistakes, and grammatical errors.	Focus on text-based presentation.

	Stage	Point of View	Presentation
5	**Pre-Sending:** Now add the title page; an abstract, if appropriate; your list of action items or recommendations; your appendices, and a letter of transmittal. Start paying serious attention to formatting, binding, presentation. Check your references and proof your text, appendices, and bibliographies.	**Reader:** Take the reader's point of view as absolute.	Get neurotic! Call in favours! Bribe your colleagues to view it from a reader's perspective.

STAGE ONE: PRE-WRITING

Pre-writing comprises several elements:

- First generating questions
- First brainstorming
- Second generating questions
- Second brainstorming
- Core sentence.

First generating questions

- **What do I want to do or achieve?** Most junior business writers try to impress their readers by telling them everything they *know* rather than answering the bosses' (or client's) question: *"What do I need to do?"*. Focus on the outcome
- **Why do I want to do it?** This question helps to put manners on your ambition, limit the scope, and focus on the outcome
- **Who are my readers?** This question further clarifies your scope by identifying what your readers know already, what you can take for granted, and how you need to pitch your argument or findings
- **How am I going to go about it?** A little neurosis here won't go astray. Before you do a belly-flop into the material, stop and think. Thirty-five percent of your time should be spent pre-writing, mostly at this stage.

First brainstorming

Free flow. Let it all hang out. Get a flip-chart, a rough sheet of paper, or whatever, to outline the possible parameters. Use a simple spiderweb cluster and flush out the many possible directions. Don't worry about relevance at this stage. Just get the issues out of your system.

Second generating questions

Look at your first generating questions again. Look at the brainstorm and identify the parts that really need to be developed to answer your first question: *"What do I want to achieve?"*.

Second brainstorming

Now put manners on your ambition. Decide what kind of organisation best suits your piece of work.

Consider the appropriate organisational device to help the development of your report or memo:

- Chronological
- Problem-solving
- Location
- Cost/benefit.

A combination of these might be best. These techniques are best demonstrated in a workshop setting.

Core sentence

This should encapsulate clearly the aim of your document. If it doesn't, go back to your generating questions and brainstorm again.

Summarise your report in one simple sentence:

"This report outlines the variable factors contributing to Ireland's level of greenhouse gas emissions in terms of four major divisions: industry, domestic, transport, ecology."

Produce a roadmap: contents page

Your readers are busy: they like roadmaps. A table of contents should act as one. Remember also that this is one of the first things a potential reader will see. Make it attractive, informative, and you will persuade them that this is worth reading and their time will be well spent.

A contents page at this stage will give you an outline that you can show to your colleagues, friends, and anyone who might help you to fill in the gaps in your thinking process (we all have blind spots). You can gain confidence that you are on the right lines, or learn that you are on the wrong lines, now rather than later.

In a first draft, a contents page will act as a guide to your own writing. In a final draft, you may need to re-phrase some of the headings to reflect what you have actually written, and also to attract your potential readers.

STAGE TWO: DRAFTING

Start wherever feels most comfortable. The *Introduction* is often the hardest thing to write, so forget it for now, except maybe in very rough draft or bullet points.

Don't worry yet about your punctuation, or presentation.

Managing your writing

Professional writers usually limit themselves to three or four hours' writing every day. After that, it becomes counter-productive. Business writers may not have the same luxury, but you can manage your environment.

Here are some tips:

- **Write free-flow:** Don't let considerations of style or grammar interfere with your thinking process. We can worry about these in later drafts
- **Leave notes in the margins for things that might be missing:** Don't stop in mid-flow to go looking for them at this stage

- **Don't start at the beginning (unless you really want to):** Just as in school examinations, you will often get your creative juices flowing if you write about the area or topic you are most comfortable with
- **Remember that you are writing with your reader in mind and that few of them will read the whole report:** Get the important facts in first, and leave long technical explanations to the appendices (unless the technical explanations are an integral part of your work)
- **Use a miscellaneous sheet:** Jot down all the things you think should be included in the report, but not in the section in which you are currently working. Sometimes you think of them on the bus, in the loo, or in the cafeteria. Never look a gift horse in the mouth. Get it down on paper
- **Write when your energy is highest, and your mind is clear:** For important documents, this may mean coming into the office an hour or two earlier than usual
- **Find a private area and/or time:** Neutralise as many distractions as possible: phones, passers by, busybodies
- **Take breaks:** Change to another writing task. Clear your desk. Have lunch. Taking breaks will enable you to distinguish between what you meant to say and what is actually now on the paper. When you get back to your work you will be reading with a more dispassionate eye
- **Don't edit as you write**
- **Don't pause to check spelling, punctuation, or minor details**
- **Don't try to get it right the first time:** You won't!

Choose a working title

Establishing a title at this stage will help you clarify your aims. It will, however, be no more than a working title since, in the course of writing, a more clear, accurate, or better title might occur to you.

In choosing a title, you need to ask the following questions:

- What title best describes the subject matter?

- Who are my readers: colleagues, bosses, clients, friends, or examiners?
- What kind of title would attract them?
- What kind of title might be too pretentious, informal, boring, uninformative?

STAGE THREE: CRAFTING

Up to now, you have been able to concentrate on your point of view: the writer. Now you have to switch gear and start thinking about who's paying you: the reader.

You have to compete for their attention, so your readers must be convinced in the opening pages that they need to read your work, and that you are going to make it easy for them to do so.

Remember what they are asking:

- Why should I read this?
- What are the facts?
- What were your methods?
- What are your findings: positive and negative?
- How do you interpret them? (Help me with some visual images)
- What do they mean?
- Do I need to act on them?
- Have you anything else original to say that might make my job easier?

Executive summary

The time-honoured device to give your readers what they need is an executive summary. An executive summary is action-oriented, unlike an abstract (for academic journals) or a summary report (mostly for government reports that have to be condensed for the media). Everything senior executives need to know should be in the executive summary. Go high on detail, low on waffle.

An executive summary serves the following purposes:

- **Extends the title:** A summary is basically an extended title, enabling the reader to capture in a glance what the report is about and whether, or why, they might need to read it
- **Marks your emphasis:** Readers may be scanning or speed-reading. Summaries allow *you* to choose what readers see immediately on approaching your work. Summaries choose key words, facts, and conclusions that *you,* the author, know to be of most importance
- **Provides a roadmap:** Summaries also provide roadmaps, enabling your readers to find their way around the project rather than setting out on a journey with no sense of direction
- **Alerts readers to key issues:** Summaries alert readers to new research in their field, new technologies their company might need to consider, or new ideas or theories that need to be taken into consideration
- **Sets priorities:** Summaries enable managers, researchers, and other readers to prioritise their reading matter. They provide potential readers with enough information to enable them to decide whether reading this report is a good use of time
- **Focuses attention:** Summaries focus attention by alerting those directly affected by the report's findings to their immediate responsibilities.
- **Aids management:** Summaries provide executives with succinct and contemporary information on what is happening throughout the firm or organisation
- **Refreshes memory:** A summary is an invaluable aid to someone who might have read the paper weeks ago and now needs to present its essence in a meeting or refer to it in his or her own report or paper.

What style is appropriate for an executive summary?

- **Focus on findings:** A summary should concentrate on presenting *findings*. It is not a précis of the report giving a blow-by-blow account of your work. Anyone who wants this can read the whole report

- **Write as news headlines:** The structure of the summary should not necessarily follow that of the report. Sometimes, it might be best to start at the end, listing the important findings. If, however, you are making specific recommendations, it may be best to start with these and then give a brief synopsis of how you arrived at this decision
- **Report, don't sell:** Summaries should be factually accurate and convey the substance of the report. They are not promotional tools designed to *sell* your work: they are intended for busy readers who must choose (whether you like it or not) what they read in the time available. Exaggeration or misinformation in a summary will reflect badly on you
- **Watch your tone:** Your summary should be consistent in tone and emphasis with the report
- **Be clear and direct:** Even though you may have been a dispassionate researcher or experimenter and, therefore, would naturally use the passive voice in your report – for example, *"... it was observed that ..."* – in a summary, revert to the usual rules of good communication: use specific verbs and nouns, active verbs, and remove any unnecessary padding
- **Be factual rather than descriptive:** Summaries should be informative rather than descriptive. They should not leave readers guessing. Tell readers *"This is what we found ... or will do"* rather than *"This is how we went about it"*. Nuances and exceptions can be made using appropriate qualifying language
- **Exclude detail:** The executive summary should not include tables, charts, diagrams, or statistics. Stick to broad generalisations, and let those who wish for detail consult the whole report
- **Be ruthless:** Write good short, succinct sentences, eliminating all deadwood and rhetorical flourishes.

FIGURE 16.2: SAMPLE EXECUTIVE SUMMARY WORKSHEET

Structure	Directions	Prompt Line *	Example
Issue This was the background, problem, issue, task, at hand	In this section, you need to focus on the ways things are or were, on what your commissioning agent wants them to be, or wants investigated.	We are writing this report because ….	*The Irish people will be asked in June to vote on a referendum, giving power to the Oireachtas to admit unlimited numbers of political and economic migrants to Ireland.*
Scope	This was the part of the action we were asked to deal with. From this point on, focus on what you *did*. In other words, let the verbs take the weight of the sentences.	We were asked/ requested/ commissioned/ required/ consulted/	*We were commissioned to investigate current public reaction to the proposed move.*
Method	This is how we went about it. Use the strongest, most descriptive verbs you can find, and let them take the weight of the sentence.	We investigated/ evaluated/ scrutinised/ compared/ analysed/ examined/ considered/ reviewed/ assessed/ appraised/ calculated/ audited…	*We devised an age-sensitive questionnaire, identified three typical demographic cohorts (North Dublin, West Cork, and South Limerick), administered the questionnaire to each cohort and analysed their responses.*

Structure	Directions	Prompt Line *	Example
Findings	This is what we found.	We found that …	*Eighty-five per cent of all demographic cohorts rejected the proposal; the results were not age-sensitive. Economic status in all cohorts accounted for an insignificant divergence in our findings.*
Conclusions	This is what we conclude.	We conclude that …	*The Oireachtas cannot implement this proposal without serious political consequences.*
Recommend-ations	This is what we recommend.	We recommend …	*The proposal should be withdrawn, or significantly modified, and subjected to further survey testing.*

* **Prompt line:** This phrase is to help you zone in immediately on the key issue. Eliminate this phrase in the final version.

Executive summary: Final version

Issue	The Irish people will shortly be asked to vote on a referendum, giving power to the Oireachtas to admit unlimited numbers of political and economic migrants to Ireland.
Scope	We were commissioned to investigate current public reaction to the proposed move.
Method	We devised an age-sensitive questionnaire, identified three typical demographic cohorts (North Dublin, West Cork, and South Limerick), and analysed their responses.
Findings	Eighty-five per cent of all demographic cohorts rejected the proposal; the results were not age-sensitive. Economic status in all cohorts accounted for an insignificant divergence in our findings.
Conclusions	The Oireachtas cannot implement this proposal without serious political consequences.
Recommendations	The proposal should be withdrawn, or significantly modified, and subjected to further survey testing.

STAGE FOUR: SHAFTING

Now bring all your editing skills into play. Develop techniques for making the document skimmable, attractive, free of embarrassing errors that could undermine your professionalism, and devoid of any words, phrases, or clichés that refuse to earn their own living.

General principles

- **Craft your text:** For professional writers, writing is most like sculpting. The first three stages are merely drafting, note-taking or outlining: real writing begins only when the overall structure is in place. Writers must draft, then craft, and shaft. As Walter Pater once said: *"All art doth but consist in the removal of surplusage"*. Then they cheat. They will often add words, strengthen verbs and nouns, and create images that act as scaffolding to hold the piece together. Indeed, this is the point of cutting in the first place: to make more room for what is essential

- **Don't get neurotic:** No one can tell you in advance how to edit your work. Nevertheless, an experienced editor spots familiar patterns immediately. At first, they will require practice; gradually, they will become second nature
- **Be concrete:** Where possible use *we* and *you* rather than abstract or impersonal constructions: instead of *"Our intention is to have this done by tomorrow"*, write *"We intend to have this done by tomorrow"*
- **Be human:** Put a human subject in charge of the sentence in the following order of precedence:
  1. I want this done by tomorrow
  2. Mr. X wants this done by tomorrow
  3. We want this done by tomorrow
  4. The team wants this done by tomorrow
  5. The company wants this done by tomorrow
- **Know your reader:** Are you writing for engineers, managers, technicians, lay people, or academics? Make the technical depth of your writing compatible with the background of your readers
- **Be concise:** Professionals are busy people. Make your writing less time-consuming for them to read by telling the whole story in the fewest possible words
- **Avoid big words**: Scientific and business writers sometimes prefer to use big, important-sounding words instead of short, simple words. This is a mistake: fancy language just frustrates the reader. Write in plain, ordinary English and your readers will love you for it
- **Use jargon sparingly:** Technical terms are helpful shorthand when you're communicating within the profession, but they may confuse non-specialist readers
- **Prefer the specific to the general:** Scientific readers are interested in detailed technical information – facts, figures, conclusions, recommendations. Do not be content to say

something is good, bad, fast or slow when you can say how good, how bad, how fast or how slow. Be specific whenever possible

- **Use visuals:** Drawings, graphs and other visuals can reinforce your text. Pictures communicate better than words; we remember 10% of what we read, but 30% of what we see
- **Use headings:** Break up the text with headings
- **Use bullet points** and parallel and rhythmic constructions
- **Use bold lead-ins**, like this.

Key questions

Business writers should cut to the chase by answering these questions:

- **What's the action?** Identify the action and the strongest possible verb that describes the action. Sometimes these appear as nouns: judgement (judge), interpretation (interpret). Let the verb take the weight of the sentence.
- **Who is doing it?** Identify who or what is carrying out the action, preferably human rather than abstract. Put them in charge of the verb, as the subject of the sentence
- **Who, or what, is receiving the action?** Ensure that the action is not hidden, or obscured, by convoluted phrases. Instead of *"The builder, who was corrupt, was sent to jail for a period of 10 years"*, write *"The corrupt builder was jailed for 10 years"*

Five key steps to power-writing

The five steps are:

- **Identify key points and make them stand out:** Your readers are busy. When you make your document skimmable, your readers can refer back easily to important points and also answer the question all readers bring to new material: *"Why should I read this?"*. Good descriptive headings will also help you avoid repetition, and cut through verbiage
- **Liberate your verbs:** Literary or academic writers focus on nouns and adjectives because they want to *tell a story*. Business

and professional writers focus on verbs because they want to *get things done*

- **Use descriptive verbs:** Let them do double duty, evoking images and describing action: instead of *"The report contains an analysis of where we went wrong last year"*, write *"The report analyses where we went wrong last year"*.
- **Get rid of passive constructions:** Instead of *"Our accounts will be subject to scrutinisation by the Revenue Commissioners"*, write *"The Revenue Commissioners will scrutinise our accounts"*
- **Stop smothering your verbs with nouns:** Replace words like "transportation", "collection", "operation" – *all nouns* – with "transport", "collect", and "operate" – *verbs*. Instead of *"The compilation of the report was carried out in June"*, write *"We compiled the report in June"*. Cut down on linking verbs: instead of *"The chief executive officer is quick to adopt new methods"*, write *"The chief executive officer quickly adopts new methods"*.

Present material in blocks

Break the writing up into short sections: Long, unbroken blocks of text intimidate and bore readers. Breaking your writing up into short sections and short paragraphs makes it easier to read.

Focus your paragraphs around one main idea. Use your word-processor to explore new ways of presenting blocks of information.

Punctuate in style

A **full stop**, or period, indicates the end of a declaration or a thought – for example: The manager wrote the report.

Commas can be used in many ways:

- A preliminary phrase – for example: *Racing to meet the deadline,* the manager wrote the report
- An inverted sentence – for example: *Because he had to rush to meet the deadline,* the manager botched the report
- An appositive (an adjective phrase embedded). Make sure that the material before, and after, the commas reads as a full

sentence – for example: Racing to meet the deadline, James Wilkins, *the manager of chemical operations,* botched the report
- Two independent clauses joined with a conjunction – for example: The technician fixed the problem, *but* the software engineer took all the credit
- Separate elements in a series – for example: A software programme must have three main features: *scalability, dependability, usability.*

Semi-colons indicate medium level pauses: there must be an independent clause on either side of the semi-colon. They can be used in many ways:
- Two independent clauses – for example: The Federal Government tried to strip Bill Gates of his assets; Microsoft hired smart lawyers
- Two independent clauses joined with a conjunctive adverb – for example: The Federal Government tried to bankrupt Microsoft; however, Bill Gates had already given all the money to good causes
- A series with internal punctuation – for example: Students intending to work in the computer industry should ensure that they gain the following qualifications: advanced degrees in humour, tenacity, and stress management; advanced certification in anthropology (for handling project managers); and advanced certificates in the culinary arts (to compensate for deprivation while on the job).

Colons indicate serious pauses: there must be an independent clause on one side of the colon. They can be used in many ways:
- Something important, dramatic or challenging – for example: I want one thing and one thing only of all my employees: honesty
- A list – for example: Our company demands three things of its employees: honesty, integrity, and flexibility.

Single dashes indicate dramatic pauses: there must be an independent clause on one side of the single dash. They can be used to direct attention backwards – for example: Careful planning, smart management, and good financial advice will lead to one thing – a good retirement pension.

Double dashes usually enclose information: make sure that the material before and after the dashes reads as a full sentence. They can be used in three ways:

- Dramatic – for example: The Planning Tribunal – exhausted, bored, and confused – finally reached its conclusions in March 2009
- Explanatory – for example: The Planning Tribunal – having met for six years – finally drew to a close
- Economical – for example: Ireland's natural resources – gas, peat, and wood – will be totally depleted in 10 years.

Parentheses (or brackets) signal minor interruptions – for example: The manager (he hadn't a clue what was happening) was treated to a visit from a Telegram Lady on his 40th birthday.

Commas, parentheses and dashes: Which to use?

If the enclosed information is a minor digression, or appositive, use commas.

> The famous financier, Maeve Hegarty, kept her money in the Cayman Islands.

For a whispered aside or an afterthought, not essential to the meaning of the sentence, use parentheses. Use this device when you want your reader to know that you are privy to certain information, but you do not want the information to distract the reader from the main topic.

> Mr. Guildfoyle (otherwise known as "The Boss") will be here tomorrow.

> **Although some people claim that the message of Jesus has been misunderstood (as no doubt it has), his followers are legion throughout the world.**

Note that sentences containing parentheses are punctuated normally, as though the parentheses did not exist.

If it adds dramatic emphasis, use a dash.

> **A dramatic event – the explosion at Canary Wharf in London – signalled the end of the IRA ceasefire.**

Using bullets

Bullets are a new grammatical device, made possible and easier to use by the advent of computer technology. The usual rules regarding punctuation simply do not apply. They are a law unto themselves:

- Don't use commas, semi-colons, or colons following a bullet
- Do, or do not, use periods after each bullet, but be consistent
- Use lower case or capitals at the start of each bullet, as appropriate.

When using bullets, ensure that each element is grammatically parallel – for example:

1. Series of nouns

> The government fell for three reasons:
> - The rate of inflation
> - The disunity between the coalition
> - The failure of the peace process.

2. Series of infinitives

> The government made three promises:
> - To combat inflation
> - To promote unity among the coalition
> - To reactivate the peace process
> - To reduce unemployment.

3. Series of present participles

> The current government stands accused on these issues:
> • Pushing through unacceptable taxation levels
> • Avoiding responsibility for high levels of crime
> • Ignoring its responsibility for education.

Platform statements

Whether you are using bulleted or numbered lists, remember that nothing should come between the verb and its object in a sentence. Your platform statement should fulfil the following requirements:

- Use full phrases, either headings or independent clauses
- Ensure that they lead logically into each item in the list
- Reduce the word count (If you find the same word repeated throughout the bulleted list, see if you can put it in the platform statement).

Craft your sentences

To grab and sustain your reader's attention in business writing, sentences should be short and varied – both in length and type. Try writing the way you speak, rather than the way you were taught in English literature classes:

- Limit your sentences to 16 words
- Let each sentence contain one idea
- Limit the number of words with more than three syllables
- Remove padding and redundancies
- Choose your words with care. Never use three when one decent hardworking word would do
- Use your thesaurus to expand the available possibilities.

Vary your sentences

Even though we have four main types of sentence, most of our sentences are declarative. We tell people the way things are, rather than what to do. Use interrogative, imperative, and exclamatory sentences to energise your writing.

Declarative sentences make statements – for example: Declarative sentences are best used to achieve formality, clarity, and objectivity.

Imperative sentences tell people not how things are, but what to do – for example: Use imperative sentences if you want to get things done.

Interrogative sentences ask questions – for example: How can you actively involve your readers?

Exclamatory sentences exclaim. Don't over use them, but try them out occasionally – for example: See what we can do!

The Jugular school of editing

Bringing together all the above skills, here's how to cut to the chase. Note the number of weak non-descriptive verbs in the original below.

> This chapter, entitled *Reference Guide*, should be **used** to look up the syntax, the description, or the examples **provided** with each command. This guide **provides** two ways to **look** up a command: by task, or by command name. The guide **begins** with a brief summary of all the commands **followed** by a detailed summary of all the commands. The brief summary of the commands **is presented** by task; the detailed summary of commands **is presented** alphabetically.

The actions are in **bold**. Note that the "is" form of the verb is weak and can usually be replaced. The original version focuses on *the guide*. The revised version focuses on *the action*.

> Use this *Reference Guide* to look up the syntax, the description, or the examples provided with each command. Look up a brief summary by task, and a detailed summary alphabetically.

Stage Five: Pre-sending

Only one rule exists for presentation: *Present the document from the point of view of your reader.* Put yourself in their shoes and imagine what you would like to see.

Ask yourself these questions:

- Have I presented the *News?* (Executive Summary: descriptive heading or subject line in an email)
- Have I distinguished between a logical and psychological presentation?
- Have I made it easy for my reader to act? (by not getting their backs up, or by sending forms, questionnaires, or other devices they can shoot back to me immediately).

Memos, email or letters

Ask a few more questions before you send them out and you will not go far wrong:

- Have I focussed on *You* rather than *Me?*
- Is my tone positive, even when presenting bad news?
- Is it libellous? Inflamatory or defamatory? Never send angry letters, memos, or emails on the day you write them. Calm down. Get a life!

Make sure that your readers are alerted early on to take note of the most important issues

When you begin, mentally say to yourself, *"Here are the News Headlines"*. Start with new interesting information or findings. Technical or descriptive papers will require other means of organisation or presentation of the hierarchies of facts.

Know what to include and what to exclude

You might have spent many months researching a particular issue, but your reader does not need a blow-by-blow account of your every adventure.

You will impress your reader far more by demonstrating your ability to abstract the essence of your research, and relegating anything else to an appendix, the dustbin, or to never-never land (the filing cabinet).

Give your readers some help

Provide them with regular pit stops along the way, in the form of helpful summaries, sub-headings, bulleted lists of information, diagrams, figures, statistics, numbering points. Use varied typefaces (but not too many!) to delineate different parts of the report.

Use visual aids

A picture is worth a thousand words. Use diagrams, tables, flow charts, line charts, bar charts, pie charts, pictograms and schematic diagrams. People without the technical background to appreciate the finer points of your work can often understand and benefit when evidence is presented visually.

But I'm no good at visuals or layout

No one's perfect. For important documents, enlist the aid of secretaries, design persons, or computer geniuses to craft the most effective layout possible, using attractive typefaces, gradated headings, and page formatting, as appropriate. Having spent so much time writing the report, don't let a poor layout or style detract from your work.

Some companies or organisations have developed an in-house layout style. These help to maintain a consistent and professional style, thus enabling secretaries and junior staff to work easily and efficiently.

Each report will be context-dependent, but bear in mind the following issues:

- **Medium and message:** Make sure that the medium supports the message and that poor presentation does not undermine the integrity of your work

- **Tier of readers:** Your readers are at several levels. Some will *have* to read the whole report; others will have to be persuaded. In both cases, give them the information they need to make the decisions as to when and why they should read it. Give them this information, the quickest, most accessible way possible
- **Your readers' questions:** Your readers will not be in front of you, so you cannot answer their questions in person. Your job is to anticipate the questions, and persuade your readers that this is worth reading. At every stage of the structuring process, bear the question in mind: *"Why should I read this?"*
  - Does it assist the reader's understanding?
  - What impression does layout convey? Formal? Informal? Technical?
  - How will the appearance impress the reader? The clarity and neatness of a report carries an unconscious message about the report itself
  - How convenient is the layout, both for the typist and reader?

Be aware of the Dos and Don'ts of layout:

- Be consistent in your headings. Use the automatic features of your word processing system
- For emphasis, use either **bold**, *italics,* or a larger font. ***Bold italics are sometimes considered to be shouting***
- Full capitals in titles are juvenile. Sentence Case is Preferable
- Do not overuse exclamation marks! Or "inverted commas"
- Underlining is considered old-fashioned – a relic of typewriter days
- Use *italics* for short quotations. She said, *get lost,* rather than She said, "get lost". Use *italics* for foreign words. Use italics rather than quotation marks for titles of books, magazines, and poems
- Use quotation marks to enclose speech when italics are not appropriate. Single 'quotation marks' are often used now in preference to "double marks". The important thing, however, is to be consistent.

One Last Step

Like any other task, writing is something that can be managed. Once you or your organisation have completed a major writing project, ask yourself the following questions:

- How could the process be improved?
- What skills do we need to be improved or acquired for the future?
- How could we better divide up the work: who showed particular aptitude for one or other task?
- How many staff should we send on the IMI's next *Business or Report Writing* course, or should we call them in for an in-company event? (Well, you should have seen that coming!)

Good luck.

PART 4

MANAGING FORWARD

While it seems obvious, the mistake some managers make is assuming others know their expertise. This is not [illegible] advocating becoming boastful about one's achievements, but done in an appropriate way, establishing your expertise or experience in a particular area can make your ability to persuade others much more effective [illegible] people in [illegible] might be [illegible] [illegible] suggesting.

[illegible]

motivated to behave consistently with that [illegible] this principle [illegible] technique. Even a small, seemingly [illegible] have a strong psychological effect on future behaviour.

Have you ever wondered what happens to petitions? In many cases, nothing. The purpose of a petition is often to get signers to make a small commitment [illegible] accordance with this in the future.

[illegible] written or made public are more likely to be complied with in the [illegible]. So if your colleague agrees in a meeting that she will [illegible] your project, getting her to [illegible] the outcome of the meeting [illegible] you will increase her likelihood of her following through on this commitment. One factor to be wary of is that the initial commitment should be voluntary. If people feel coerced into the initial commitment, they are much less likely to honour it or may feel resentful about doing so.

The principle of reciprocity

There are societal norms that obligate people to repay what they have received. Free samples of food in supermarkets, test-drives

17: Managing in Changing Times

Tom McConalogue

Key Learning Objectives

- ☐ Appreciate why resistance to change is no longer an option for most organisations.
- ☐ Understand the different levels of change and why the real benefits of change are often in the long term.
- ☐ Have a clear understanding of the process as it applies to any level of change.
- ☐ Have a range of tools that can be applied in your own area.
- ☐ Understand why resistance to change occurs and how best to recognise and manage it.

While change and transition have become bywords in many organisations today, it is still a difficult and hazardous process to manage. At one level, change is going on all the time – as Cardinal Newman once suggested:

"To live is to change – to live a long life is to change many times".

But, in the decade of the Celtic Tiger, while many organisations experienced a great deal of change, in many cases it was handled badly, left a residue of bad feeling or simply failed to produce the expected results.

This chapter explores the conditions necessary for healthy change, whether in introducing continuous change or managing periodic realignments. It will also examine the role of the manager in times of change where the critical responsibility for implementation lies.

An Environment of Change

By and large, organisations or individuals don't change because they want to change but because they have little choice if they are to stay healthy. It is the environment that drives change, and how sensitive and responsive organisations are to the demands of their environment determines how well they survive and develop. As the environment becomes more uncertain and turbulent, so organisations will have to develop the capacity to make quicker, and sometimes more radical, responses to change.

Examining the Irish environment over the last few decades clearly illustrates the evolving nature of change. In the 1950s and 1960s, as Ireland began its fledgling journey as an industrial country, the environment was relatively stable and protected by trade barriers. Most organisations engaged in long-term incremental planning, with the focus mainly on improving internal efficiencies and keeping costs down. In the 1970s and 1980s, we joined the EEC and experienced the first oil crisis, an influx of foreign-owned multi-national companies and changes in employee and customer expectations. It was clear that organisations, unable to predict the long-term, had to become better managed and more flexible in the shorter-term.

Since the early 1990s, the Irish economy has experienced new and dramatic changes in the environment with major developments in information and communications technology, global marketing, and changing social demands that have driven a need for contingency and scenario planning and building the capacity to make rapid responses to change. Also in this decade, the main focus in organisations has moved away from administrative efficiency and short-term results to a consumer- and competitor-driven agenda for change. The dramatic level of change experienced in the last decade, which is likely to continue for the future, albeit at a reduced level, also demands not just leadership at the top but proactive change leaders at all levels in the organisation – as John Kotter said:

> *"... you can't manage people into battle".*

As the environment for change shifted, so has the need for organisations to structure themselves differently and to adopt mindsets and cultures appropriate to the new conditions. Rosabeth Moss Kanter predicted some time ago that, in response to the changing environment, organisations would have to become more flexible, focused, flatter, faster, and friendlier, if they were to survive the new conditions. At the same time, a number of books, such as *In Search of Excellence* and *The Art of Japanese Management*, identified the competitive advantage for many companies as increasingly lying in the softer areas identified by the McKinsey 7S model as Staff, Style, Skills and Shared values.

Against the backdrop of a rapidly changing environment and rapid economic growth, how well have organisations and managers responded? In his book, *The Living Company*, Aries de Gues highlighted the fact that most organisations have a life span of less than 50 years and that even mature organisations will have to become learning communities, if they are to survive in the longer term. Not only have some mature Irish organisations experienced decline in the last decade, but many of the newer and developing organisations have been less than successful at learning how to manage their own changes.

A study carried out by the Harvard Business School found that over 30% of change programmes had little effect on bottom line results, while other research indicates that 40% of IT projects are abandoned, most quality programmes don't work, and less than 30% of attempts at business process engineering (BPR) are successful.

WHY CHANGE EFFORTS FAIL

While there are many reasons for the poor success rate of change initiatives, one of the main causes lies in the way that it is perceived. Managers are still inclined to see change as something that is planned, installed or implemented, a "programme" view that downplays the people implications and ignores the fact that change is a messy, rather than a rational, process. Part of the reason for managers continuing to hold this view is that change is initially defined in overt or tangible terms such as introducing technology, changing systems, realigning the product range or reducing costs.

FIGURE 17.1: THE ICEBERG MODEL

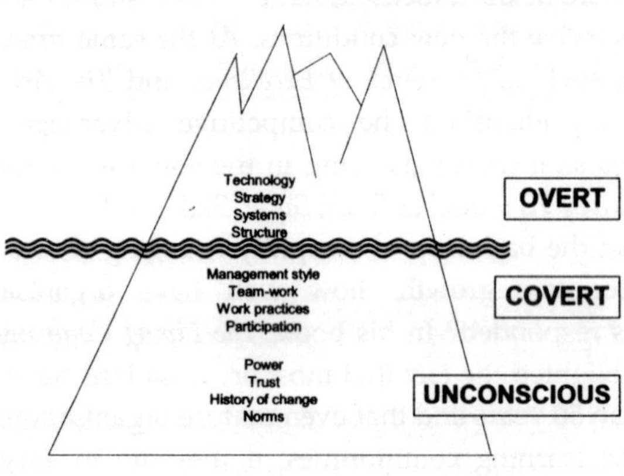

The iceberg model of change (**Figure 17.1**) suggests that achieving the real benefits of change also means changing the less tangible things such as teamwork, leadership style or work practices, often described as the culture of the organisation. What frequently blocks change efforts from being successful are things that are deep in the collective subconscious of the organisation, such as dysfunctional norms, bad relationships, closed mindsets and baggage from the past that needs to be surfaced and dealt with, if change is to take place.

STRATEGIES FOR CHANGE

While most managers have experienced change in their current or a previous organisation, the strategies with which they are familiar are often determined by the conditions in which these changes have taken place. The main strategies for dealing with change can be distilled into three approaches:

- Power coercive
- Rational empirical
- Normative re-educative.

The *power-coercive* approach (clout) is generally associated with crisis turnaround, where there is an immediate threat and where new leadership is often brought in to rescue a failing organisation. In these circumstances, the staff are usually expecting radical change and the process often involves significant restructuring, divesting and cost-cutting. The benefit of this strategy is that it is swift and clinical, while the main downside is that it can generate resistance and cannot be repeated too often.

The *rational-empirical* strategy (consultants) is usually associated with using external experts, who are seen as having an unbiased and informed view. The benefit of this approach is that it is easier for external consultants to convince those people who need to be convinced, while the downside is that consultants' reports often say little about how to implement the changes they propose. In addition, there is often little real ownership for the findings by the real clients (those who need to be on board or could stop it from happening).

The *normative re-educative* (consensual) approach emphasises a participative view of change, highlighting the importance of changing norms and behaviours and educating the staff to new values, mindsets and models. Although this approach emphasises the importance of ownership and commitment through involving the key players, the main downside is that it takes time, a luxury the organisation may not be able to afford.

In practice, many organisations use a mixed model, sometimes front-ending a change process by replacing the top leadership or using consultants to make the hard decisions to reduce staff or cut costs and then using a more consensual process to bed down the new business model or changes in work practices.

However, over time, many organisations and managers have come to see the benefits of anticipating change and the value of creating a change-able culture through a process of educating and involving staff, so that any change is a part of an agenda for continuous improvement. In many organisations, structures have been introduced at all levels of organisation to facilitate more consensual approaches to change such as performance management, continuous improvement programmes (CIP), communications/culture audits, and business literacy programmes, reflecting change as an increasing feature of organisational life. In a recent survey of 130 middle managers, over 75% of the respondents expected to be involved in a major change effort within the next two years and 95% expected it would occur within the next five years.

CHANGE AS A PROCESS

At a most basic level, any change, whether strategic, operational, technical or cultural, is about getting from where you are now to where you want to be for the future. As such, there are three stages in any change process (see **Figure 17.2**):

- Readiness
- Transition
- Institutionalisation.

Creating readiness for change is similar to the importance of readiness in other situations, like losing weight or giving up smoking – it is often half the battle. A study by Arthur J. Little identified lack of buy-in from staff as the most critical obstacle to change, with over 64% of managers seeing it as the most serious obstacle.

FIGURE 17.2: PROCESS ISSUES IN CHANGE

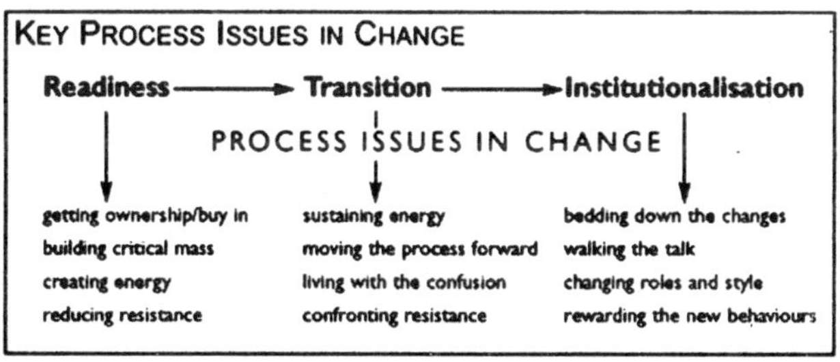

While building readiness is often critical to getting ownership and commitment to change, so ultimately is managing the transition. In the same way that fat people don't resist being thin but the process of getting there, so people tend to resist any journey that is uncertain and uncomfortable. While the old saying, *"a change is as good as a rest"*, sounds reasonable in theory, in practice, the human condition is that people prefer certainty and stability and tend to resist anything that makes them anxious.

Also critical to managing transition is keeping up the energy over the duration of the journey. Examples such as going back to study or losing weight illustrate how difficult it is to take on things that are long-term and uncertain and that people often lose energy when they don't see results in the short-term.

The third stage in any change process can be equally challenging, institutionalising or bedding down the changes in the culture. While it may be easy to get an improvement in customer service or quality for a day or two, the real challenge is to embed change in the values, practices and behaviours of the organisation so it becomes part of the way of working. And much in the same way that medical science has battled to overcome the issue of rejection in organ transplantation, so too there is a tendency for change to be rejected, unless there is constant auditing, review and renewal.

At each stage of a change process, there are critical issues that need to be managed as indicated in **Figure 17.2**. But while it is important to manage the process issues, it is tasks, events and projects that drive any transition forward. At each stage, this means identifying tasks and events sufficient to redirect people away from their day-to-day concerns. Some of the tasks that can help to drive a change process include:

- Have an off site meeting with all those involved under one roof
- Set up task groups to examine aspects of the change
- Generate and share data through surveys, interviews, benchmarking
- Set measurable targets for the change
- Track and publicise what you are trying to change
- Train staff in new skills – for example, computers, quality, auditing service
- Put change on the agenda of all meetings
- Break the change process into projects and assign project leaders
- Celebrate milestones on the journey
- Fast pilot the change in one area
- Set up and train audit teams

- Benchmark best practice in other areas or plants
- Hold regular workshops on issues related to the change.

TOOLS, MODELS & FRAMEWORKS

For most change processes, the place to start is with generating and sharing data as a way of getting staff to buy into the need for change and for reaching a consensus on the issues that need to be addressed by the change. However, whether the data is generated by consultants, or in a more participative way, it is important that those who need to be on board have ownership of the data – as the saying goes *"if they haven't bought the problem, they surely won't buy the solution"*.

In sharing data with staff, it often helps to have frameworks or models to assist them in making sense of information that, on the surface, may be confusing and contradictory. Some practical models that help people to share data for change include:

- Prouds and Sorrys
- Force field analysis
- Blocks to effectiveness
- Open systems planning.

Prouds and Sorrys

As a simple way of opening up around any change issue, the Prouds and Sorrys exercise is best done at a meeting and requires a flip-chart. Start by giving the group 10 to 15 minutes to brainstorm all the things they are proud and sorry about in relation to an issue for improvement, whether quality, service or simply the effectiveness of the department. Having completed the brainstorm, give them a further 10 minutes to identify two or three main issues on both sides and to action-plan some first steps towards enhancing the Prouds and reducing the Sorrys.

A similar exercise that can be useful at the beginning of any change process for encouraging discussion on attitudes and feelings is called Hopes and Fears. Before the brainstorm, give the participants some time to reflect on their own personal hopes and fears for the change. Getting feelings out into the open early on in any change process is useful for helping people to get in touch with their worst fantasies and providing information that focuses them on the best possible outcomes for the change.

Force field analysis

The concept of Force Field was developed by Kurt Lewin, who suggested that, in any unresolved issue, there are equal forces pushing for a solution and blocking a resolution. Mapping and defining those forces is often useful in understanding the possibilities for moving forwards. There are a number of stages in completing a force field analysis (FFA), which are best done in a group or with several groups sharing their results.

First, list all the forces that are driving the change on one side of a flip-chart and those that are restraining or preventing it from happening on the other. Now identify the relative strength of each force by rating each item from 1 to 10. This will help participants to acknowledge that not all data is significant in relation to an issue and that some is stronger than others.

Next, examine the actionability of each item. While an item may be important to an issue, it may be something over which the group has little control and as such it is not worth trying to influence. Finally, focus on the strong, actionable, restraining forces. Usually, it is easier to remove the blocks to progress than to push harder for change, which often invites an equally strong reaction. Follow up the FFA by doing a short term action plan to influence the top three actionable forces.

As a tool for sharing data for change, FFA is useful when working on the initial stages of large transition processes, periodically during the process or for analysing particular issues in detail. While it has face validity, in the sense that it is easy for people to identify with FFA, it also permits groups of people to work on the same issue together and thus is useful for creating ownership.

Blocks to effectiveness

Based on an early model by Marvin Weisbord, this framework assumes that most organisations or systems would be effective, if they were not blocked in some way.

The framework is based on a view that any organisation, department or team is simply a group of people who get together in order to carry out a common task and that they typically run into trouble, either through lack of direction or because they are not working as a team. Eight areas where organisations frequently get blocked include:

- **Direction:** Unclear or not shared
- **Leadership:** Lack of proactive management at all levels
- **Energy:** Misdirected energy or low morale
- **Relationships:** Lack of openness, honesty or trust
- **Reward:** Lack of monetary and non-monetary recognition
- **Skills:** Individual skill or core competencies deficiencies
- **Structure:** Inappropriate, complex or divisive
- **Integration:** Poor systems or mechanisms for integrating the effort.

As a vehicle for identifying areas of weakness in a department or a team, blocks to effectiveness is a simple and reliable tool. It can also be used in groups to rate the group, to share those ratings and to dialogue where the main blocks exist.

Open systems planning

As a way of representing an organisation as dynamic and interdependent, open to and affected by its environment rather than as a sterile organisation chart or set of boxes, the notion of open systems planning (OSP) emerged from systems models in biology.

While it is tempting to see the environment in which an organisation exists as amorphous, OSP suggests that, in reality, it is made up of a set of domains, which make demands on the system. Some of those domains are tangible, such as the shareholders, competitors or financial institutions, while others are less tangible, like social attitudes or the age structure of the market.

In carrying out an OSP for your department, first list all the domains that influence your area and identify the three or four key domains. For each domain, spend some time answering the following questions:

- What is this domain demanding from us?
- How well are we currently responding?
- How could we make better responses?

As part of a strategy review or operational improvement initiative, OSP can be a useful tool in looking at the forces for change in the environment as a counterbalance to the internal strengths and weaknesses of the department.

The critical purpose in using these models is to get a shared sense of the real problems or vision for the future that those affected by the change can buy into. And increasingly, the benefit of using consultants during a change process is not so much for their expert solutions but for providing models, frameworks and designs.

Planning Transition

While getting readiness is a critical stage in any change process, so is managing the journey from A to B. In managing transition, there are two main approaches or models:

- Planned change
- Action research.

As the name suggests, planned change emphasises the importance of agreeing the vision for the future and identifying a series of detailed events, projects or activities to drive the process from where you are now to where you want be in the future.

Action research, on the other hand, highlights the importance of having a shared sense of the problem but focuses on identifying the first steps in the process and using the outcome to plan for the next stage. As an emerging process, it recognises that, as you do things in any change process, the end-state or even the next step may change as tasks reveal more certainty about the direction of the change.

In practice, most change efforts are a combination of both models. Staff and senior management often do want the certainty of a planned process, particularly if there is a need to budget for resources. But detailed plans can also straightjacket the process and attract high levels of resistance to the detail as well as to the end-state. The action research model, while less systematic, is probably more representative of the way that change actually takes place, as a serendipitous process that often runs into unforeseen obstacles and is affected by the outcome of individual events along the way.

WHY PEOPLE RESIST TRANSITION

Some commentators view the management of transition as the management of resistance, in the sense that, if there were no resistance, it would be simple enough to announce change. But people resist change, because it threatens the certainty or comfortable niche that they may have been allowed to assume over time.

Typically, when people feel threatened, they respond in one of two ways, either by running away or standing and fighting. The fight or flight syndrome is a primitive response to anxiety, part of the human condition that dates back to when we were faced with possible attack by wild animals or a human enemy. While the observable signs of resistance are generally more obvious, others are less visible and hard to read such as cynicism, confusion, busyness or head-nodding. It is fair to assume, however, that most of the symptoms of resistance have their root cause in the same underlying emotions of anxiety, loss of control and grieving.

While a number of strategies are useful in dealing with resistance, the first step is to recognise it as legitimate. We all resist change in one way or another – as the saying goes, *"people prefer the certainty of misery to the misery of uncertainty"*. But, rather than allowing resistance to simmer below the surface, it is usually more productive to bring it out into the open through finding ways to let people share and discharge their concerns.

Some of the following strategies are useful for managing resistance during any transition process:

- **Inform:** Let people know what is going on. One business leader summed up successful change as requiring two ingredients: planning and communications. Increase the amount and range of mechanisms for communicating with staff and find ways to repeat the same messages that are often difficult for people to hear when the emotions are high
- **Include:** Identify the key staff affected by the changes, or those who need to be involved if the change is to be successful. Bring them on board by including them in the process, whether on task groups, as leaders of project teams, on implementation groups or steering committees. Involve as many of the players as possible, on the basis that people who are involved are usually more committed to making things work
- **Train:** In order to develop their capacity for using new systems, changing work practices or understanding the new business model, training is still one of the most practical strategies in change. While some training may be in the nature of conferences, briefing sessions or updating on technology, it can also include coaching, mentoring, counselling, peer review or self-learning
- **Reward:** As parents learn in getting children to adopt good habits, or to accept new circumstances such as a new school, there is often a need to affirm new behaviours and celebrate progress towards the desired state. Organisations with a history of successful change find many ways to affirm the process through celebrating milestones, setting short-term targets, rewarding achievement, making presentations, giving awards and recognising change champions at all levels

- **Slow it down:** Resistance to change is often a by-product of moving too fast on change and the resistors can often play a positive role in slowing the process down until people are on board. However, at the same time as slowing the process down, there is a need to keep the energy high because there are always those who want to see the process go into terminal decline. The way to keep the energy high while slowing down the process is to load people with activities, tasks, and projects that relate to the change while, at the same time, making sure there is sufficient time for people to deal with their anxieties.

CHANGE MANAGERS OF THE FUTURE

Any predictions of where change management is going for the future are necessarily based on changes in the environment, current trends in organisation design and the emerging literature. While it is tempting to suggest a number of possible scenarios, the certainties for change management (CM) in the next decade will be in three areas:

- Change management will increasingly focus on mindsets, teamwork, work practices, management styles and values as well as technology, systems and strategies
- While the direction will continue to be set at the top, CM will increasingly involve managers and staff taking major responsibility for working together to improve both the hard and softer areas of the business
- Change management will shift its focus to building organisational capacity for change, rather than simply responding to crises or implementing programmed approaches to change.

Although it is early days to assess the extent to which Irish businesses have become learning or change-able organisations, there is a sense that many are beginning to manage their agenda for change in more mature ways than in previous decades. This is due in large part to companies operating in more open and competitive environments, benchmarking their activities against industry leaders, managers gaining international experience, more investment in management education, and managers learning how to deal with change through the school of hard knocks.

Overseeing the shift in the way that companies are dealing with change are developments in the manager's role. While traditionally managers have performed a custodial or managerial role associated with control and short-term results, increasingly they are being asked to take on more strategic functions that include responsibility for implementing and supporting change. As they become more strategic, managers have assumed a vital bridging function between the top management's vision for the future and the implementation of change.

Related to the development of strategic leadership at all levels of the organisation, many Irish organisations have moved along a continuum of managing change by decree and negotiation in the direction of change by consultation, involvement and consensus, which means managers strengthening their skills at getting results through staff. If a major competitive advantage for the future is the ability of organisations to make rapid responses to changes in the environment, it assumes that managers will have to use their staff as the key resource their businesses often espouse.

While many of the human systems concepts advocated in the 1960s, such as autonomous work groups, socio-technical work design, participation, job enrichment and industrial democracy never realised their promise, a new relationship between workers and management has begun to emerge in this decade. It has seen practical moves towards participation and involvement that are driven, not by humanistic values, but by a real need for customer-friendly design, dedicated knowledge-workers, better people management and the shortage of skilled staff.

SUMMARY

The environment drives change. In the current turbulent and uncertain environment, healthy organisations are those that anticipate and manage change before it becomes a crisis. Many change efforts fail because the technical and systems issues are given too much attention over the human aspects of the change.

There are three basic ways to bring about change:

- Through power
- Through the use of consultants
- Through a re-educative process involving those responsible for implementation.

There are three elements in any change process:

- Readiness
- Transition
- Institutionalisation.

Resistance to change is natural and legitimate and can often be a positive force for change. Organisations of the future will require all levels of management to become more proactive, strategic and transformational.

FURTHER READING

Beer, M. and Nohria, N. (2000). Cracking the Code of Change, *Harvard Business Review*, May / June.

de Geus, A. (1997). *The Living Company*, London: Nicholas Brealey.

Kotter, J. P. (1995). Why Transformation Efforts Fail, *Harvard Business Review*, March / April.

Little, A. D. (1994). *Management Study, Managing Organisational Change: How Leading Organisations are Meeting the Challenge.*

McConalogue, T. (2003). *Dealing with Change: Lessons for Irish Managers*, Cork: Oak Tree Press.

Weisbord, M. (1987). *Productive Workplaces: Organising and Managing for Dignity, Meaning and Community*, San Francisco, CA: Jossey Bass.

18: MANAGING OUTSOURCING

Deirdre Garvey

Key Learning Objectives

- ☐ Understand the types of outsourcing taking place in business today.
- ☐ Learn how outsourcing can be used as a strategic tool.
- ☐ Appreciate the issues that arise in the management of outsourcing.

Outsourcing has been described as one of the major organisational and industry shifts of the 20th century. Outsourcing is a term that is often misused, overused and abused, when it is used to refer to an element of subcontracting or to describe a procurement activity. Outsourcing is more than this. It is best defined as:

> *"... the transfer to a third party of the continuous management responsibility for a provision of a service governed by a service level."* (Gay and Essinger, 2000)

The long-term nature of, and transferral of management responsibility for, an activity are key in outsourcing. Outsourcing can be oversimplified and done too hastily. We will see how there are many strategic issues relating to the outsourcing decision and that the skills and coordinating mechanisms required to manage outsourcing are different to those for performing the same activities internally.

BACKGROUND

From the 1960s to the 1980s, large successful corporations like IBM and Digital pursued strategies of vertical/backward integration. The rationale behind this strategy was that many key components of such companies contained proprietary elements. They also believed that, by performing activities in-house, they limited rival access and created a barrier to entry. Although this strategy worked well at that time, the worst performers in the computer industry in the 1980s were those companies that had pursued this strategy.

The 1980s "stick to your knitting" or "back to basics" approach saw a return to focus on core activities. This advocated concentrating on doing a few things well and acquiring the rest from outside service providers. This started the interest in outsourcing as a business concept. **Figure 18.1** summarises how it has since developed.

FIGURE 18.1: THE DEVELOPMENT OF OUTSOURCING

First wave (pre-1997)	Second wave (1997-2001)	Future wave (2002+)
Contract manufacturing	On-line platform (Digital Insight))	Real-estate-management services
Fulfilment	Application service provider	Design to manufacturability services
Card processing	Human-resources services	Supply chain and logistics services
Call centre	Internet-banking software and hosting	Procurement services
Country-payment systems	Mortgage processing	Direct-marketing services
	Decision-information services	Credit risk management
	IT services	Financial-advisory services

Source: Adapted from Byron *et al.* (2002).

One of the key developments in outsourcing has been the change from asset-intensive outsourcing to knowledge-intensive outsourcing (**Figure 18.1**). James Brian, who has written extensively on outsourcing, describes it as:

> *"... one of the greatest organisational and industry structure shifts of the century".*

In 2000, according to Dun & Bradstreet, third party providers of operational services had worldwide revenue of $1 trillion. In Ireland, an Accenture report on outsourcing highlighted that the value of outsourcing in Ireland in 2003 was set to reach €209 million and is estimated to reach €319 million in 2007. However, the biggest trend in outsourcing since its inception is the growing use of *offshoring* (outsourcing to other countries, usually for a labour cost and/or skill advantage), particularly in the IT sector. Some key factors that have been driving offshoring in the wider business environment are:

- Global access to outsourcing service providers
- Decreasing interaction costs
- Developments in information technology and communication links.

Some of the key drivers for outsourcing within organisations themselves are an increasing focus on:

- **Flexibility:** Organisations need to be flexible to respond in a fast-changing environment. Large organisations that own all parts of the value-chain may not be conducive to fast change and, therefore, outsourcing provides the structures and response mechanisms to the changing environment. In addition, increasingly short product life-cycles are driving companies to improve continually on time to market
- **Specialisation:** Many companies are seeing the benefits of specialisation in an activity, particularly those activities where there are economies of scale, knowledge-intensive activities and activities that can benefit from continuous updating of technology
- **Innovation:** The need to innovate continually around products/services, processes and customer needs. Markides (2000) describes this focus in innovation at a strategic level as finding a new *who* (customer), a new *what* (a customer need) and a new *how* (a way of meeting this customer need). Outsourcing has become one of the tools companies can use to allow them focus their efforts on finding more innovative ways of meeting customers' needs.

This gives us some perspective on the importance of outsourcing and some of the factors driving both the level, and types of, outsourcing.

WHY COMPANIES OUTSOURCE

Research presented at the 2002 Outsourcing World Summit by Corbett & Associates, a global company that has completed considerable research and training on the topic of outsourcing, ranks the key reasons why companies outsource as:

- Reduce operating costs (35%)
- Focus on core business (32%)
- Create a variable cost structure (13%)
- Increase speed to market (5%)
- Improve quality (5%)
- Conserve capital (5%)
- Foster innovation (2%)
- Grow revenue (2%).

The reasons for a company to develop outsourcing strategy are many, though they can be summarised as:

- Financial
- Business
- Technical
- Political.

Financial reasons for outsourcing

- **Reduce costs:** Many companies expect that outsourcing will save money. The perception is that suppliers' costs are lower due to economies of scale and specialisation.
- **Improve cost control:** There is a view that cost allocation will be more visible and controlled than if these costs were incurred internally
- **Restructure budgets:** Some companies get involved in outsourcing to restructure from capital-intensive budgets to more flexible operating budgets. Outsourcing also provides the ability to purchase resources as needed, rather than investing in capital.

Business reasons for outsourcing

- **Help at start-up:** When companies are starting up, they simply cannot afford large capital investment. In particular, we have seen the growth of service providers in Ireland as many US multi-nationals starting their European operations pursue an outsourcing strategy
- **Devolution of management structures:** Many organisations use outsourcing as a means to reduce or maintain headcount
- **Cyclical demand:** Where an industry is exposed to peaks and valleys of demand, outsourcing reduces the risk of having high overheads in times of inactivity.

Technical reasons for outsourcing

- **Access to specific skills:** An organisation may need access to specific skills that they either cannot, or it is not strategic for them to, build skills internally
- **Access to new technology:** Service providers may have invested in R & D, providing a way for the client company to access emerging technology without the investment or risk involved
- **Focus on higher value activities:** It allows internal resources to move on to higher value work while they outsource work where their business knowledge or skills do not add value to the product.

Political reasons for outsourcing

- **Reaction to the bandwagon:** Just as with any fad in the business world, businesses move to outsourcing because of the favourable reports and success stories. Also, some are influenced by the failure of the vertical integration strategies of the 1970s
- **Eliminate a troublesome function:** Outsourcing is sometimes a solution to a continuous problem area, if it cannot be managed successfully internally. Outsourcing may be valid, where a client company does not have the skills to manage a specific

function; however, if the real source of the problem is not analysed, one may be merely moving the problem elsewhere by outsourcing.

Many organisations have outsourced for the wrong reasons. They have learnt, with much pain, that outsourcing does not cure all ills and that the efficiency imperative and troublesome functions may still remain. Research by Corbett & Associates (2002) has shown that the top inhibitors to outsourcing specifically for small businesses are:

- Fear of loss of control
- An activity is viewed as too strategic
- The company's unique culture
- Difficulty in measuring the value.

When I work with managers from different companies on outsourcing, I usually divide the group into two:

- One which currently is engaged in outsourcing (group 1)
- Another (group 2) which is not engaged in outsourcing.

I ask group 1 why they outsource and group 2 why they don't. Interestingly, top of both groups' list is "control". Group 1 believe they can achieve greater control over an activity by outsourcing it, while group 2 are concerned that they will lose control over an activity if it is outsourced.

This prompts the questions as to what activity a company should outsource and **why**, and what activities a company should ***not*** outsource and **why**?

The next section looks at taking a strategic approach to outsourcing and the key steps in that process.

A Strategic Approach to Outsourcing

"Outsourcing isn't an end in itself but rather a strategic tool for enhancing overall performance ... If outsourcing isn't strategic, it probably shouldn't be used at all." (Doig *et al.*, McKinsey report, 2001)

The starting point in developing a strategic approach to outsourcing is identifying why a company wants to outsource in the first place. The strategic approach to outsourcing allows managers to leverage their company's skills and resources by:

- Concentrating on the firm's set of core competencies, where it can achieve pre-eminence and provide unique value
- Strategically outsourcing other activities for which the firm does not have a critical strategic need or special capabilities.

In this way, companies can:

- Maximise returns on internal resources
- Leverage full use of external suppliers' investments, innovations and specialised assets.

The strategic outsourcing process is presented in **Figure 18.2**.

Figure 18.2: The Strategic Outsourcing Process

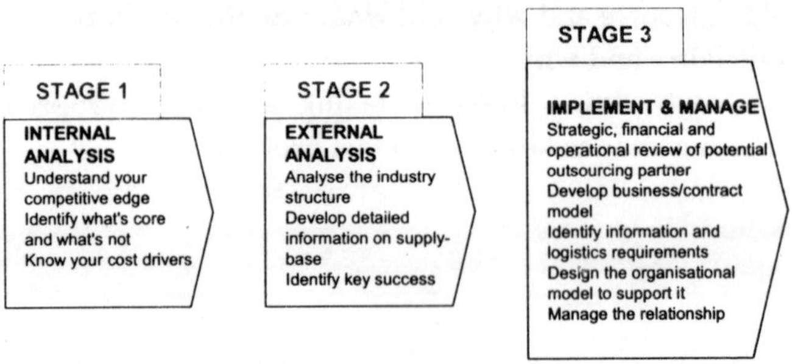

Stage 1: Internal analysis

In order to combine core competency and strategic outsourcing to maximum effectiveness, a company needs to:

- Analytically select and develop the core competency that will provide the firm's competitive edge and the basis of value creation for the future
- Determine strategically, rather than in an *ad hoc* or short-term fashion, which activities to maintain internally and which to outsource
- Assess the risks and benefits of outsourcing in particular situations and be strategically selective.

To do this, a company must look at two decisions: what to keep internally and what to outsource. It must be understood that the opportunity cost of not outsourcing a non-core activity is the resources dedicated to the core activity itself – for example, the opportunity cost to Microsoft of not outsourcing international product manufacturing activities is software development, its core value activity.

Much has been written about the area of core competence and criteria identifying core competence are generally seen as skills or knowledge sets, flexible long-term platforms, limited in number and providing unique sources of leverage within the value chain. In addition, one might add that core competencies are areas where the company can dominate. True focus in strategy means the capacity to bring more power to bear on a selected sector than any other competitor. In the past, this meant owning and managing all elements of the value chain, termed *vertically* integrated. However, companies like Dell are now integrators of a *virtual* value chain, where they do not own all parts of the value chain but only their core competence and rely on specialist organisations to deliver the rest. In this way, they can achieve scale without mass.

There are four key areas to question in relation to keeping an activity internally:

Market power

- Does owning all activities build barriers to entry?
- Do companies in adjacent parts of the value chain have more power?

Specificity

- Is investment in specialised assets required?
- Is technical specialisation required?

Quality

- Does one need to own this activity to maintain control over quality?

Technology

- Is the technology at the early stages of development and unstable?
- Is there an interactivity between design and the customer?

In relation to all of the above, as technology stabilises and industries mature, the answers may change and therefore drive a selective outsourcing process.

To decide on outsourcing an activity, there are also a number of key questions to be answered:

- **Competitive edge:** To maintain a competitive edge, is it necessary to perform an activity internally?
- **Vulnerability:** What is the potential vulnerability that could arise from the failure of the activity outsourced?
- **Control:** What can we do to alleviate our vulnerability by structuring arrangements with outsourcing service providers?
- **Flexibility:** What flexibility do we need?

Focusing then on an individual activity, a company must be able to meet three conditions for that specific activity:

- It must be able to specify what attributes it needs
- The technology to measure the attributes must be reliable
- The technology must be accessible to both the company and the supplier company.

In addition, if there is a variation in delivery, the company needs to know what else has to be adjusted in the overall delivery system.

Using these criteria to decide whether an activity is a good fit for outsourcing may help to eliminate outsourcing for political reasons. Alternatively, it may require a company to meet these conditions first in its internal performance, before outsourcing the activity.

On completing the internal analysis, a company should have established what it identifies as its core competence and why it should remain internal to the company. It should understand why, and what, it will achieve by outsourcing an activity. It should analyse individual activity in relation to the three criteria above. Finally, the company should understand the cost structures and have completed a risk assessment. If outsourcing an activity also means a changing relationship for employees with the company, then it is important to understand the legal impact and requirements at this stage.

Stage 2: External analysis

At a higher level, a company needs to understand the structure of the industry in which it competes. One element of industry structure is an analysis of the supply base. An assessment of the competencies, skill sets and cost structures is critical information and one should not assume that these will be similar to those of the buyer in the industry. This analysis should also indicate key forces shaping the structure of the supply base, who are the key players and the capabilities that companies are developing for the future supply base.

Companies need to understand at the outset what the supply base can bring in relation to:

- **Cost benefit:** Due to activity scale, lower labour costs, lower capital intensiveness, etc
- **Process benefit:** Process technology of skill that is difficult to access or replicate otherwise

- **Specialist benefit:** Shareable expertise and learning that has been acquired from other similar customers or markets
- **Production benefit:** A benefit in production capacity management that can manage peaks and valleys better.

On the other hand, the supply company needs to understand how it can create value in having an economy of scale that a customer cannot achieve internally and an economy of skill by leveraging process innovation from customer to customer. At the same time, the supplier has to balance the need for a customised solution and the need to standardise and transfer learning.

It is also important to be clear at this stage what the approach to supply base will be. Different approaches to the supply base include:

- Single supplier
- Dual supply model
- A tiered model.

The tiered model provides flexibility to differentiate service providers according to activity, volume, quality level, geography or strategic nature of the activity. It is the most complex, but can be the most effective in managing diversity.

Following a wide review of the supply base, an important part of the outsourcing process for a company is to develop its **selection criteria** and measurement, in advance of a detailed evaluation of the supply base. These selection criteria should be based on the company's business objectives. Outsourcing is a commercial decision, not a personal individual one. By having clear criteria at the outset, the basis of the selection decision is a commercial one and minimises the risk of personal/emotional issues.

The next stage of the outsourcing process is gathering detailed information about supplier companies. How companies approach this depends largely on the nature of their outsourcing and the competitive dynamics within the industry. For example, if the supply base is at a mature stage and consolidation has taken place resulting in a small number of large players, a company may use a competitive bidding process which tends to focus on ensuring cost competitiveness. If a company has a specific project/activity to outsource, it may use a Request for Proposal (RFP). Developing comprehensive profiles on a number of potential service providers is a useful starting point in the process. This can be done by developing a basic questionnaire, which includes but is not limited to the following areas:

- **Legal structure of the company:** Is it a publicly quoted or private limited company, consortium or partnership?
- **Financial:** Request the last three years' audited accounts and analyse the financial dynamics of the activity or market in which you specifically look to outsource
- **Company policy and procedures:** Quality management, health & safety, security, etc.
- **Company skills:** Permanent and contract staff, by functional area, competency areas, information on staff turnover, etc.
- Current client profile, details of work undertaken and whether any contracts have been terminated (and, if so, why)
- Management structure within the company, performance management systems and the development of staff
- A reference client in a similar industry sector or scale of work.

From the questionnaire, you should then be able to develop a shortlist of supplier companies on which you can focus to make the final decision(s).

It is very worthwhile at this stage making a site visit to the potential service providers, not only to validate information but also to understand the culture of the company. Cultural fit is essential to success – and the only way to understand this is to experience it in a company setting.

Stage 3: Implement and manage

The final stage in outsourcing as a strategic decision is understanding how it will be managed. This involves developing the business model and the organisational model by which to manage outsourcing.

Developing the business model

Within the business model are two key related areas:

- The pricing structures
- The contractual arrangement.

At this stage, having completed internal analysis, one should have a clear understanding of the appropriate cost drivers for the activity. Also, having completed an industry-wide analysis, the cost structure of the supply base should also be clearly understood. As Chrysler (1994) highlighted:

> *"My enemy is my supplier's costs, not my supplier's margins. Therefore, what can I do to help my suppliers reduce their (and ultimately) my costs?"*

Accepting that supplier companies must be profitable, pricing structures are developed to balance the need for profitability with the drive for cost efficiency and providing adequate incentives for same. Pricing structures in use include:

- Fixed price
- Gain-sharing
- Cost-plus
- Bidding.

A fixed price model may be appropriate where there is a stable environment and little variation in inputs or requirements, and has the advantage of often being less costly to negotiate.

A gain-sharing model has equitable advantages, but requires considerable effort in establishing the parameters and measuring against them.

A cost-plus model may be appropriate in the very early stages of outsourcing an activity, or in the early stages of technology development, where costs and productivities are not easily quantified. It has a downside in its lack of incentive for cost efficiency or innovation.

A bidding model may be an appropriate mechanism in a particular competitive environment or at a mature industry stage. It focuses the decision primarily on cost and, therefore, overlooks other critical factors like quality and service.

Recent research by the *Outsourcing Institute* on key factors for successful outsourcing indicates that cost should only account for 30% of a decision. Commitment to quality and flexible contract are also key factors. It is also important to recognise that different pricing mechanisms work better for different types of services.

Key issues of control & vulnerability

As a company makes the decision to outsource, based on the internal analysis of their core competence and competitive edge, it needs to deal with the potential exposure it could create in outsourcing an activity. To do this, it must understand:

- What is the potential vulnerability that could arise from the failure of the activity outsourced?
- What can we do to alleviate our vulnerability by structuring arrangements with service providers to provide appropriate controls, yet provide for necessary flexibilities in demand?

The contract should provide for both control and flexibility but one needs to balance these perspectives. I find the following model (**Figure 18.3**) useful in making the decision around what level of control is required and what level of flexibility is needed. There are a wide range of control/flexibility options available to managers and between the extremes of either are opportunities for developing special incentives in contractual arrangements to address this.

FIGURE 18.3: MAKE *VERSUS* BUY DECISIONS

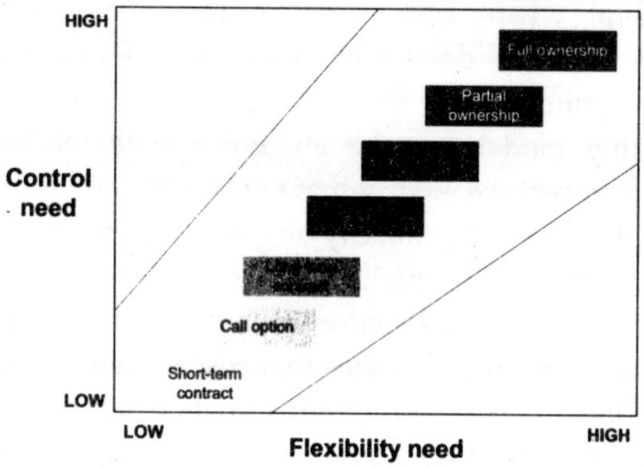

Source: Quinn, (1995).

The organisational model

If a company is embarking on an outsourcing strategy, there are two important points to note:

- Managing outsourcing is not the same as performing an activity internally
- If it's going to work, it needs to be a partnership approach with the supplier from the beginning.

The work of outsourcing really begins after the contract is signed, as the relationship needs to be managed, and without management it will fail. Organisations need to adopt new management approaches – they need to change focus from controlling inputs to specifying outcomes, a shift from **how** things are done to **what** needs to be done. This may require changes in organisational structure, changes in roles and responsibilities and development of new skills. In some companies, this may also involve changing and relocating staff. All of this makes outsourcing a major change initiative for companies and thus key to doing this is the involvement of, and communication with, staff.

This involvement should start at the earliest part of the decision-making process:

- In the initial internal analysis
- At the supply-base, review and development of selection criteria
- Participation in supplier auditing and selection
- Provision of training on the legal and business model aspects, if necessary.

If staff are involved in the process throughout, they are part of the decision-making in the outsourcing strategy and have both the responsibility and commitment to make outsourcing work with the selected supplier partners.

Successful management of outsourcing requires the same energy, enthusiasm and professionalism found in management anywhere. It is the systematic application of good management principles: communication, managing performance, creating an environment of continuous improvement and innovation.

A study by the *Outsourcing Institute* (1994) identified the following skills in managers that were required to successfully manage outsourcing:

- **General management skills:** The manager becomes a broker, a facilitator and an integrator of resources
- **Communications skills:** The manager creates the bridge between the organisation and the supplier
- **Business skills:** Strategic, managerial and tactical thinking is required
- **Financial skills:** The ability to draw implications from financial information.

Real-time accurate information is also critical to managing the outsourcing process. Technological developments within the supply chain make critical information in relation to product, process or performance visible and real to all elements of the supply chain. In general, companies implementing an outsourcing strategy need a greatly enhanced logistics information system to track, monitor and co-ordinate activities throughout the supply chain in real-time.

FUTURE TRENDS IN OUTSOURCING

As outsourcing has increased significantly worldwide over the past number of years, and as companies have become more experienced, for many it has now become a question of *how best* to outsource rather than *whether* to outsource.

Outsourcing as business transformation tool

Having a more variable cost structure has become a real priority for many companies. Outsourcing has become a way to take a fixed cost structure and turn it into a variable one that responds to the business environment. In other cases, outsourcing is a means of getting better use of capital by selling existing assets of a company to an outside service provider.

Offshore sourcing

Offshore sourcing has been described as the biggest event since outsourcing inception. The move to outsource to countries like India and China is affecting every area of outsourcing. Gartner research (2003) estimates that 10% of jobs in US tech companies and IT service providers will be relocated offshore by 2004.

India is fast becoming a global hub for back office services as US and European companies increasingly shift their IT services, call centres and other business processes to India. In the last 10 years, Ireland's automotive jobs have moved largely to Eastern Europe and textile facilities have relocated largely to the Far East, giving way to more high tech industries.

Now, Ireland is having difficulty competing in the high tech area with countries like India, given India's supply of highly qualified and low cost labour. India's technology services sector grew to $10 billion in 2003, indicating the demand for the sector's value proposition. It is estimated that offshore companies can maintain this advantage for potentially 15 years or more.

Business process outsourcing

Business process outsourcing is continuing to increase, with the market segmenting into full service and transaction-based, according to an *Everest* survey in 2003 (Bender-Samuel, 2004). One of the bigger industries driving this is the insurance industry, which is outsourcing third party administration and claims processing.

SUMMARY

Outsourcing is a strategic decision. It therefore takes considerable time and consideration to make decisions about what the organisation does, and does not do, in the medium-term to long-term. Having decided on outsourcing an activity, it also takes considerable effort in managing that process for optimum performance. The following summarises what choices need to be made and how the organisation can implement these decisions:

- Identify what's a core activity and what's not
    - Competitive Edge: To maintain a competitive edge, is it necessary to perform an activity internally?
    - Vulnerability: What is the potential vulnerability that could arise from the failure of the activity outsourced?
- If an activity is to be outsourced does it meet the criteria of:
    - Specificity: Specify what attributes it needs
    - Measurability: The technology to measure the attributes must be reliable and accessible to both the company and the vendor
    - Predictability: If there is a variation in delivery, you must be able to identify what else will be impacted
- Understand the cost drivers of the activity to be outsourced
- Understand the legal requirements
- Develop clear selection criteria

- Understand the industry assumptions and the role of the supplier in your industry. Generate detailed profiles of the supply base from your analysis
- Understand the management, the culture and the operational capabilities of the company that will become your partner
- Develop a contracting model to manage
  - o Flexibility
  - o Control
- Manage the relationship, make it work.

REFERENCES & FURTHER READING

Accenture report (2003). *Guide to Strategic Outsourcing in Ireland,* Dublin: Accenture.

Bender-Samuel, P. (2004). Outsourcing in 2003: How offshoring is changing the industry, *Outsourcing Journal,* www.outsourcing-journal.com/jan2004-everest.html.

Byron, G. *et al.* (2002). The Other side of Outsourcing, McKinsey Quarterly, No.1.

Christensen, C. (2001). The Past and Future of Competitive Advantage, *MIT Sloan Management Review.*

Doig, S. J. *et al.* (2001). Has Outsourcing Gone too Far, *McKinsey Quarterly,* No. 4.

Gay, C. L. and Essinger, J. (2000). *Inside Outsourcing: The Insider's Guide to Managing Strategic Sourcing,* London: Nicholas Brealey.

Herman, J. (1996). Outsourcing Your Work Means Managing Your Outsourcers, *Business Communications Review,* Vol. 26.

Hill, C. W. L. and Jones G. R. (2001). *Strategic Management Theory,* Boston: Houghton Mifflin.

Kumra, G. and Sinha, J. (2003). The Next Hurdle for Indian IT, *McKinsey Quarterly,* Special Edition.

Markides, C. (2000). *All the Right Moves,* Boston: Harvard Business School Press.

Quinn, J. B. and Hilmer, F. (1995). Make or Buy, *McKinsey Quarterly,* No. 1.

Rothery, B. and Robertson, I. (1995). *The Truth about Outsourcing,* Aldershot: Gower Publishing Limited.

Saunders, M. (1994). *Strategic Purchasing and Supply Chain Management,* London: Pitman Publishing.

Websites

www.corbettassociates.com

www.gartner.com/s_about/press_releases/pr24july2003a.jsp

www.outsourcinginstitute.com

www.outsourcing-journal.com

19: DOING BUSINESS STRATEGY

Robert Galavan

Key Learning Objectives

- ☐ Understand what strategy is.
- ☐ Get an introduction to the key tools of strategy.
- ☐ Identify the key elements of the strategy planning process.
- ☐ Learn what contributes to successful (and unsuccessful) strategy implementation.

Let me start by nailing my colours to the mast and stating that strategy is an essential element of all organisational success. Now some will easily agree with that statement, while others will provide a ferocious challenge in the name of luck and serendipity. Those who argue against strategy as an essential element of success will put forward the case of some organisation they know of that had no idea where they were going, but got lucky and made it big.

One fundamental flaw in this, and many other, arguments like it, is an assumption that you can have "no strategy". It is certainly conceivable that an organisation may have "no explicitly shared plan", but individuals will always have some sense of what they want ... dreams of the future count as plans. The other fundamental flaw in the argument is the belief that "a plan" means "a strategy". Certainly plans form part of many strategies, but the absence of a plan does not mean the absence of a strategy.

Even in an organisation that does not plan, every action taken is a step in implementing a strategy. The guidance for strategy in such circumstances comes not from a view of the future, but from the experience of the past and the ingrained cognitive characteristics of the strategic leaders. Even without plans, people and organisations do not behave randomly. They follow a course, which may not be linear or obvious, but which does follow a pattern. In the absence of a plan, it is that pattern that describes the strategy. The implication is that, if executives are to understand strategy better, they need to deal with strategy not only from the perspective of the future (where they want to go), but also the past (where they have been and what they have done) and the present (who they are and where they are).

Ultimately, the goal of strategic leaders is to help their organisations find a fit with the environment within which they operate. This can be done from the outside-in or the inside-out:

- From the outside-in, organisations identify a desired position in the environment and build the capabilities to compete successfully

- From the inside-out, organisations clarify their capabilities and identify new positions in which those capabilities will allow them to compete successfully.

Either way, strategy from the perspective of the future requires executives to make tough decisions about the allocation of resources. At the same time, they must recognise that their success will be measured not on the quality of their plans, but on the results of their actions.

While doing strategy, some will get lucky. But I like to remember the golfer Arnold Palmer's response to a journalist, when asked about the number of lucky putts he had in a round of golf. He said:

"It's like this, the harder I practise, the luckier I get".

If adapted a little, this gives my definition of luck for organisations: the point where preparation meets opportunity. Strategic planning in this context is not about coming up with the right answer, it is about preparing for an uncertain future. In other words, the plan is not an end in itself, the planning is equally important. Giving executives the time, the skills and the motivation to engage in strategic thinking is part of the organisation's preparation for tomorrow's opportunities. What follows in this chapter is a framework that should help you with your practice.

A Strategy Framework

I have to confess that I like the idea of roadmaps or models or frameworks (which is no doubt a result of my experiences and so I continue the pattern). I think a framework, and I mean "a" framework, not "the" framework, helps to provide a starting point. Some will argue that strategy has no start point or indeed end point, that it is a continuous and iterative process through which executives develop their organisation. Of course, that is correct, but not very helpful, because if you are reading this book, you are probably looking for a start point. So I offer a framework (**Figure 19.1**) in the same way as I would offer a map to a climber on the side of a mountain. Not really to get you started, you have already done that, but to help you understand better where you have come from, where you are now and the implications for where you intend to go as you start the rest of your journey.

FIGURE 19.1: A STRATEGY FRAMEWORK

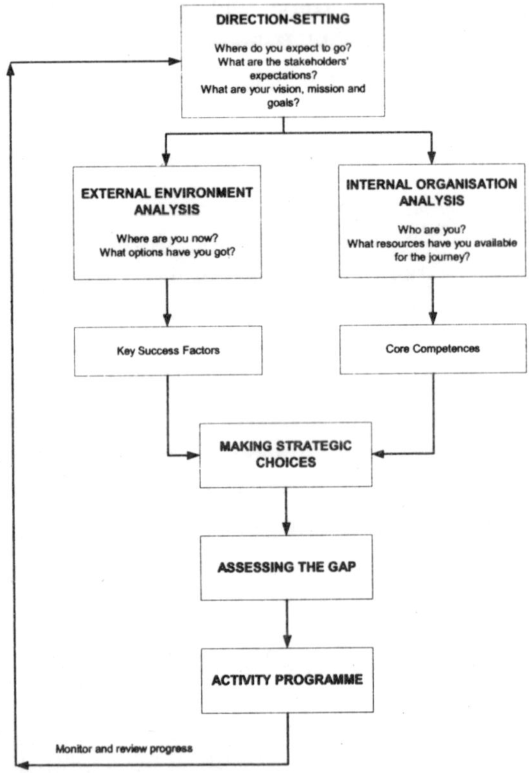

DIRECTION-SETTING

Direction-setting helps by providing the organisation with a target that is the equivalent of giving a sailor a point on the horizon. It doesn't tell you how to get there but it makes it much easier to recognise when you are going off-course.

Organisations articulate their direction in a variety of ways and over a variety of time horizons. To add to the confusion, you will see organisations use terms like vision and mission interchangeably. For our purposes, let us define direction-setting as a complement of business definition, values and goals (**Figure 19.2**).

FIGURE 19.2: DIRECTION-SETTING

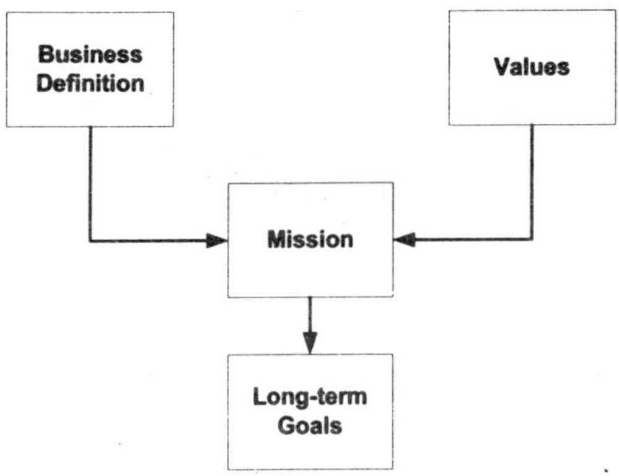

Defining the business

Defining the business plays two important roles:

- It encourages managers to discuss what business they are in. This may seem like such a basic point, but I am regularly told by workshop participants that they never actually thought about what business they are in. More worrying for me is the implication that they never thought about what business they are not in

- A clear business definition provides the basis for strategic focus. When I work through this process, even with relatively small businesses, executives are often surprised to see how fragmented their organisations really are. A fragmented approach is usually an indicator that managers will be unable to give the focussed energy that is required to be the best and to win.

Business definition (**Figure 19.3**) requires you to answer three simple questions.

- Who are my customers?
- What products or services will we offer them?
- What organisational processes will we use to deliver the above?

FIGURE 19.3: BUSINESS DEFINITION

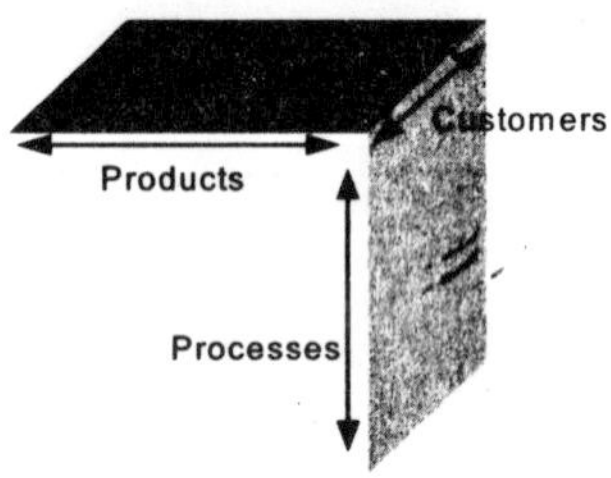

For example, you may define your business in terms of larger commercial organisations, to which you sell big-ticket proprietary technology, using qualified engineers in a relationship marketing approach. Alternatively, you may focus on medium-sized business customers, to whom you sell a range of branded products through a branch network. The broader the definition, the more difficult it is to provide the focus necessary to be the best. As a rule of thumb, you know you are making progress when you can state clearly the customers you will not sell to, the products you will not sell, and the processes you will not use.

Identifying the values

Value statements have become essential for most modern organisations. Yet, at the same time, very few seem to understand why they have them. Many organisations will publish them on their websites and in their corporate literature, but have little idea of their true value.

The cynical approach to organisational values is to create a list of all those values that would make the organisation a great place to work, then publish the list in the belief that you have delivered on your obligations. The problem is that, within an instant of the staff seeing the list, they know whether the organisation lives the values. If you get the list wrong, they know it, they see it for the cynical exercise it is, but worse, they now see your entire strategy process tainted in the same way.

You must be clear about why you want to identify and codify your organisation's values. A valid approach is to identify values that underpin the behaviours that provide an economic rationale for your organisation's success. The purpose of a value statement then is to capture the feeling, emotions and deeply-embedded principles that guide the human energy in your organisation.

But what if you don't like the values as they are, what if you want to change them? My simple advice is go ahead and talk with people about your concerns and the need for change. Identify the behaviours that will change as a result of the new values. Show people, by example, how they bring success. When you can point to the changed behaviours of the strategic leaders, when you can show people the values in action, when you can show people the results of those actions, then and only then can you publish the "new" organisational values.

Setting the goals

Collins and Porras (1996) suggest setting BHAGs (pronounced *beehags*) or *Big Hairy Audacious Goals* for your organisation. These are goals with a very long-term horizon, up to 30 years, that set the tone for everything to follow. For example, Sony's BHAG from the 1950s was to become *"the company most known for changing the world-wide poor quality image of Japanese products"*. Goals like this stretch and challenge the organisation to step up to the mark, they tug at people both on the cognitive and the emotional levels.

Not all organisations will set goals with such a distant horizon or indeed at such lofty heights. However, all organisations do need to set long-term goals with at least a three-year to five-year horizon. Even in today's fast-moving economy, long-term goals are essential to provide that mark on the horizon. Long-term goals provide the means by which you will judge progress on your strategic journey.

External Environment Analysis

The purpose of an external analysis is to help managers understand the world that exists around their organisations. We have many tried and tested tools to help make sense of the business environment, so well tried and tested in fact that many managers will discuss these tools as though they were of themselves all that is needed to do strategy. Please don't fall into that trap: strategy is a living process, not just a set of well-defined tools.

Getting to grips with the business environment requires the orchestration of a vast amount of information and there are two key difficulties associated with this part of the process:

- The breadth and diversity of the information
- The dynamic ever-changing nature of the information and understandings formed.

The first difficulty is overcome by organising the analysis in stages. The second difficulty can only be overcome by ensuring that strategy formation is part of an ongoing iterative process.

To help make sense of the world around our organisations, it is necessary to stratify the analysis and try to get a sense of the different pressures that operate at each level of the system. For the purpose of clarity, we will deal with only three levels in this chapter:

- The broad macro-environment
- The industry
- The organisation.

In other cases, it may be necessary to identify specific sectoral level pressures or pressures specific to competitive groups within the industry (**Figure 19.4**).

FIGURE 19.4: EXTERNAL ENVIRONMENT ANALYSIS

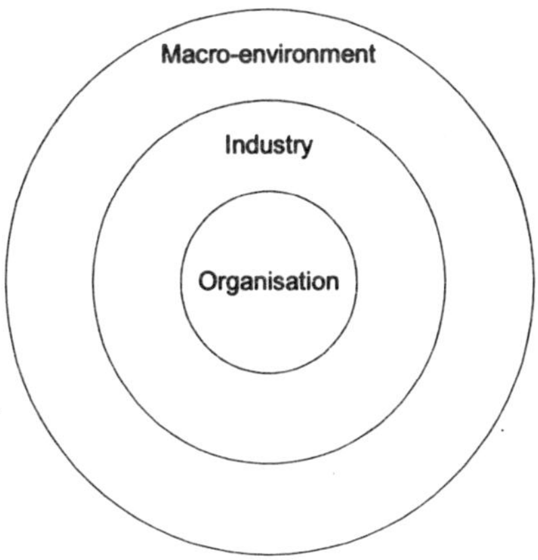

The macro-environment

A macro-environment analysis is carried out to identify forces in the business environment that are likely to have a significant influence on the industry. This is not about understanding the competitive forces in the industry – that comes later – but is about identifying those forces that will drive change in the industry.

A macro-environment analysis can be carried out using the PESTLE framework: an acronym for **P**olitical, **E**conomic, **S**ocial, **T**echnological, **L**egal and **E**nvironmental. **Figure 19.5** shows a list of some of the items to be considered under these headings.

FIGURE 19.5: THE PESTLE FRAMEWORK

POLITICAL	ECONOMIC	SOCIAL
Govern stability and initiatives Taxation policies Privatisation policies Regulation policies Social welfare policies	Business and economic cycles GNP trends Interest rates Unemployment Inflation Disposable income	Attitudes to work Lifestyles Demographics Education Social mobility
TECHNOLOGICAL	**LEGAL**	**ENVIRONMENTAL**
New technologies Improvements and developments Information technology Basic research investment Technology transfers	Health and safety Employment law Monopolies legislation Trade restrictions	Waste disposal Pollution control Transport Energy supply Spatial planning

When conducting a PESTLE analysis, there is a great temptation to list as many issues as possible. The objective should be to include only those issues that will materially influence the industry and then to identify how the changes will differentially impact your industry and organisation.

The PESTLE analysis seeks to address two broad questions:

- In the future, what macro-environment changes will be particularly important to the industry?
- Will these changes differentially impact your organisation?

The first question is answered more or less directly through the analysis. The second requires an understanding of the structure of the industry and your organisation's position within that industry.

Industry analysis

The point of an industry analysis is to identify sources of competition that will affect profitability. While your organisation's immediate competitors should obviously be included in this analysis, it is necessary to go beyond this limited group. Our understanding of competitive industry forces has been greatly enhanced by the work of Porter (1980), who argues that industry competition is dependent on the industry's underlying economic structure, which he describes in a framework of five forces (**Figure 19.6**).

FIGURE 19.6: THE FIVE FORCES FRAMEWORK

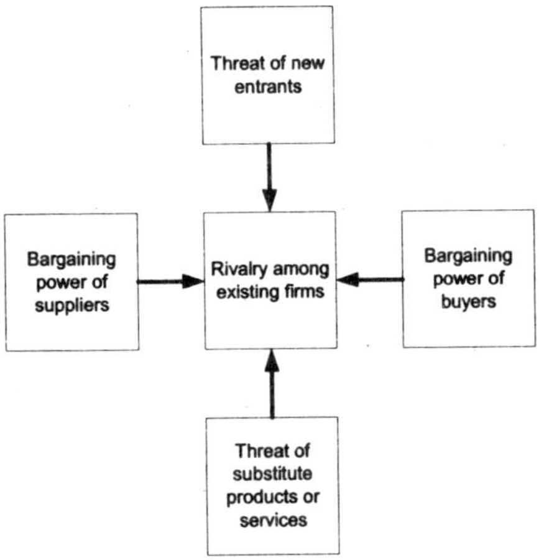

Source: Adapted with the permission of The Free Press, a Division of Simon & Schuster Adult Publishing Group, from *Competitive Advantage: Creating and Sustaining Superior Performance* by Michael E. Porter. Copyright © 1985, 1998 by Michael E. Porter. All rights reserved.

Threat of new entrants

The threat of new entrants to the industry is dependent on the barriers or hurdles that the industry places in front of potential entrants. Typically barriers include:

- A need for economies of scale
- Access to distribution channels
- High capital costs
- Specific experience
- Legislation or regulation.

The logic is that, if the barriers are low, new entrants can easily access the industry's profits to the disadvantage of the incumbents.

Threat of substitute products or services

Substitutes allow customers to switch to alternative sources from outside the industry to satisfy their requirements. It could be as simple as product substitution, where somebody decides to drink milk rather than a carbonated drink. It could be substitution of a delivery channel, where perhaps on-demand satellite television substitutes for video rental outlets. It could even be that improved quality in the production of a product substitutes the need for a service network.

Bargaining power of suppliers

Bargaining power of suppliers is likely to be high when the suppliers are larger in scale and smaller in number than the buyers. Examples of where this happens include:

- Where a buyer has integrated a supplier's proprietary technology into their products
- Where the supplier has a strong brand
- Where there is a credible threat of the buyer integrating forward if they do not achieve an adequate price.

Bargaining power of buyers

Bargaining power of buyers is likely to be high when buying in the industry is concentrated with a few major players. Buyers grouping together to form buying groups sometimes achieve this concentration. Buyer power will also be high where there are many alternative sources of supply, as is often the case in commodity industries with undifferentiated suppliers. Buyer power can be high when the product or service is a large part of the buyer's total cost, causing them to pay particular attention and shop around. Switching costs and a threat of backward integration also come into play here.

Rivalry among existing firms

Rivalry among existing firms will cause competitors to compete more fiercely, usually with a cost to the industry's profitability. Rivalry is increased when an industry has:

- Slow, no or negative growth causing an excess of capacity
- Relatively equally-sized competitors, so there is no leader in the market
- High fixed costs, so that any reduction in volume is costly
- Little differentiation among products or services, encouraging a focus on price competition, and
- High exit barriers, making it costly for firms to leave the industry and apply their resources elsewhere.

The key question to address having completed the analysis is: how well are you positioned to protect yourself from the forces?

Organisation impact and key success factors

Throughout the external environment analysis, you work in ever-decreasing circles to identify the impact of the issues identified on your organisation. The outcome of the analysis should be opportunities or threats, possibly described in the form of key success factors for your organisation.

One of the simplest approaches to identifying the opportunities and threats is to produce an organisational impact grid (**Figure 19.7**) to identify how the changes in the macro economic environment will affect the industry, which will in turn affect your organisation.

In the top grid, you identify how the PESTLE factors will change the forces in the industry. From that analysis, you move on to identify the specific opportunities, threats and key success factors that result from these changes.

FIGURE 19.7: THE ORGANISATIONAL IMPACT GRID

	Threat of New Entrants	Threat of Substitutes	Power of Suppliers	Power of Buyers	Existing Rivalry
Political					
Economic					
Social					
Technological					
Legal					
Environmental					

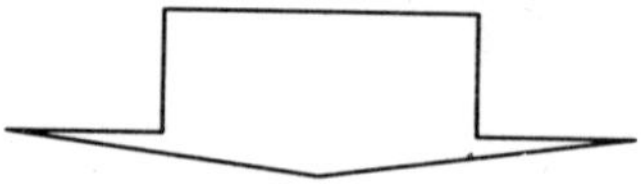

Opportunities					
Threats					
Key Success Factors					

INTERNAL ORGANISATION ANALYSIS

From the perspective of a design or planning approach to strategy, the internal organisation analysis is conducted following the external environment analysis to identify the resources and competences that we have available to support us on our strategic journey. The presumption is that, once you have identified the opportunities and threats, you can change the organisation to meet these challenges – that is, strategy from the outside-in. This view was popularised by an article by Levitt (1960), titled "Marketing Myopia", where he called on organisations to "think" differently about their organisations and their definition of the business. The assumption was that, if you thought about it differently, you could broaden the organisation's options and prosper. However, Levitt missed the point that, while it is easy to conceive a new and broader business definition, doing it is much more challenging.

Before redefining the business, managers must assess whether they have the appropriate resources and competences to be successful. While resources and competences can be developed to deal with new circumstances, their development is by no means a simple matter. An organisation's competences – those things that truly make it better and different – are often deeply embedded in the organisation's history and social systems.

By all means analyse the external environment and identify opportunities, threats and key success factors. But do not fall into the trap of thinking that changing the organisation to meet these challenges is either a simple option or the only one. A different approach is first to identify the resources and competences that exist within the organisation. Then conduct an environment analysis to identify opportunities to exploit them – that is, strategy from the inside-out.

Whichever approach you start with, the end result should be a combination and the tools are similar. A word of warning: the internal organisation analysis is a much more messy process than the external environment analysis. Apart from the tangible resources, the analysis is trying to capture intangibles in the form of competences that often form from processes and social interaction.

Value chain analysis

The purpose of a value chain analysis (**Figure 19.8**) is to allow managers to represent and structure their knowledge of a business in a format that gives them new perspectives on value creation. It should help managers understand how value is created in the current configuration and also provide them with an opportunity to conceive new ways of configuring the system to deliver value to the customer.

FIGURE 19.8: VALUE CHAIN ANALYSIS

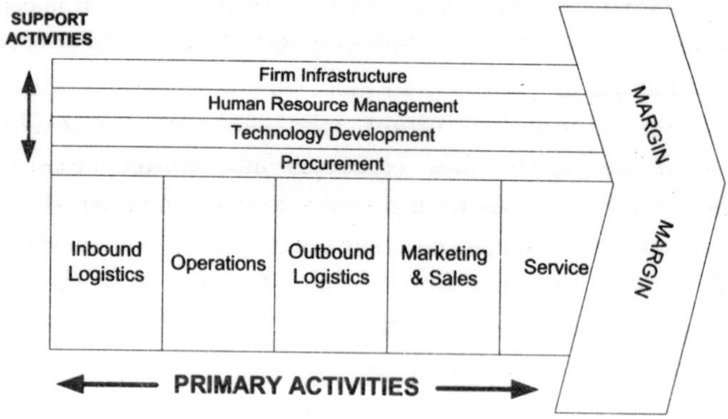

Source: Adapted with the permission of The Free Press, a Division of Simon & Schuster Adult Publishing Group, from *Competitive Advantage: Creating and Sustaining Superior Performance* by Michael E. Porter. Copyright © 1985, 1998 by Michael E. Porter. All rights reserved.

The primary activities consist of those activities involved in the production of the product or the service. The support activities are those aspects of the business that, while not serving the customer directly, support the activities of those that do.

In addition to using the tool to conceptualise the chain of value delivery, other information can be added such as the build-up of firm costs through the value chain and making an assessment of whether the cost-build matches the value-build in the eyes of the customer. This focuses the minds of managers on the most critical areas.

It may be that not just reconfiguring the value chain is in order, but part of the chain could also be out-sourced (see **Chapter 18**). Companies like the furniture designer and retailer, Ikea, and the fashion clothing company, Zara, both have reconfigured the value chain within their organisations and, by outsourcing significant parts of the operations, like manufacturing, they have reconfigured the industry value chain.

Core competences

The purpose of identifying and analysing your organisation's core competences is to understand better the strengths that your organisation brings to its current markets and consequently may be able to bring to new markets. In our rapidly-changing world, products and services have increasingly shorter life-cycles. Typically, product-cycles are less than the three to seven years that would be considered a strategic planning cycle. In such cases, products cannot form the basis of a strategy. The challenge is to go beyond the product to identify the competences at the core of the organisation on which competitive advantage is built. With a better understanding of the core competences that create competitive advantage, managers can make more informed decisions about which products, services and markets can be addressed effectively. By concentrating on the development of the competence rather than the product, managers provide the organisation with a sustainable base from which new products can be developed as the requirements shift.

The identification of a core competence is not a simple task. In fact, its very nature – an embedded multifaceted capability – makes it difficult to identify. Many core competences stem from tacit social knowledge that cannot be codified and exists in no one place but emerges from the ongoing and living process that is the organisation. This has the advantage of making it difficult for competitors to imitate and the disadvantage of making it difficult to manage.

FIGURE 19.9: IDENTIFYING CORE COMPETENCES

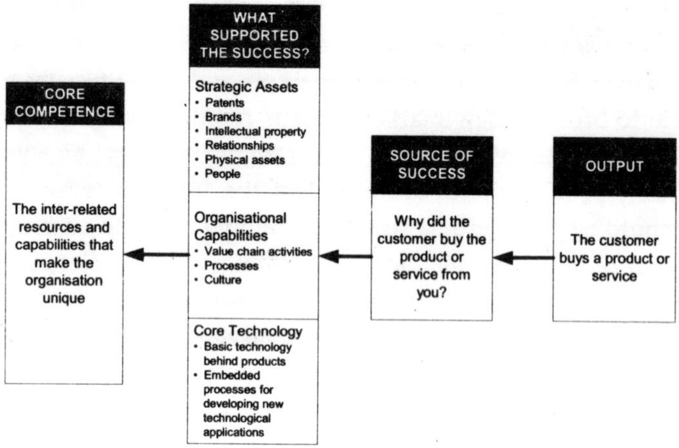

Identifying a core competence is a process that begins with the customer and works back through the organisation. The purpose of focusing on the customer in this process is to identify *why* they bought the product or service. What was it in the mind of the customer that provided the difference that convinced them to buy from your organisation over that of a competitor? Once you have a sense of the reasons why customers buy from your organisation, you can identify how the organisation's strategic assets, organisational capabilities and core technologies support that success. This is much more difficult than it might seem at the outset, because the capability or asset that supports the success may not be the obvious one. It may be that customer responsiveness is a source of success but that it is supported, not only by a customer service process, but also, for example, by the unintentional under-utilisation of a key physical asset.

Ultimately, the goal is to identify the fundamental components of success and how they are interrelated. It is this interrelated mix of assets and capabilities that defines the organisation's core competences. Once identified, they can be developed and nurtured in preparation for them to deliver the next wave of organisational success.

At this point in the analysis, it may be helpful to conduct a SWOT (an acronym for Strengths, Weaknesses, Opportunities and Threats) analysis, where we consider the opportunities and threats identified in the external environment analysis and compare them to the strengths and weaknesses derived from the internal organisation analysis.

Strategy from the outside-in suggests starting with the opportunities and threats and then assessing strengths and weakness relative to them. Strategy from the inside-out suggests that we start with our strengths and weaknesses to identify how to build on competences to exploit opportunities and to deal with the threats.

A practical difficulty I have found with SWOT analysis is that it is almost too easy to do. Managers often believe that they can intuitively identify opportunities, threats, strengths and weaknesses without doing the fundamental groundwork in the analysis. The result is all too often a long list of potential opportunities, threats, strengths and weaknesses that have never been properly assessed. This has led to SWOT being described by my colleague, Cliff Bowman, as a "Substantial Waste Of Time".

I think the practical difficulties associated with SWOT can be overcome by concentrating on Key Success Factors (KSFs) and Core Competences. The concepts are very similar but the language helps managers to focus on the really important aspects that make a difference. Essentially, the process asks managers to identify key opportunities and threats and core strengths and weaknesses, removing the tendency to provide lists that add no real understanding and that have no analytical basis.

STRATEGIC CHOICES

Strategic choices are made in the context of the direction set for the business and the analysis of both the external environment and the internal organisation. The purpose of understanding these three key influences is to inform the strategic decisions that managers must make.

Generic strategies

Most strategic choices will involve a decision about the positioning of the organisation relative to its competitors.

Porter (1980) identifies three potential generic strategies that organisations should follow:

- The cost-leadership approach focuses on being the lowest cost producer in the industry
- The differentiated approach focuses on providing a product or service that is both different and better than your competitors
- Porter's third generic strategy comprises a focussed, or niche, approach in a limited market to either of the above.

An intuitive reaction from managers to the generic strategy argument is often "Why can't we aim for a differentiated strategy, while at the same time doing it cheaper than everyone else?". The simple answer is that being the lowest cost and being differentiated is likely to require very different skill sets or competences in the organisation. Trying to do both together is likely to result in achieving neither and ending up stuck in the middle with competitors that are either lower-cost or better-differentiated. A more valid approach is to build one position and then to think about how to improve on the other.

Competitive position map

To help understand where your organisation sits relative to your competitors, it is useful to map the positions. There are two important dimensions to consider:

- The relative value of your product or service to the customer
- The relative cost of your product or service to the customer.

This is very similar in concept to the price/performance trade-off used by many marketing practitioners. A key difference is that we are using the concept of value *in the eyes of the customer*. In this assessment, it is only better when the customer values the particular aspects of the performance. So we may have a product that is better-performing, but performs in ways that the customer does not value.

The other difference is that we are interested in is the customer's perception of the price, which may or may not include the total cost of ownership. This will depend on the buyer and their mindset. In fact, the same product with an identical ticket-price to two different customers may be perceived as more or less expensive by either. This could be because of something basic, like a brand perception, or something more complex, like a need to reorganise internal systems to accommodate a new service offering. So knowing the customer extremely well is important at this point. In fact to help things along, it is often useful to have a particular customer in mind when working through this process with a management team. Sometimes plotting the views of new and existing customers separately offers an interesting insight. I find we can get a great impact from this assessment when we get the management team to produce their map of the positions and then go and get some customers to provide their own assessment. The gaps between the two will often generate an immediate action agenda.

The purpose of preparing the map is to identify the options that we have for repositioning. So the first step is to identify your position and the second is to identify where you want to move. Organisations, except in the case of a monopoly, will not choose point C (Figure **19.10**). However, many previously excellent organisations find themselves at that point – not because they increased their costs or reduced their value, but because others reduced their own costs and increased their own value relative to them. The point of the competitive position map is that the positions are relative. So, as others move up and to the left, anybody not changing and improving automatically moves down and to the right.

FIGURE 19.10: THE COMPETITIVE POSITION MAP

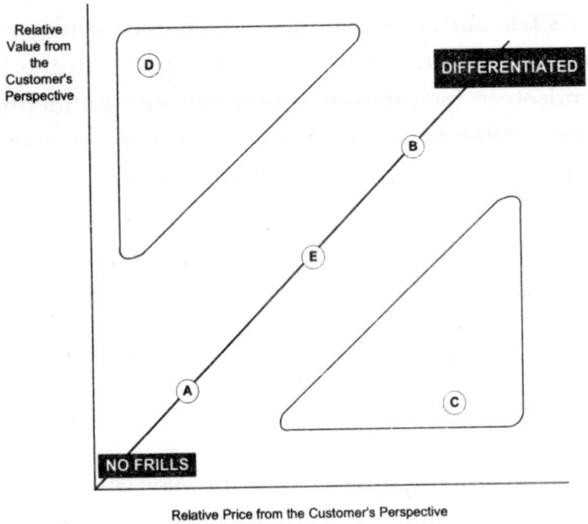

A very attractive location is point D, outperforming the industry – delivering both value and price ahead of the industry. Of course, this is the point that Porter's generic strategy warns about. By trying to achieve point D, most organisations get stuck in the middle at point E. Worse still, because they cannot focus in the long-term on both axes for development, they end up drifting towards point C, unable to do anything particularly well.

Point A and point B are the objectives for the lowest-cost leader and the differentiator respectively. The logic behind these positions is that they afford an opportunity for protection against industry forces. Choosing a position, therefore, is not just about choosing a position that you like the sound of, it is about choosing a position that will afford you the best protection in your industry.

Having chosen a preferred position, the question follows as to whether the organisation has the resources and capabilities to support it. Differentiators will require resources and capabilities that support different and better products. I think it is worth emphasising the point that differentiation does not mean "different". It means achieving competitive advantage through being different *and better* than your competitors. All too often, managers tell me they have a differentiation strategy, when all they mean is they have something different, but not necessarily better than the competitors. For those aspiring to the lowest-cost leadership position, they need to recognise that it is the "lowest" cost position, not just a low-cost position, that is the target. This will also require very particular resources and competences to be achieved.

Pulling it all together

The point of our direction and analysis phases is to ensure that we have the necessary information and understanding of our situation to inform the choices we make. In practice, we need to make choices, then reflect on competitor reactions, and review the whole process over and over until a clear and cohesive picture emerges.

Some of the issues that should be addressed include:

- Have we adequately defined the scope of the business?
- Are we clear who our customers are?
- Have we identified the specific part of the industry value chain that we will address?
- Do we know what production/service delivery technologies we will use?
- On what basis will we compete?
- What position will we target?
- Is the target position supported by our resources and cost structure?
- Will our stakeholders support our choices?
- Will our values support the required behaviours?
- Does our story make sense in the eyes of the customer?
- Is there a viable economic model and are we clear about the KSFs that support it?

ASSESSING THE GAP

Given that we now have a clear view of where we need to go, we need to assess the gap that exists between our current state of operation and the desired future state. A simple framework of description is often the most useful tool and quite easy to apply. Yet experience shows that it is around this point that most strategies start to come apart. This is because the senior management team, so impressed with their work to date, forget to bring the rest of the organisation with them. This is the point at which the strategy must be broadened out to include the maximum number of people who will ultimately be responsible for the implementation of the plan. Remember all you have to date is a plan – until you get some action, it has no real value.

The challenge for the senior management team is to describe the strategy to those who will need to implement it and to work with them as they take the first few key steps. Explaining the strategy to a group and watching them perform a gap analysis can be an enlightening experience. You find out very quickly how unclear they are about certain aspects and how even the clearest aspects get misinterpreted. But this is natural and all part of the learning process, for the organisation has to learn its new strategy and the consequences it has for the behaviour of all its implementers.

There are many frameworks in the literature to help with a gap analysis, but **Figure 19.11** is a good starting point. Strategy and structure play an interdependent role in the development of the other. But both need to be clearly described in terms of the old and the new. With this in place, as many people as possible should be involved in the development of a gap analysis based on people, skills, culture, systems and processes. It often seems like a daunting task to set out on a gap analysis (another good reason to involve as many people as possible), but keep in mind that the purpose is to create an action agenda, not a detailed action plan.

FIGURE 19.11: ASSESSING THE GAP

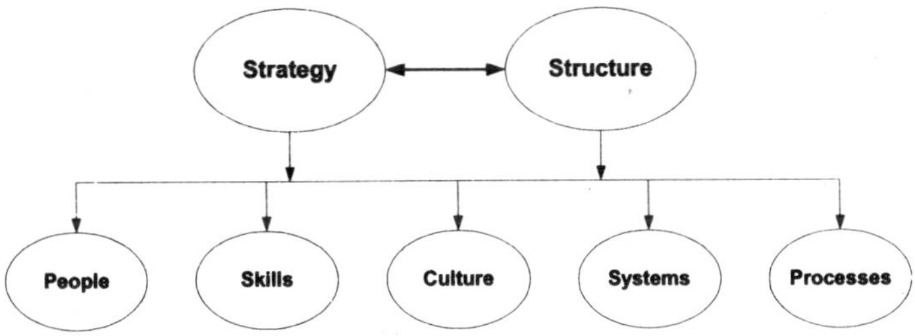

ACTIVITY PROGRAMME

Following from the gap analysis, a number of particular work streams are likely to emerge to challenge the organisation. In some cases, the work streams will fit neatly into existing structures or possibly some of the new structures that are about to be implemented. In such cases, it may make sense to include the action programme for those issues in the normal business planning cycle for the organisation. In other cases, it will be necessary to engage in a fully-fledged organisational change programme which is beyond the scope of this chapter.

There are some cases where it is useful to separate the work stream from the normal line planning programmes. For example:

- When the work programme requires significant cross-functional co-operation
- When the work programme requires senior management involvement to ensure it gets priority attention
- When the work programme is not in alignment with the normal work of any particular group or function
- When the intensity of the change requires the attention of staff significantly above and beyond their normal workload over a sustained period.

The nature of the action planning methodology will be driven by the complexity of the projects at hand. There is, however, a tendency to overcomplicate the process to a point where it is very difficult to identify what is actually happening. In times of change, people respond well to simple and clear requirements – the subtleties can be sorted out later. The early stages of a change programme should be used to get some early wins and help to convince people to lend their support to a successful programme.

I have used variations of the following action planning sheet to implement some quite large change programmes with success (**Figure 19.12**).

FIGURE 19.12: AN ACTION PLANNING TEMPLATE

Organisational Unit			
Key Goals	**Description**		
1.			
2.			
3.			

Goal:			
Objective (What)	**Action** (How)	**Lead by** (Who)	**Deadline** (When)
Key Performance Indicator: (How to measure progress)			

AND FINALLY

This chapter has given you some insights into the area of strategy, with all its complications, contradictions and challenges. It should have given you a feel for strategy in the real world ... a difficult, messy, ongoing learning process.

It's not that we don't know a lot about how industries work, we do. It's not that we don't know a lot about how to analyse and critique, we do. It's not that we don't have managers with the talent to envision the future, we do.

The problem is that, at the end of the day, the strategy that matters is the one we deliver – that's why I called the chapter, *Doing Business Strategy*. So the final word goes to Mintzberg (1999) when he questions:

"... why can't strategy be everything a company does ... ?".

REFERENCES & FURTHER READING

Abell, D.F. (1980). *Defining the Business: The Starting Point of Strategic Planning,* Englewood Cliffs, NJ: Prentice Hall.

Ambrosini, V., Johnson, G. and Scholes, K. (1998). *Exploring Techniques of Analysis and Evaluation in Strategic Management,* Essex: Pearson Educational.

Barney, J.B. (1991). Firm resources and sustained competitive advantage, *Journal of Management,* 17, 99-120.

Bowman, C. (1995). Strategy workshops and top-team commitment to strategic change, *Journal of Managerial Psychology,* 10, 8, 4-13.

Bowman, C. (1998). *Strategy in Practice,* Essex: Pearson Education Limited.

Bowman, C. and Faulkner, D. (1997). *Competitive and Corporate Strategy,* London: Irwin.

Campbell, A. and Yeung, S. (1991). Creating a sense of mission, *Long Range Planning,* 24, 4, 10-20.

Collins, J.C. and Porras, J.I. (1994). *Built to Last: Successful Habits of Visionary Companies,* New York: Harper Business.

Collins, J.C. and Porras, J.I. (1991). Organizational vision and visionary organizations, *California Management Review,* Fall, 30-41.

Collins, J.C. and Porras, J.I. (1995). Building a visionary company, *American Journal of Political Science,* 37, 2, 80-100.

Collins, J.C. and Porras, J.I. (1996). Building your company's vision, *Harvard Business Review,* September-October, 65-77.

Hambrick, D.C. and Fredrickson, J.W. (2001). Are you sure you have a strategy?, *Academy of Management Executive,* 15, 4, 48-59.

Hamel, G. (1996). Strategy as revolution, *Harvard Business Review,* July-August, 69-82.

Hamel, G. and Prahalad, C.K. (1990). The core competence of the corporation, *Harvard Business Review,* May-June, 79-91.

Heracleous, L. (1998). Strategic thinking or strategic planning?, *Long Range Planning,* 31, 3, 481-487.

Kaplan, R.S. and Norton D.P. (1996). Using the balanced scorecard as a strategic management system, *Harvard Business Review,* January-February, 75-85.

Kotter, J.P. (1995). Leading change: Why transformation efforts fail, *Harvard Business Review,* March-April, 59-67.

Levitt, T. (1960). Marketing Myopia, *Harvard Business Review,* July-August, 45-56.

Mintzberg, H., Ahlstrand, B. and Lampel, J. (1998). *Strategy Safari: The Complete Guide through the Wilds of Strategic Management,* New York: The Free Press.

Mintzberg, H. and Lampel, J. (1999). Reflecting on the strategy process, *Sloan Management Review,* Spring, 21-30.

Mintzberg, H. and Waters, J.A. (1985). Of strategies, deliberate and emergent, *Strategic Management Journal,* 6, 257-272.

Porter, M.E. (1980). *Competitive Strategy: Techniques for Analysing Industries and Competitors,* New York: Free Press.

Porter, M.E. (1985). *Competitive Advantage: Creating and Sustaining Superior Performance,* New York: Free Press.

Porter, M.E. (1996). What is strategy?, *Harvard Business Review,* November-December, 61-78.

20: LEADERSHIP

Michael Shiel

Key Learning Objectives

- ☐ Understand what constitutes leadership.
- ☐ Learn how to develop leadership in your organisation.
- ☐ Identify the organisational elements that contribute to effective leadership development.

The problem with leadership is that it sounds like it is a good thing in itself: a worthy thing to develop sometime, but right now we have a business to run, and so we pay little real attention to it.

This is because leadership is often described in heroic terms: a demi-god is inspired with a vision of the way forward, which is unavailable to the rest of us. This vision is then transmitted in a kind of supersalesmanship to grateful recipients (known as followers) who, overawed by its brilliance and originality, gladly put it into effect.

There is just one little problem: life is not like that. This is the cartoon version of leadership. Real day-to-day leadership is a lot more mundane and, at the same time, a lot more complex.

WHAT IS PRACTICAL LEADERSHIP?

To figure out what real practical leadership is, it is helpful to understand what it is for. Think about this: your shareholders are concerned that their money is achieving the best possible return, bearing in mind the level of risk they are taking. So, one of the measures they might use to judge the performance of your firm is return on capital employed (ROCE). They want to be assured that they are getting the most out of the firm's assets, which they have already paid for. If you want to get more capital for the firm, you will have to convince them that they will get an adequate return on that too.

The people in your firm constitute another asset, but it does not appear on the balance sheet and so we are tempted to pay less attention to the return the firm gets on them. If you look at your sources of competitive advantage, you may see a strange irony in this practice. In the 21st century, access to financial capital is seldom a real competitive advantage; with global capital markets glutted and constantly in search of opportunity, it's a buyer's market; it's the people with the ideas who are in demand. Equally, access to capital equipment is no real source of advantage either; for example, the most profitable airlines in the world have access to the same aircraft from the same two major manufacturers as do the chronic loss-makers. So what makes the difference? Over the course of the last century, the competitiveness of firms has increasingly depended on the people in them, and correspondingly less on privileged access to finance, machinery or raw materials.

This is almost a reversal of the situation in the great industrial era; at that time, the idiosyncratic and individualistic nature of workers was an impediment to the efficient functioning of the enterprise. Employees had to be homogenised, controlled and, above all, measured. In effect, they became a commodity. Management thinkers at the start of the 20th century believed in the necessity of standardising work and removing the opportunities for creativity and individual initiative; this was the sole preserve of a superior being at the "top" of the organisation. By the start of this century, finance and equipment had been commoditised and the role of people had become critical to the survival and prosperity of firms.

The problem that this poses is that many of our approaches to management belong to an earlier era. We still pay attention to measures such as return on financial capital, and rightly so. But the big strategic question for any company boss is:

> *"Are you paying attention to your principal competitive asset? To the one aspect of your firm that can set you apart from all the others in your market, and prevent you from being a 'me too' firm with, at best, average industry returns?".*

Of course, you may say that superior products and service are what will create superior performance, but where do you think they come from? Where do you think the next generation of products and services will come from, as your competitors imitate the best aspects of your current offering and, in the process, threaten to "eat your lunch".

The question for you now is this: you know, with some degree of accuracy, the return on financial capital in your business. But what is the return on human capital? To what standard of performance do you hold yourself and your firm in this respect? This is not a trivial question; it is probably at the heart of whether you will prosper in the coming years, or follow so many chronic underperformers in a slow (or fast!) decline, measured, for example, by market share or (often more alarmingly) profitability. To put the question clearly: can you say that everyone in your firm is bringing to bear every available ounce of intelligence, imagination, effort and collaboration? There are plenty of "cop out" answers to this question, ranging from the "hygiene factor" approach ("I'm not stopping anyone from performing") to the truly pathetic ("We do our best at this – honest!").

Your organisation is your principal competitive weapon. Just like a sportsperson or a soldier, if it is not toned, skilled, agile and ready to meet its challenges, your business is already starting out at a disadvantage. It is unlikely to get an acceptable return on its capital, financial or human. This is not a new thought; much of the management literature of the 20th century was concerned with channelling the efforts of workforces to be more productive. The emphasis was principally on compliance. The difference between now and 100, or even 50, years ago is that there is a different emphasis on what we need from a workforce. Businesses require workers at all levels to be not only physically present, but increasingly, also "psychologically present". That is to say, firms need employees to make available aspects of themselves that are part of who they are as people, in order to be flexible; to make an extra effort; to deal effectively with highly complex, unpredictable situations; to be imaginative in developing new products, services and approaches to problems; to be sensitive in dealing with customers and colleagues.

These qualities cannot be commanded to appear; they cannot be conjured up in compliance with some organisational *diktat*. As far as these human qualities are concerned, all employees are volunteers. At a deep level within themselves, they can decide, consciously or unconsciously, how much of themselves they will bring to the service of the business. Whether, or how much, they do bring this energy to bear is affected by individual personality and history. But it is also strongly affected by the context in which they find themselves; that is to say, it depends on the daily (or yearly) lived experience of the employee. What is it like to work, to make an effort, in this business?

Practical leadership is focussed on two things:

- Making the best possible contribution by the organisation to the performance of the firm today
- Creating the organisation that can ensure the prosperity and growth of the business in different future conditions.

Leadership is a fundamental aspect of putting strategy to work. It is a non-optional imperative in creating the future. Put another way, poor leadership is a millstone around the neck of your business. Poor leadership constitutes an unacceptable overhead cost in your financial reckoning; your business is failing to get the return on human capital for which it has *already paid.*

If that is what leadership is about, how do you actually do it on a daily basis? What should you think about in order to have a real impact on your firm? The following ideas should help you start on your path to the development of real practical leadership.

THE SEVEN "A"S OF LEADERSHIP

Attitude

You have to start by deciding within yourself that you want to make a real difference. One of the distractions from this is vanity; you want to look like a leader, like a character in a film. If your focus is on yourself, rather than on the organisation, your impact will be merely cosmetic. Effective leadership, while powerful, is also quite an act of humility. Do you have enough self-confidence not to need to be "pumped up" by the job you're doing?

Colloquially, managers are sometimes seen as being in one of three groups:

- The first group, the real leaders, are restless and curious, wanting to look outside and over the horizon to take advantage of the constantly varying landscape; they make change happen

- The second group simply react to what is already happening and do what is necessary to survive for another day; in effect, they watch change happen
- The third group, obsessed with themselves, their organisation, or perhaps just their golf handicap, get run over by the future; they ask *"What happened?"*.

Real leadership is about getting out into unfamiliar parts of the landscape, because that is where you think you belong.

Attention

One of the scarcest commodities in life, and especially at work, is attention. There is so much to distract you, so many claims on your time, so many competing priorities. It is not hard to be busy. If you spent 24 hours a day at work, you would probably still not get it all done. The most important thing you will do tomorrow at work is to decide where to place your attention. For many managers, their agenda is decided by what is happening right now; in effect, they are managed by events, rather than the other way around. So how do you choose where to place your attention? You have to ask yourself: *"What will move our business forward today? What can I do that will make a real difference?"*

The next most important thing is to direct the attention of your colleagues (please don't call them "followers", they are leaders in their own ways too). The most powerful ways in which you can direct their attention is by asking relevant questions and then engaging with them when they respond.

The job of leadership is to get people thinking about the right things, and doing it creatively. As any teacher will tell you, the best way to get a student to think is not to *speak at them,* but to get them to *speak to you,* to explain their views. As they are speaking, they are thinking and developing their ideas. So get your people talking, and talking about what is really important for the firm. Focussed, lively conversation, guided by relevant questions, is at the heart of a creative agile organisation. As your disciplined conversation proceeds, new areas for attention will become apparent. Skilled dialogue is at the heart of daily leadership. Monologues and similar pseudo-leadership communications deaden vital interaction.

Added value

The important point here is that there is a big difference between *counting* money, and *making* money. To use a sporting analogy, it is the difference between playing the game and simply keeping the score.

The purpose of leadership is to add value. It is clear how workers at the front line add value, and it quickly becomes clear if they are destroying value. It is much more difficult to know whether managers are adding value or whether they are, in fact, destroying value. The notion that a manager could destroy value is alien to many managers – but simply occupying an office and ensuring compliance with established procedures is hardly adding value. To explore this, think about company performance with this question: *"Would you invest your personal savings in your own firm? Would you invest in you?"*.

To answer this question, one of the things you would probably do is to look back at recent performance – for example, at profitability, growth, etc. These are so-called "lagging indicators" – in other words, they are only known *after* the event. But, if that is all you would do, it would be like driving a boat by looking back at the wake. How would you know there is not a rock ahead?

So, to see whether there is a future for your business, a potential investor would look also at the viability of the current strategy, how well the business plan was being implemented and, above all, would make an estimation of the quality of the management. What new ideas are they contributing? What are they creating that was not there before? Or do they simply try to improve the present, like an army getting perfectly prepared to fight the last war instead of the next? Adding value means that you bring something unique to your work, something that moves you forward. If everyone in the management team thinks the same way, then most of you are redundant and you're getting a free ride! Practical leadership means making sure that everyone understands that they have to add unique value somehow, and that there is space to do it.

Agenda

This means developing and agreeing goals for *everybody*. It may be stating the obvious, but the most important thing about personal goals is that it should be clear what they have to do with the overall goals of the business. In the "cartoon" version of leadership, employees happily take on personal goals because of the awesome character of the "great leader". This is the trap of personalisation – making it seem that people are there to serve the "leader" rather than the mission of the organisation. This approach seldom works out in real life, because real people are smart and aware.

As humans, we seek meaning in the situations we meet and in the actions we are asked to undertake. Think about the laws you have to obey when driving a car – for example, in relation to drinking, or speeding. It is more difficult to obey those laws if they seem pointless than if they clearly appear to serve a goal that is important to you, like saving lives. Equally, the actions you are asked to undertake at work have to serve some overall goal that you understand and value.

In most organisations, intelligence is randomly distributed among the employees (although many managers behave as if the folks at the top had all the smarts!). The implication of this for you as a manager is that half of your staff may be smarter than you (what a thought!). They need to understand what is happening and why. You shouldn't mistake this for saying that they have to *like* what is happening. People will put up with a lot of difficulty, if their tasks make sense.

The agenda should, as far as possible, be the *collective* creation of everybody involved. Have you ever tried to paint a picture, or make anything with your hands (even just a snowman)? Have you noticed how, despite all the imperfections of your artefact, you became attached to what you had created? People can really only become committed to things that they have participated in creating, whether these are physical artefacts, abstractions such as a new idea, or deeply personal things like a relationship. The task of leadership is to stimulate and support your colleagues in creating an agenda for action that is relevant to your organisation and meaningful for them. You are assisting them in creating their lives at work. This comes about through challenging them to come up with goals and engaging them in dialogue to refine and agree where they are going to put their energy.

Available

This is a true story told to me by a manager.

> A supermarket chain was about to construct a new store in the centre of a small historic city. The architect proudly showed the plans to the owner of the chain, and was particularly pleased with the views from the large office proposed for the store manager. The owner promptly drew a line across the manager's office on the drawing and asked the architect to build a wall there. "But it will be too small, and he won't like being in there" objected the architect. "That's right", replied the owner, "but that's not where we make the money, nor where we meet our customers, our suppliers or our staff".

It's too easy to hide away in your office and believe you know what's going on in your business through reports and meetings. By the time information reaches you in your "lair", it is usually too late to do anything about it, and it has probably been "sanitised" anyway. Real leadership requires you to get out into the mainstream of the business and not get stuck in a backwater where you only get to know a pale caricature of the real business.

Getting out in the action forces you to pay attention and think about what is really important. One of the most alarming things about businesses that fail is that, very often, the information that could have saved them, or at least alerted them early to their difficulties, was *already present* in the organisation, just not in the place or in the form where it could be noticed by those with the authority to do something about it.

The checkout staff in a supermarket usually know more about customer sentiment, and know it a lot earlier, than management. Cabin attendants in an airline gain a lot of information very quickly from passengers about their competitors, and especially about their comparative strengths and weaknesses.

A CEO of a bottled gas company once told me that, when he got unsure of what was happening in his business, he donned a pair of overalls and steel toecap boots and spent a day helping one of his truck drivers to deliver gas around the country. He met customers, chatted with the driver about the business and always discovered that the people at "ground level" knew a lot more about the business than he did. He also had time to reflect and set his agenda anew.

Action

Have you ever spent the first waking moments of a day just thinking about all you needed to get done that day? And after exploring your options in increasing detail, you suddenly realise that you're still in bed and have actually done nothing yet! There is a similar hypnotic quality to discussions in organisations; it can feel as if simply discussing action is the same as taking it. There comes a point when you have to insist on some action, lest you fall into this trap. The reasons for not taking any action include *"we're not ready ..."*, *"we need more data ..."*, etc. The belief is that there is some ultimate form of analysis that will make it comfortable to take action.

The big myth of "cartoon leadership" is that leaders somehow have access to some certainty about the future that lesser mortals do not. The truth is that, having learned as much as possible, and gained a "good enough" view of the situation, capable leaders insist on some kind of action to avoid being stuck in the present.

In Buddhist teaching, the highest form of knowledge is "wise action". The commitment to action focuses energy and attention.

It calls on skills and insights of which you might not have been aware – or points to the lack of these. It begins to test agreed assumptions and to point to unconscious assumptions that may have to be examined in the cycle of action and learning. Action is the most powerful form of "reality check" – but you have to be paying attention.

The experience of taking action can give rise to significant and deep learning, provided the discipline of learning is followed. A rescue helicopter pilot once told me that a mission was not finished until all those involved in an operation went into a room to understand what had just happened and to share their learning with colleagues. This "After Action Review" takes place immediately after an operation while all the insights and feelings (in other words, motivation to learn) are still fresh and available. The purpose is learning to do it even better next time – not to blame or to brag. Many of these discussions are difficult, but the motivation is clear. This is practical leadership, shared by all involved. In rapidly changing industries, where there is a lot of uncertainty, the capacity to act and learn from action by reflecting, alone or with others, is what sets real leadership apart. In many cases, action/learning cycles can be very rapid – for example, in the financial markets.

Action is one side of the leadership coin – reflection is the other. Action without reflection is busyness; reflection without action is paralysis. The development of a leader demands a growing capacity for both.

Practical leadership requires a capacity for awareness while engaging in action – a kind of "reflection-in-action". To develop this ability, you have to have the discipline to take a few seconds to stop regularly and ask yourself some simple questions: *"What is happening now? What is* not *happening now? What is happening that was not planned, or that strikes me as strange? How do I make sense of this? What should I do differently as I commit to further action?"*

Agility

The secret of corporate survival lies in understanding an important distinction about organisations. Companies go out of business because they do not evolve as fast as their industries. Shock changes in industries test the capacities of businesses to change fast enough to keep up. For example, witness the changes in the airline industry in recent years: previously high-performing firms find themselves trailing recent arrivals in measures, such as profitability and shareholder returns.

The reason is that most companies are built to *perform*, not to *evolve*. The mere fact that a company is performing well right now tells you nothing about its ability to change to take advantage (or at least survive) a new set of circumstances, although this assumption is often made. The ability to perform right now, and the ability to adapt for the future are very different. Being the incumbent, the industry leader, matters less and less in many industries as change is forced on a company. The "king of the castle" assumes he will always be the king and does not gain the important learning that only comes with the struggle to survive. In this sense, nothing fails like success, and nothing succeeds like failure.

The focus of leadership in an organisation requires two perspectives:

- One is present-day performance
- The other is future survival and growth.

Both are tests of leadership. Agility is the opposite of atrophy: it is the capacity to learn and grow to take advantage of changes in any of the circumstances affecting your business. However, simply *knowing* this does not make you any more agile than before you knew it, in the same way that an athlete who knows she has to be fit and skilled does not become so just by *knowing* it; she must undertake focussed, disciplined development in order to have a chance of winning the "big prize". Agility in an organisation has to become a target in itself.

What are the elements of agility? You have to assess honestly how agile your business really is. What changes have you undertaken in the last 12 months? What were the effects of those changes? What were the real difficulties? The only real test of agility is actual change; most companies claim that they are ready to take on the future; only events can test this claim. Many organisations are disagreeably surprised at how difficult they find change. Would you be surprised at how difficult you found it to run a marathon if you had not undertaken any real training?

In attempting to develop the agility of your organisation you are mainly working against three types of habit:

- Habits of action
- Habits of thought
- Habits of feeling.

Habits of action arise because we are accustomed to doing a certain range of things, and doing them in a characteristic way. We only become aware of our habits when they are challenged. Take a test: fold your arms. Now open them and fold them the other way round, with the other arm on top. Does this feel strange? Try writing with your left hand (if you are right-handed, or *vice-versa,* if left-handed) and see how strange that feels. Our habitual range of action is often much narrower than we like to imagine but, because we stay within that range, we believe ourselves to be quite capable of a lot more. The only way to extend your capability is to challenge it continually, to try new things. In your organisation, look at the rituals that have become part of the culture; look at people and groups who have become settled into doing just one type of activity, or doing it in just one location. You have to find ways of varying and enriching these patterns of action. For this reason, many organisations ensure that their people change responsibilities regularly.

Habits of thought mean that we have characteristic ways of looking at the world and making sense of what we see, before deciding what to do about it. This results from the training and experiences we have had up to this point. Show a business problem to an accountant, a production engineer and a marketeer and they will probably come up with different versions of what the actual issues are – and all will have some validity, but none will be the total picture.

The role of leadership in this situation is to create a setting in which the interchange of these players will result in a richer and more useful perspective and basis for action. What is important in this process is not to attempt to homogenise views but to use differences in perspective to point to the things you really need to work on and understand.

Differences in outlook and conflict of opinion are not flaws in the system; they are the very things that enable you to break out of habitual thought patterns that can trap you in the present while your competitors create the future. What matters is how you deal with this level of strategic debate. Many "pseudo-leaders" feel intensely uncomfortable in this type of productive conflict and attempt to flee from it by suppressing real discussion, often replacing it with "pseudo-issues" that may be more familiar or appear more manageable. You really don't have time to waste on this type of avoidance.

One business leader of my acquaintance has a rule-of-thumb when deciding where to direct attention: *"Go where it's hottest"* – in other words, deal with the real issues, however tough. Your authenticity and credibility as a leader will be strongly tested in situations like this, but this type of approach is the only authentic way of helping an organisation to break out of habits of thought.

The great motor manufacturer Henry Ford said:

> *"If you think you can do something, or if you think you can't, you're probably right".*

We are familiar with the idea that our thoughts can affect our feelings. For example, if you think about an unexpected bill you have to pay, you might feel a little unhappy. What we are less familiar with is the idea that it can work the other way round also: our feelings can affect our thoughts. One of the commonest feelings experienced in the face of change or a new challenge is anxiety, which is that vague feeling of unease or non-specific fear that is difficult to allay. It may also be experienced physically as the familiar knot-in-the-stomach, which typically occurs before a big event. The uncomfortable feelings that often accompany facing up to tough issues, such as anxiety, anger, fear of loss, or vulnerability, can easily affect our thinking without our knowing it. For example, a salesperson who wants to avoid the discomfort of possible rejection in making a sales call may find plausible reasons for putting off a call; this is the well-known phenomenon in sales management called "door-knob fever". Our minds are very creative at finding plausible reasons to avoid situations that make us feel uncomfortable, such as facing an uncertain future. What is important to recognise here is that it is the feelings that give rise to the thoughts and this mostly happens outside of our awareness. As long as we are unaware of this, we cannot do anything about it. As we continue to face situations of challenge, we may develop similar feelings, which then engender similar responses. A habit is born, and this cycle continues to be reinforced.

If, in a time of change, or even of the prospect of change, you encounter behaviour that seems a little inexplicable, see whether you can sense what feelings may be at play, even if they may seem a little inappropriate to the situation. It may be helpful to inquire, but not too forcefully, what feelings may be around. It is important in doing this not to appear to judge or reject anyone's feelings. There are no right or wrong feelings - all that matters is what *is*. The first step in helping others to move on from unpleasant feelings that may constrain their thinking or their effectiveness is simply to acknowledge those feelings. People feel reassured by the feeling of being understood and accepted, not by being told that everything will be fine.

The deepest work of leadership is done with the feelings of those who work with you; as they experience the authenticity of your interaction with them, however difficult it may be, they are more likely to be able to escape from the limiting cycles of habits of feeling.

And finally, a bonus 'A'...!

Alone ... Don't be! Leadership is not the outcome of individual brilliance and glib salesmanship portrayed in the Hollywood version beloved of popular management journals. In reality, it is the outcome of an intensely interactive and collaborative practice. Leadership development is not focussed on the growth of one person's mythic charisma but on what an organisation needs to be able to perform today and to survive and prosper in a different future. It is not the display of one person's undoubted talents, but the process of developing and putting to work the talent and drive of everybody in the organisation. Leadership is not a glorious virtue in its own right but is needed to serve the real purpose of the organisation. Leadership is not the agglomeration of power to one person who reigns over "followers" but the development of talent, skill and courage – that is, leadership ability – in others as well. It is *not* your job to have all the bright ideas, all the useful information. It is your job to ensure that there are bright ideas and useful information. Leadership is as much about what you enable as what you cause directly.

Therefore, in taking up your role of leadership there is no need to isolate yourself from others and their ideas and personalities. Leadership takes place in interaction with colleagues, customers and other stakeholders. So get out there and lead!

FURTHER READING

Bennis, W., Parikh, J., and Lessem, R., (1994). *Beyond Leadership*, Oxford: Blackwell.

Gerstner, L. (2002). *Who Says Elephants Can't Dance?: Inside IBM's Historic Turnaround*, London: Harper Collins.

Heifetz, R. A. (1994). *Leadership Without Easy Answers*, Cambridge, Mass: Belknap Press and Harvard University Press.

Kotter, J. (1999). *John P. Kotter on What Leaders Really Do*, Boston: Harvard Business School Press.

Schein, E.H. (1995). *Organizational Culture and Leadership*, San Francisco: Jossey-Bass.

Weick, K. and Sutcliffe, K. (2001). *Managing the Unexpected: Assuring High Performance in an Age of Complexity*, San Francisco: Jossey-Bass.

INDEX